D1283567

EXPLAINING
Hindu Dharma

A GUIDE FOR TEACHERS

EDITED BY DR NAWAL K. PRINJA

First Edition (1996) published by RMEP of Chansitor Publications Ltd.
Second Edition (1998) published by VHP (UK)
Second Edition - Reprint (2001) published by VHP (UK)

Vishwa Hindu Parishad (UK)
Registered address:
48 Wharfdale Gardens, Thornton Heath, Surrey
CR4 6LB. Tel: 0181-684 9716 Fax: 0181-679 7515
Also at:
Karam House, 79 Lever St, Manchester M1 1FL.
Tel: 0161-236 8621 Fax: 0161-228 0056

First published by RMEP 1996   ISBN 1 85175-118-1
Second Edition published by Vishwa Hindu Parishad (UK) - Soft Back   ISBN 0-9534354-0-7
Second Edition Reprint - Soft Back   ISBN 0-9534354-0-7
Second Edition Reprint - Hard Back   ISBN 0-9534354-1-5

Editorial Board:
Dr Nawal K. Prinja
Shri Dharam Vir Dhanda
Shri M.C. Satyanarayana
Dr Shankar Rao Tatwawadi

Contributing authors:
Dr Bal Mukund B. Bhala (Hindu International Medical Mission)
Dr Girdhari Lal Bhan (Kashmiri Pundit Association)
Professor Surendra Nath Bhardwaj (Arya Samaj London)
Mr Amritlal Chandegra (Shree Ram Mandir, Birmingham)
Dr Raman Gokal (Gayatri Parivar)
Swami Dayatmananda (Ramakrishna Mission)
Mr Dharam Vir Dhanda (SCAA Working Group, Nottingham SACRE)
Dr Vinod Kapashi (Institute of Jainology)
Mr Lakshmidas Kotecha (President, VHP UK)
Mr Joniah Parathasarathi (Hindu Education Council & VHP Yorkshire)
Dr Nawal K. Prinja (SCAA Working Group, Trafford, Salford and Manchester SACRE)
Dr H.V.S. Sastry (Bharatiya Vidya Bhavan, London)
Mr M.C. Satyanarayana (President, Hindu Swayamsevak Sangh UK)
Pundit Ramsarran Sankar (Greenwich University)
Mr Suresh Singhal (Brahamkumaris of UK)
Dr Shiva Subramanya (VHP USA)
Professor S. Tatwawadi (Banaras Hindu University, retd, HSS UK)

Acknowledgements
VHP (UK) wishes to acknowledge the help and guidance received from the Religious Education material published by the following people/organizations:
Hindu Council of Kenya
Veda Niketan of South Africa
Dr B.K. Modi of India
Hinduism Today newspaper, Hawaii, USA
The editors also acknowledge helpful suggestions received from Eira Meadowcroft, RE Conference Administrator, and Dot Ingham, RE Advisor, Manchester City Council Education Department.

Illustrations provided by:
Invu Photographic Services, UK, Miss Anupa Gokal, UK, Kiran Ratna Co., UK, *Hinduism Today*, USA, Mr Brijesh Jaiswal, India, Mr Nana Wagh, India, Dr B.K. Modi, India, Mr Bikas Rauniar, Nepal, ISKCON, The Bhaktivedanta Book Trust, UK and USA, Swaminarayana Hindu Mission, UK, Mr Jagdish Sharma, Mr Brij Kalia, Mr Sudhir Shah

Advisors
Mr Dhiraj D. Shah (Hindu Council of Birmingham)
Mr Kishore Ruparelia (General Secretary, VHP UK)
Mrs Saraswati Dave (Inter Faith)
Mr Gopal Gupta
Mr Hasmukh V. Shah (Public Relations)
Mr Tarsem Lal Gupta (Finance)

Standing Advisory Council for Religious Education (SACRE) Advisors:
Joniah Parathasarathi – Bradford
Dharam Vir Dhanda – Nottingham
Uttam D. Mistry – Bolton
Kulbhushan Joshi – London Borough of Redbridge
Vinod Wadher – London Borough of Brent
Anand Vrat Chandan – Birmingham
Prabendan Dave – Newham Borough Council
Nawal Prinja – Manchester, Salford and Trafford

Printed in Great Britain for VHP (UK) by
Chatham Printers Limited,
32 Chatham Street, Leicester LE1 6PB.
Tel: (0116) 255 6696 Gax: (0116) 255 6571.
E-mail: info@chatham.co.uk
ISDN NO: (0116) 247 0011

PREFACE

This book has been prepared by British Hindus with the main objective of presenting an accurate picture of Hinduism both for teachers of Religious Education and for students studying Hinduism as part of their Religious Education course. There are many noteworthy publications already available on the subject, but most of them tend to present just one author's perception of Hinduism and even that is often a non-Hindu's point of view. This in itself is not objectionable, but what is more desirable is an authoritative and comprehensive view of Hinduism as a living faith. This is only possible in a book such as this one, in which a group of Hindu authors living in Britain explain about their own faith.

Hinduism by its nature defies simple definition. Modern researchers have discovered texts in ancient Hindu scriptures that refer to astronomical events dating Hinduism earlier than the conventional view of human history. Owing to its very ancient history and gradual development over many thousands of years, Hinduism has acquired a great deal of diversity, to such an extent that sometimes one can come across views within Hinduism that appear to contradict each other. This has created many misunderstandings which have been further perpetuated by authors attempting to explain Hinduism in the West; as a result, Hinduism has become the most misunderstood of all religions.

A sincere attempt has been made in this book to correct some of the misconceptions about Hinduism often found in Religious Education books. For example, the statement that Hindus worship many gods is factually wrong: Hindus believe in one and only one God who is worshipped in many different ways and is given a variety of different names. Some books wrongly present Hinduism merely as a collection of old myths and legends full of superstition and offer little explanation of the scientific and spiritual nature of Hinduism. An attempt has been made in this book to provide correct factual information and an accurate interpretation of Hindu traditions.

The six chapters of the book cover all the topics specified in the syllabuses issued by the School Curriculum and Assessment Authority, Northern Examinations and Assessment Board, Southern Examining Group, Independent Schools Joint Council and a number of local education authorities. Teaching material is provided for different primary and secondary age groups within the age range four to eighteen, covering Key Stages 1 to 4 and 16-plus students. Each topic includes a brief introduction for the teacher and, where possible, links with other topics are indicated. Suggestions are given on ways of introducing the topic in the classroom, along with some useful material in the form of examples, stories, pictures, exercises and typical questions.

The British branch of the World Council of Hindus (Vishwa Hindu Parishad, UK) has undertaken the task of producing this book, the aim of which is to combine the scholarly expertise and personal experiences of Hindu authors from various religious traditions to produce material suitable for teachers and students. The editors selected the topics and arrangement of material after consultation with professional RE teachers, school inspectors and the relevant examination boards. Above everything else, the book has been approved by world-famous Hindu scholars and religious authorities, namely, H.H. Jagadguru Shankaracharya Shri Swami Vasudevanandaji Maharaj of Badrika Peeth and ex-Shankaracharya Pujya Swami Satyamitrananda ji Giri of Bharat Mata temple, Haridwar, India.

The first edition of the book published by RMEP received excellent reviews and has been sold out. The second edition has been produced with some addition and amendments to the text with four additional pages of colour illustrations. The editorial board is grateful to the members of the Hindu community and the professional RE teachers who have made suggestions to further enhance the educational value of this book.

Out of hopelessly intricate mythology must come concrete moral forms; and out of bewildering Yogi-ism must come the most scientific and practical psychology – and all this must be put in a form so that a child may grasp it.

SWAMI VIVEKANANDA

CONTENTS

CHAPTER ONE
INTRODUCTION

⁞ *Satyameva Jayate – Truth alone triumphs*

(MANDUKYA UPANISHAD 3-1-6)

'Hinduism' is now generally accepted as a generic term to identify the religious practices of the people of India. No ancient Hindu scripture has given any specific definition of Hinduism. In the absence of an authoritative definition, some confusion about the meanings of the words Hindu and Hinduism has arisen and is still prevalent. Therefore, the purpose of this first chapter is to provide clarification of these important terms in order to help teachers engaged in teaching Hinduism as part of religious studies.

In the judgement of the Supreme Court of India, dated 11th December 1995, it was stated: 'When we think of Hindu religion we find it difficult, if not impossible, to define Hindu religion or even adequately describe it. Unlike other religions in the world, the Hindu religion does not claim any one prophet; it does not worship any one God; it does not subscribe to any one dogma; it does not believe in any one philosophical concept; it does not follow any one set of religious rites or performances; in fact, it does not appear to satisfy the narrow traditional features of any one religion or creed. It may broadly be described as a way of life and nothing more.' This way of life consists of the religious, spiritual, cultural, moral, ethical and every other aspect of life. The vastness and variety of this knowledge has led to an extensive literature and a great variety of customs, traditions and practices over centuries of unending quests.

Hindu Dharma – Sanatana Dharma

One of the major living religious traditions of the world, Hinduism is also recognized as the most ancient. It is different from most others because it was not started by any single individual, seer or prophet, and its origin cannot be traced to a particular period of human history.

It is not based on one single book or a set of dogmas; on the contrary, it allows a great deal of freedom of thought, faith and worship. Hinduism is not a single religious faith system because it does not insist on any fixed set of doctrines. There are a variety of religious sects or traditions in Hinduism. However, in spite of this diversity, there is a certain unity among all the various doctrines and schools of thought because their basic principles are based on the 'eternal laws of nature' which can be rightly defined as Sanatana (eternal) Dharma (laws of nature). These are based on the teachings of the Vedas, Tripitakas and the Jain Agamas. The Vedas are now recognized by many scholars as the most ancient literature in the world. The term 'Sanatana' is often used to highlight this quality of being ancient and eternal. The knowledge of the universe and the laws contained in the Vedas and in the subsequent scriptures is considered to be applicable at all times and places. As these laws bind the universe and its components together, it is called 'Dharma', i.e. that which keeps all together.

The terms Vedic, Buddh, Jain and Sanatana are always appended by the term 'Dharma'. It is one of the most intractable terms employed in the Hindu philosophy and is derived from the root 'dhru', meaning to uphold, sustain or support. The most apt description of the comprehensive, broad-based nature of Hinduism is therefore 'Hindu Dharma'. It comprises a medium, an instrument or an integrated scheme of life by which one is prevented from falling down and is uplifted spiritually. It is thus more a way of life or a value system than a religion. However, the term 'religion' is used here for the sake of convenience and also because of the lack of a better synonym for 'Dharma'. Usually, 'Dharma' is translated as righteousness, morality, religious code and duty.

The impression may be given that Hinduism is a 'federation' or a 'commonwealth' of many religions, but it is more than that; it is a way of life and culture in which several religious practices are harmoniously blended and bound by the common bond of 'Dharma'. In the words of a Hindu scholar and writer, Ram Swarup: 'it is the name of one religion or one truth lived at hundred points in hundred ways by men of different capacities and preparedness. Unity of Hinduism is not external and geographical; it is deep, subtle, spiritual; it has multiple expressions; it lives in them all; it also exceeds them.'

The development of Hindu religion and philosophy shows that from time to time saints and religious reformers attempted to remove from Hindu thought and practices elements of corruption and superstition and that led to the formation of different sects. Buddha started Buddhism; Mahavir founded Jainism; Basava became the founder of Lingayat religion; Dhyaneshwar and Tukaram initiated the Varakari cult; Guru Nanak inspired Sikhism; Dayananda founded Arya Samaj, and Chaitanya began Bhakti cult; and as a result of the teachings of Ramakrishna and Vivekananda, Hindu religion flowered into its most attractive, progressive and dynamic form. If we study the teachings of these saints and religious reformers, we would notice an amount of divergence, there is a kind of subtle indescribable unity which keeps them within the sweep of the broad and progressive Hindu religion.

(EXTRACT FROM THE JUDGEMENT OF THE SUPREME COURT OF INDIA, 11TH DECEMBER 1995)

Each soul is potentially divine. The goal is to manifest this divinity within, by controlling nature, external and internal. Do this either by work, or worship, or psychic control, or philosophy – by one or more, or all of these – and be free. This is the whole religion. Doctrines, or dogmas, or rituals, or books, or temples, or forms are but secondary details.

(SWAMI VIVEKANANDA)

The Word 'Hindu'

History is mostly guessing; the rest is prejudice.

(WILL DURANT)

The word 'Hindu' has its origin in Sanskrit literature. In the Rig Veda, India was referred to as the country of 'Sapta Sindhu', i.e. the country of seven great rivers. The word 'Sindhu' refers to rivers and sea and not merely to the specific river called the Sindhu (Indus), now in Pakistan. In Vedic Sanskrit, according to ancient dictionaries, 'sa' was pronounced as 'ha'. Thus 'Sapta Sindhu' was pronounced as 'Hapta Hindu'; similarly 'Saraswati' was pronounced as 'Haravyati' or 'Harahwati'. This is how the word 'Hindu' came into being. The ancient Persians also referred to India as 'Hapta Hind', as recorded in their ancient classic 'Bem Riyadh'. That is why some scholars came to believe that the word 'Hindu' had its origin in Persia. The Greeks who invaded India under Alexander the Great, dropped the 'H' completely and used the name Indoos or Indus which later led to the formation of the word 'India'.

The Origin and Other Names of Hinduism

As explained above, there is no equivalent word for 'Dharma' in English. Dharma is not confined to the performance of religious rituals and ceremonies but is used in a much wider sense. It is a synthesis of worship, morals, a code of conduct and duty. It is based on the laws of nature. Buddhism, Sikhism and Jainism all come within the fold of this Sanatana (eternal) Dharma (laws of nature). Because the earliest known Hindu scriptures are the Vedas, it is also known as the Vedic Dharma. As depicted in the family tree of Hindu scriptures (see p.126), the Vedic literature is the root of almost all Hindu scriptures.

Some Hindu scholars and philosophers have defined Hinduism as a noble way of life. The Sanskrit word for 'noble' is 'Arya', hence Hinduism is also called Arya Dharma. In fact, the ancient name of India found in many Hindu scriptures is 'Aryavarat', meaning the abode of noble people. Some scholars have misunderstood the use of the word 'Arya' in Hindu scriptures, and have made the mistake of thinking that 'Arya' is the name of a race which came from outside India. Hindu scholars reject these ideas based on the evidence from recent archaeological findings. The Aryan invasion of India is at best an unproven theory and at worst a myth.

There is a period in Hindu history during which Hinduism is often identified as 'Brahmanism' by some Western scholars. This is the period when the true teachings of the Vedas were forgotten and ritualism propagated by some Brahmin (priestly) classes became popular. Whilst it is true that Hinduism went through a period of experimentation or perhaps some degradation, it would be illogical and incorrect to assign to Hinduism the name of just one class within the whole Hindu community.

Often followers of a particular sect or movement may use a name to identify themselves. For example, generally non-reformist adherents of the ancient Hindu traditions and rituals are known as 'Sanatanist'. The followers of a reformist movement, Arya Samaj, may call themselves 'Arya Samajist'. Many other names, like Vaishnavite, Jain, Lingayat, will also be found.

The most important point to remember is that Hinduism is not founded by any one person and it is not based on any one book. Its name as well as its traditions have changed throughout its long history.

Finally, it should be noted that whilst the term 'Hinduism' is popular in the English language, Hindu religious leaders prefer to use the name 'Sanatana Dharma' or Hindu Dharma instead of Hinduism. The General Secretary of the World Council of Hindus, Shri Ashok Singhal, has explained that in spite of

the rich diversity of religious sects and traditions in Hinduism, there is a certain unity because their principles are based on the 'eternal laws of nature' which can be rightly defined as Sanatana Dharma. This name also signifies unity in diversity.

The Land of Hindus: Hindusthan

Etymologically, what is Sindhu in Sanskrit is Hindu in Persian and India in English. This establishes the simple fact that Hindus originate from the country now known as India. In the present Indian Constitution, the country is referred to as 'India that is Bharat'. Before it

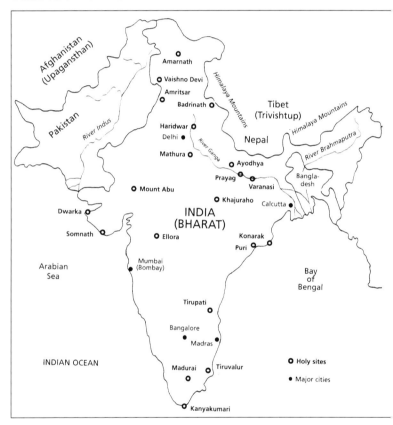

Map of India (Bharat), showing important holy sites

was termed India, the country was known as Hindusthan, i.e. the land of Hindus and Hinduism. In the Baarhaspatya Shastra (400 BCE), Hindusthan was described as the vast stretch of land spreading between the Himalayas and the Indian ocean. Prior to that it was Bharat Varsha, named after Bharat, the son of Rishabhdev. Some people believe that the country was so named because it is the land of the Vedas, which are called 'Bharati', meaning

Ancient seals from the Indus Valley

dedicated to the pursuit of knowledge and wisdom. The ancient name for India is 'Aryavarat', literally meaning 'abode of the Aryans'. Unfortunately, in the Western mind the term Aryan has negative connections with Nazism, but in the Sanskrit language the root 'Arya' means 'worthy, holy, noble'.

Some scholars believe that Aryans invaded India from some other part of Asia or Europe. A German scholar, Max Muller, first proposed the hypothesis that conquering legions of white 'Aryans' invaded North India on horseback around 1500 BCE and ultimately displaced India's Dravidian tribes. This theory of Aryan invasion of India is now strongly contested by many scholars on the grounds that the internal evidence in the scriptures like the Vedas points to India as the immemorial home of the Hindus (Aryas). Furthermore, no one has been able to fix the starting point of this imaginary journey, which some believe to be propaganda by German nationalists, whilst others have alleged that the Aryan-Dravidian split provided a convenient precedent for British subjugation of India.

New astrological and archaeological evidence has come to light which suggests that the people who composed the Vedas called themselves Aryan and were indigenous to India. Evidence to discredit the invasion theory comes from Rig Veda which mentions in verses 6-51-14/15 that the winter solstice occurs when the sun rises in Revati nakshatra (Aries); this was only possible in 6000 BCE, long before the alleged invasion. Carbon dating has confirmed the presence of horses in Gujarat (a state in western India) in 2400 BCE, disproving the hypothesis that Aryans brought the horses to India. NASA satellite photographs prove that the Sarasvati river basin is real, not a myth. Kunal, a new archaeological site in Harayana (another state in India), has revealed the use of writing and silvercraft dating from about 7000 BCE. Finally, six seals excavated from the Indus Valley depict animals and indicate that some form of early Hindu yogic arts existed there more than 4000 years ago.

The Time Line, depicting the chronology of Hindu history, published by the newspaper *Hinduism Today* (December 1994, London edition) and articles in *The Organiser* (Vol. XLV No.25, January 1994, published in New Delhi, India) present the views of contemporary researchers which, in short, conclude that the Aryan invasion of India is at the most an unproven theory and in all likelihood just a myth.

IN THE CLASSROOM

1. Display the map of India and locate the River Indus.
2. Play the word game shown below by changing/adding/deleting one letter at a time to create the words 'India' and 'Hindu', starting from the word 'Sindhu'.

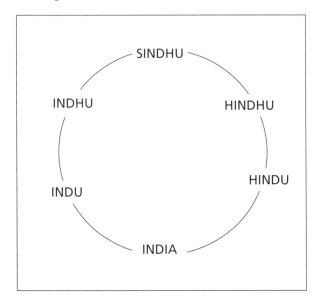

Religious Education and Hinduism

The teacher is an enlightened person and does not suppress the inquisitiveness of the students.
(ATHARVA VEDA, 20-21-2)

The legal position

Religious Education (RE) has been a compulsory element in the schooling of all pupils in county and voluntary schools in the UK since 1944, and this requirement was reinforced by the 1988 Education Reform Act. Under this Act, every Local Education

Authority (LEA) shall have a Standing Advisory Council for Religious Education (SACRE) which shall advise the LEA on matters related to religious education and collective worship. SACREs have the power to require LEAs to set up an Agreed Syllabus Conference. The 1988 Act clearly states in clause 8.3 that all agreed syllabuses adopted after 29th September 1988 must 'reflect the fact that the religious traditions in Great Britain are in the main Christian whilst taking account of the teaching and practices of the other principal religions represented in Great Britain'. Normally, the five other principal religions considered are: Hinduism, Buddhism, Sikhism, Islam and Judaism. At the request of a parent, any child in a maintained school may be excused from receiving Religious Education. Teachers may also withdraw from teaching RE.

Generally, most teachers will find that Hindu parents are willing to work with the new Education Act, provided that the school's policy on RE is explained to them and Hinduism is included in the agreed syllabus..

Hinduism as a subject is so flexible that teachers and headteachers responsible for developing RE lessons and/or collective worship will find it easy to blend Hinduism into their plan of work. The following paragraphs explain how Hinduism can easily meet the proposed aims and objectives of RE.

Aims
There are basically two main aims of RE:
(a) Understanding the teachings and practices of Christianity and other world religions;
(b) Encouraging the development of pupils' own beliefs and values. Educationalists believe that a right balance between the two areas will contribute to the spiritual, moral, cultural and intellectual development of pupils. A teacher can readily fulfil both aims by teaching Hinduism for two main reasons.

First, teaching or discussing other faiths as an educational subject has been an accepted part of the educational process in Hindu tradition. For a Hindu, the God of his neighbour is not false. On the other hand, anyone is free to question and study any part of Hinduism without causing any offence.

Secondly, the moral and spiritual development of a student is considered an essential part of a child's education. In Hindu scriptures, there is a clear distinction between education leading to knowledge about the physical world and education leading to ethical and spiritual knowledge. The former, whilst considered to be essential for professional/vocational qualifications, is considered to be lower knowledge, while the latter is given more importance and called higher knowledge. Many stories can be found in the texts which synthesize materialism and spiritualism.

Concepts
It is expected that the contents of a locally Agreed Syllabus will vary from one LEA to another. However, some common concepts, such as beliefs about God, founders of religions, worship, sacred texts, festivals, traditions and ethical teachings, will be found in most of the syllabuses. None of these is alien to Hinduism. Plenty of suitable material is provided in this book to explain these concepts to pupils of all ages.

Attitudes
Most RE teachers will wish to encourage certain attitudes, including curiosity, self-confidence, open-mindedness, critical ability, respect for the views of others and so on. But the development of such attitudes is worthwhile only if pupils are presented with reliable information, since the analysis of incorrect or incomplete information can lead to false conclusions. The material in this book has been prepared keeping in mind the questioning style of teaching that is likely to take place in the classroom. The rich diversity of Hinduism is proof that there is freedom of thought and belief, and therefore, the teaching of Hinduism will encourage open-mindedness and critical ability.

Questions
Most of the RE syllabuses will be centred on finding answers to some of the questions which are of universal human concern. Responses will be sought to questions like: Who am I? Why am I here? What is the purpose of life? Why did the universe begin? What is a soul? What happens after death? Reflection on such topics will cover aspects of spiritual development by inducing a sense of

awe, wonder and mystery. This form of learning by questioning is found in the famous Hindu texts called Upanishads. In addition, pupils will be encouraged to search for answers to moral and ethical issues faced by modern society. Such an exercise will enhance the value of RE. Material has been provided in Chapter 6 of this book to help teachers find the right interpretation of Hindu views on contemporary issues.

Balance between faiths

There are six principal faiths to be taught. The law specifies that Christianity should be the main faith, but the allocation of time for each faith remains the responsibility of each school. Some teachers may prefer to put more emphasis on the faith shared by the majority of the pupils in the class, but such an approach may not be of much educational benefit. It is recommended that RE is best taught, like other subjects, with total impartiality and equal weight given to all faiths.

If time constraints force teachers to select fewer faiths to study, it will be helpful to note that, based on geographical, historical and philosophical links, the six main faiths can be placed into two categories: the first category comprises Christianity, Islam and Judaism; the second category comprises Hinduism, Buddhism and Sikhism. The links between Hinduism, as the founding faith, and other faiths like Sikhism, Buddhism and Jainism cannot be denied. The material in this book has been prepared so that coverage of Hinduism will provide opportunities to link with other faiths of Indian origin that come within the fold of Hinduism.

Key stages

The teaching material in this book includes suggestions for introducing the topics to various age groups. The age groups are referred to by key stages: KS1 (5–7 years), KS2 (7–11 years), KS3 (11–14 years), KS4 (14–16 years) and KS4+ or Post-16 (16–18 years).

CHAPTER TWO
CONCEPTS, TRUTHS AND VALUES

*T*he study of any religion must start with the development of an understanding of the key concepts, an appreciation of the fundamental truths and an understanding of the important values which are held by the adherents of the faith. In this chapter, information is given on all those principal items which are likely to be covered under this topic in an RE syllabus.

Teachers are warned that instances of factually incorrect information about Hinduism have been found in some RE books. In this book, therefore, the opportunity has been taken to correct this. Attention is drawn particularly to the concept of one God (below); distinction between the words Brahman, Brahmaa and Brahmin (p.34); Yoga and its four main branches (p.44); historical truth about the links with Buddhism, Sikhism and Jainism (p.47); and the correct interpretation of the concept of non-violence (p.53).

Hinduism is not a closed book and does not believe in purging ideas. It has always welcomed, from time to time, new interpretations creating new concepts and values. In case of any conflicting interpretation, it is recommended that the explanations given in this guide should take precedence on the grounds that this book presents living Hinduism. Religion must be explained by the people practising in the faith, not by academics observing the faith from outside.

One God

The fundamental concept in Hinduism is that God is one but as he has many attributes and many functions, he is called by many different names. Hinduism gives freedom to believe that God is formless and also allows him to be worshipped in diverse forms. These forms include complementary attributes of male and female deities, some in human and some even in animal form. These various forms are described on pp.21–26.

Hindu scriptures also point out that whilst God is one, he cannot be fully defined. To define is to limit. Whatever is limitless defies definition. Total knowledge about God is beyond human comprehension, so for this reason Hinduism allows use of various terms, names, symbols and images to allow people to discover God in whichever way they want to. This freedom of thought and form of worship is unique to Hinduism and it is this that has been misunderstood by those authors who claim that Hindus worship many gods. One western author, H. T. Coolebrooke, in *Essays on the Religion and Philosophy of the Hindus*, has warned about this kind of misunderstanding: 'Hindu theology is consistent with monotheism, though it contains seeds of polytheism and idolatry'. He further observes that Hindu texts which declare the unity of Godhead have been misunderstood and he dismisses arguments about multiple Gods as vain disputes probably arising from misinterpretation of Hindu mythology, which personifies the abstract and active powers of the divinity, and ascribes sexes to these mythological beings.

The Vedas, recognized as the supreme scriptural authority of Hindus, declare that:

They call him Indra (the resplendent), Mitra (the surveyor), Varuna (the venerable), Agni (the adorable), and He is the celestial, well-winged Garutmat (the great). The Truth is one but the learned call it by many names as they speak of the adorable as Yama (or-dainer) and Maatarishvana (cosmic breath).

(RIG VEDA, 1-164-46)

The key concept of 'Ekam sat viprah bahuda vadanti', meaning 'the truth is one but the learned call it by many names', has been repeated in many other scriptures.

> *This is the Lord of all, this is the omniscient of all, this is the source and this is the beginning and end of all beings.*
> (MANDUKYA UPANISHAD, 6TH MANTRA)
> *One who rules over every single source*
> (SVETASVATARA UPANISHAD)

IN THE CLASSROOM

The concept of one God having many names can easily be taught at Key Stage 1. A teacher can start by taking an example from daily life, where one person is given different names by different people. For example, ask children how their father or mother might be introduced by other relatives. Their father will be known as husband, son, grandson or uncle by different people. Similarly, God is one but is known by many names.

At Key Stage 2, the discussion can be further extended to show how different names are associated with different qualities and functions. The story of 'The Elephant and Six Blind Men' may be helpful.

At Key Stages 3 and 4, pupils can be asked to find out why Hindus felt it necessary to give so many names to one God, and why this freedom of choice has been mistaken for worship of many gods. The material on forms of God (pp.21–26) and religious symbols (pp.28–31) will be helpful. Vocabulary like Parameshwar, Paramatma, Ishwar, Prabhu, AUM, Brahma and Bhagwan can be introduced to KS4 students. Though these terms have slight differences in meaning, in English they are all roughly translated as god or goddess.

A-Level students may start to discuss the definition of God. Why does Hinduism say that God cannot be fully defined? Do human beings need freedom to worship God in whichever way they want to? What choices are available in Hinduism?

Typical questions/discussion points
1. How many Gods do Hindus worship?
2. Why do Hindus give different names to one God?

The Elephant and Six Blind Men

Once six blind men came across an elephant. They had no idea what an elephant looked like, so they started to explore. The first blind man moved his hand around the elephant's side and exclaimed, 'The elephant is like a big wall.' The second, who was holding one of the legs, disagreed, 'No, it is like a thick pillar.' The third interrupted, 'I think it is like a big flag.' He was near the elephant's big flapping ears. The fourth, who had caught the tail, insisted that it was like a rope. The fifth felt the tusks and announced that it was like a pestle. Finally, the sixth could not remain silent and yelled, 'You are all wrong. The elephant is really a hose-pipe.' He had felt the animal's trunk. They all started to argue about the shape and size of the elephant, until a sighted person came along to show them around it. They then realized the truth.

330 Million Gods

It is often said that Hindus believe in 330 million gods. This is incorrect because in Hindu Dharma there is only one God. The different forms or qualities of the one God are represented by different 'Devatas'. In the Vedas and other Hindu scriptures, 33 different classes or types of qualities (Devatas) are mentioned. In Sanskrit, the word 'koti' is used for class but it is also used to describe a number equal to 10 million. Some scholars have misinterpreted the word 'koti', claiming that there are 330 million gods.

Hindu Values

As explained in the first chapter, Hinduism contains a wide variety of beliefs and religions. While all these different sects and religions are free to select their own mode of worship and their own name of God, amongst this diversity Hindus have some common values and rules of behaviour. This section provides a brief description of common Hindu values.

Respect for mother and mother earth

This earth is my mother and I am the son of this earth.

(ATHARVA VEDA, 12-1-12)

Hindus have raised the status of mother to the level of goddess. The first value that a Hindu child learns from his or her family is respect for the mother. Hindu scriptures such as the Mahabharata state that adoration of one's mother is equal to the adoration of God. In Hindu families, it is a common custom to bow down to touch the feet of elders and parents. This traditional custom emphasizes the value of elders. The concept of Mother Worship is deeply ingrained in the Hindu way of life and the mother is considered to be the first guru of the child.

This concept of respect for the mother is extended to other natural phenomena which provide sustenance for life. For example, the cow, the provider of milk, is considered holy and worshipped as a mother; similarly, the earth and nature are treated with great respect. Chapter 12 of the Atharva Veda is full of prayers for the earth.

The Earth on which grow foodgrains, rice
*   and barley,*
On which live all types of men, our homage be
*   to her,*
Who mellows with the rain.

(ATHARVA VEDA, 12-1-42)

In Hindu tradition, everything good, blissful, protective and evil-destroying is associated with a mother-image.

Respect for father and ancestors

In Hindu families, respect for parents and elders is emphasized. Hindus believe that bringing up children is a religious act – the Dharma of every parent. For children, the parents are therefore divine. Hindus consider

The Story of Shravankumar

Thousands of years ago there was a thick forest on the banks of the River Sarayu which flowed close to the city of Ayodhya. One night the king of Ayodhya, Dasharath, came to the forest to hunt. Dasharath was a good marksman and could shoot in the dark by merely following the direction of the sound made by animals.

Dasharath waited under a tree. He heard a gurgling sound. Thinking that an animal had come to drink from the river he shot an arrow in the direction of the sound. A moment later there came the cry of a human being. The anxious king ran to the place and found a youth writhing in pain on the bank of the river. The arrow was stuck in the youth's heart.

The youth's name was Shravankumar. He was a caring person and was dedicated to his parents, who were old and blind. It was their wish to visit holy places in their last days. Shravan carried them from shrine to shrine in two baskets which hung from a sling. While on their pilgrimage the three had came to the banks of the River Saryu for a short rest and a drink of water.

With difficulty Shravan told the king about his parents who were waiting for him not far from the river. He requested the king to take the pot of water to them and then he died. Dasharath carried the pot of water to Shravan's parents. They said, 'Son, why are you late? Where did you go?' Dasharath did not reply. Then the mother asked, 'Why don't you speak? What is wrong?'

With tears in his eyes Dasharath told them about their son's death. He was willing to take them to his palace and look after them. But the old people were not interested in his offer. They only cried for their son. The mother dashed the pot of water to the ground. Then she cursed the king, 'One day you too shall lose a son and die crying for him.'

Many years later, Dasharath's son Rama had to go into exile for fourteen years. The pain of separation from his son was so great that it lead to Dasharath's death. His only fault was that he had unintentionally prevented a son from serving his parents.

the service of one's parents to be a pious and divine duty and preventing anyone carrying out such a duty is considered to be a sinful act. The story of Shravankumar, who was dedicated to serve his parents, is often recited.

Respect for teachers

There is a great guru and shishya (pupil) tradition in Hinduism. The Hindu scriptures say that, like parents, the teacher is also worthy of worship. A guru is not just a teacher. A true guru is believed to be a divine gift to man because such a guru does not only impart education but also gives inspiration and passes on experience and knowledge. There are stories describing how Shri Krishna and Shri Rama showed total obedience towards their respective gurus. For a Hindu, a guru can be a person, a symbol or a book. For example, in the Sikh faith, the holy book 'Granth Sahib' is treated as the Eleventh Guru. Millions of Hindus belonging to the organiz-ation called the Rashtriya Swayamsevak Sangh (RSS) in India, known to be the largest volunteer group in the world, consider the Saffron Flag (Bhagwa Dhwaj) as their guru. Further discussion on gurus and disciples is given on pp.31–33.

Truth

Hindu scriptures state: 'Truth alone triumphs' (Satyameva Jayate). This saying also appears in the national emblem of India. The story of King Harishchandra illustrates the value of following the truth irrespective of any obstacles and difficulties.

Righteous living

In Chapter 1 it was explained that 'Hinduism' is the term often used for 'Hindu Dharma', and one of the meanings of the term 'Dharma' is righteousness. Therefore, righteous living is an

The Story of Muni Sandipani

In ancient days sages in India built their hermitages far from towns and cities. Sage Sandipani ran a gurukula (residential school) in his ashram. Sandipani was a very well-known teacher who gave equal opportunity to all, whether a pupil was the son of a king or a pauper. All pupils had to share the work in running the school. They were required to take part in the religious ceremony, collect firewood, sweep the ashram, cook and wash, look after the cows and work in the gardens and orchards. They obeyed their guru, who acted as their guardian, and the teachers.

One of the students of Sandipani was a prince called Krishna, son of Vasudev, who studied with another student, Sudama, the son of a poor Brahmin. A great friendship grew up between Sudama and Krishna. They went about together and did their work jointly.

One day, when Sandipani was away, his wife, who also lived in the ashram, ordered Krishna and Sudama to bring firewood from the forest. So, with axes in their hands, they set off. They had to go deep into the forest to find suitable wood but just when they were about to bundle it, there was a sudden storm. The sky became dark and heavy rain began to fall and soon the young boys lost their way.

When the guru returned to the ashram he noticed that Krishna and Sudama were missing. Accompanied by older students, with torches in their hands, he went in search of Krishna and Sudama. The party eventually found the two boys shivering and wet to the skin. The guru praised them for the courage and the love they had shown towards him and the school.

essential part of Hindu values and way of life. The Hindu scriptures say: 'If you protect right-eousness, the righteousness will protect you.'

The story of a young boy named Magha is often used to illustrate this value (see p.18).

(see p.18)

The Story of King Harishchandra

Many thousands of years ago, King Harishchandra lived in Ayodhya, a city in northern India. He was a good king and always spoke the truth. He would never break his promise.

The king's fame as a ruler spread far and wide. In those days, there lived a sage whose name was Vishwamitra. He heard of the king's truthful nature and decided to test him. Vishwamitra arrived at the court of the king. When the king enquired if he needed any help, the sage asked, 'Will you give me whatever I ask?' The king said, 'Yes'. Then the sage asked him for his entire kingdom.

Harishchandra had never gone back on his word, so he gave his whole kingdom to the sage. The sage demanded, in addition to the kingdom, his dakshina (a gift given to a holy person). Harishchandra had nothing left now, so he asked the sage for some time in which he could find the dakshina. Then, Harishchandra, his queen Taramati and his son Rohitaswa took off their royal robes, dressed themselves as ordinary people and went to look for work.

After much searching Taramati found a job as a maid in the house of a Brahmin. Rohitaswa stayed with her, but Harishchandra had to go away. Eventually he became a guard of a crematorium where he earned a small sum of money cremating dead bodies. Whatever wages Harishchandra received were given to Vishwamitra as part payment of his dakshina.

One day Rohitaswa was bitten by a snake. When Taramati saw her son she thought he was dead and with great sadness took his body to be cremated. There she recognized that the keeper of the burial ground was none other than her own husband. She burst out crying, 'Has Dharma vanished from the world? Have our prayers been in vain? Look at us, we are reduced to such a pitiable plight.' But there was no time for sentiment. Harishchandra had a duty to perform and demanded the fee for cremation. Taramati had no money and paid the fee by giving him a part of the funeral cloth. As they prepared a funeral pyre for their son, they decided to end their lives. Then a surprising thing happened. Vishwamitra appeared at the crematorium. He had witnessed all that had happened and he was impressed by the patience, honesty and dutiful way in which Harishchandra and Taramati conducted themselves. Appearing before Harishchandra, he said, 'I took your kingdom because I wanted to test you. You have proved to me that you are the most truthful king on the earth. As I am pleased with you, I hand back the kingdom of Ayodhya.' The sage applied some medicine on Rohitaswa's wound and the boy became well again.

Harishchandra returned to Ayodhya with his family. His son became king and once again the kingdom was ruled with justice, wisdom and truthfulness.

(Source: Markandeya Purana)

The Story of Magha and the Elephant

The king of Magadha was always indulging in pleasures. He gave no attention to the administration of the country. He was interested only in the amount of money that came into his treasury. The civil servants took advantage of the situation and stooped to corruption and bribery. The people too became indolent and spent most of their time in gambling and drinking.

There lived in one of the districts in Magadha a youth whose name was Magha. He was a kind, simple fellow who derived great pleasure from giving service to his people. He swept the roads and pathways and saw to the needs of the sick. If a bullock cart got stuck in a ditch he pushed it out. If he saw a dead animal he made suitable arrangements for its disposal.

The people made fun of Magha and called him a fool. They often bullied and taunted him. But Magha, undaunted, continued with his humanitarian work and gradually the public's opinion of him changed. The young people became impressed by his service and one by one they came to give him assistance. Magha formed a society and the youths became its members. In the name of the society they began to give assistance wherever it was required. Magha made five rules to be observed by the members of his society. These were:

1. There must be no violence.
2. No one must steal.
3. No one must tell lies.
4. Women should be respected.
5. No one should drink alcohol.

The whole district began to be impressed by the good work of Magha and his society. Slowly the people started to reform. They no longer fought or stole and stopped drinking. But Magha's reforms did not please the governor of the district: his revenue was affected because fewer fines were paid. The governor went to the king and complained that Magha was a traitor who incited the people not to pay taxes. The treasury had become empty.

On hearing the complaint, the king became angry. He ordered that Magha and his friends be trampled by an elephant. Magha remained calm and silent. He had faith in truth and righteousness, and he addressed his friends thus: 'With firm conviction and devotion we have done our work. We have to die one day. Therefore all of you get ready to receive cheerfully the punishment imposed by the king. Bear no malice or hatred against the king or the elephant.'

Magha and five of his companions were made to lie on the ground. The soldiers tried their best to drive the elephant over the body of Magha and his companions but the elephant would not move forward. It came as far as Magha and stopped. The king was astonished. This event demonstrated the strength and value of righteous conduct.

(Source: Jaatak Kathas)

Forgiveness and fearlessness
There are numerous stories in Hindu scriptures which convey the message that the development of qualities like non-violence and forgiveness require fearlessness and strength, as shown by Swami Dayananda.

The Story of Bold Swami Dayananda

Swami Dayananda was a sanyasi who dressed in orange robes. He was a great reformer and the founder of Arya Samaj (one of the modern Hindu reformist movements). He was also an intellectual and spiritual giant and he possessed an athletic body. He was fearless and he felt for the poor. He wanted to reform Hindu society through the strength-giving and holistic message of the Vedas. In his discourses he propounded his views about education of women, abolition of child marriage, eradication of untouchability and similar prevalent dogmas that weakened the social fabric.

Some seemed to understand his teaching, but there were many who were angered by it. They threatened to harm him, but the Swami was afraid of no one.

Once, during one of his discourses, a misguided influential man called Karansingh was present in the crowd and he approached Swami Dayanand in anger. Swami Dayanand greeted him and asked him to be seated, but the man demanded, 'Why do you speak ill about our customs and traditions?' Dayanand replied, 'I do not speak ill about our true and enlightened customs and traditions, I try to reform only the degenerated and perverted ones among them.' The man retorted, 'We do not accept your interpretation of these things.' Swami replied, 'You might go ahead with your ill-conceived notions, but I have to do my social and spiritual duty.'

Dayanand's words annoyed the man even more. From his waist he drew a sword and rushed at the Swami. Dayanand quickly grabbed Karansingh's arm and wrenched the sword from it. He broke it by pressing its point into the ground. The man felt ashamed and hurriedly left the place. Swami Dayanand's friends asked him to charge the man. But Dayanand said, 'Even though the man forgot the duty of a warrior, how can I forget the duty of a Swami? A Swami does not harm anybody. When it comes to actions or Dharma, he cannot forget truth, even if the king gets annoyed. Besides God, he fears no one.' Swami Dayanand was a fearless man.

Honesty

Here is a short story from the Upanishads which illustrates the value of honesty.

In Search of Wealth

In the past, students went to live with their master to gain education. Such places were called gurukuls. In one gurukul, the master wanted to test his students, so he gathered them around and said, 'I need some money urgently. Can you go and bring some from your family? But please be careful. I do not want anyone to know about this, so only bring the money when no one is looking.'

All the students went home and came back next morning with some money, except for one boy. 'Why have you come empty-handed? Couldn't you pick up some of your parents' money when no one was looking?' enquired the master. The boy replied that in spite of many attempts he kept on failing. 'Why?' questioned the master. 'Surely there must have been a moment when no one was looking?' 'Yes, master,' replied the boy, 'I did come across many chances when no one else was looking, but I always found myself looking at my own wrong deeds.' The master then declared that he was the only student who had gained any real education because he knew the value of honesty.

Service to mankind

Hindus consider that service to others is a virtue; giving pain to others is a sin. Giving and sharing with others is one of the values preached relentlessly in Hindu scriptures.

The Story of a Bhikhuni and Lord Buddha

Once upon a time the village of Shravasti was stricken by drought. No rain fell and all the crops failed. Because of the shortage of food, the poor began to die. People started to hoard food and no one gave to charity. Gautama Buddha could not bear to see the suffering, so he gathered the people of Shravasti together. He asked, 'Who will take the responsibility of feeding the hungry?' The wealthy merchants and prosperous people just found one excuse or another. In the end, one of the women, a bhikhuni (one who begs for a living) named Supriya, came forward. She said, 'O Lord, with your blessings, I shall take upon myself the task of feeding the hungry.' Everyone was amazed. How could a beggar feed the hungry! Supriya explained her plan: 'I will come with my begging bowl to every household. If each one of you gives me a small amount, I shall have enough to feed all the hungry.' By her action Supriya saved the lives of many people by encouraging them to learn to share.

Non-violence

Hindu scriptures preach the value of non-violence. Hindus believe that all life is sacred, to be loved and revered, and therefore they practise non-violence. Many Hindus are vegetarians because they believe that the lives of animals should also be protected. More information about the concept of non-violence is given on p.53. The following story illustrates how one has to be fearless in order to be non-violent.

Gautama Buddha

Mahavira Jain

Preachers of non-violence:

The Story of Gautama Buddha and Robber Angulimal

A robber named Angulimal lived in a forest just beyond the borders of Shravasti. Angulimal not only robbed people but also murdered them, then he cut off the fingers (anguli) of his victim and made a garland (mala) of them for himself. This is how he got his name, Angulimal. People shivered at the mention of his name and everyone moved away from the neighbourhood.

One day Gautama Buddha went through the forest. When Angulimal saw the Buddha, he lifted his axe and ran towards him. 'If you proceed further I shall kill you,' he said. But Buddha, cool and collected, continued to walk. Angulimal threatened again and sprang forward to attack. Buddha showed no signs of fear. The robber held back and began to think, 'No one ever dared pass this way alone and unarmed. What kind of man is this who comes alone and without a weapon? At sight of me people tremble with fear and fall at my feet and beg for mercy. This monk shows no sign of fear!'

Buddha, with his serene and peaceful look, just smiled at Angulimal. And as Angulimal looked into the monk's eyes he became overpowered by the spiritual strength in them. Buddha created a great impression on the robber. He was transformed and all his evil desires and habits left him. He lay down his axe and fell at the Buddha's feet and asked for forgiveness. Buddha lifted Angulimal up and embraced him. At his request, Buddha accepted Angulimal as his disciple. From that time Angulimal accepted the teaching of non-violence and never again harmed anyone for his own selfish purposes.

IN THE CLASSROOM

Use the stories to introduce the Hindu values described in this section. Talk about the values that are important in the pupils' own homes. How do parents like them to behave? What are they expected to do/not do, especially in relation to other people? How is respect shown to others and how is respect gained from others? How do they show respect towards their parents, teachers and classmates? Tackle the question about the need to speak the truth. Is it wrong to tell lies?

Typical questions/discussion points
1. What does it feel like when people behave badly towards us?
2. What qualities do you need to have to forgive others?
3. Why do Hindus respect the earth and the cow as mother figures?

Forms of God

Hindus are not polytheistic. The different gods and goddesses are mere representations of the powers and functions of the one Supreme God in this manifested world. Hindus believe that God can be worshipped in diverse forms or in his formless state. There is, therefore, a general misunderstanding that Hindus have innumerable gods and goddesses. The rationale for the various forms and representations of the one God is as follows:

The mind of man is in a chaotic state and helplessly runs in all directions seeking fulfilment of all its desires. It thus becomes agitated, rendering the mind unfit for meditation (see pp.114–117), an important path to self-realization. The great Hindu sages and seers saw divinity in everything in this world and set out in a scientific, logical and practical manner, a way of life to achieve union with God. Hinduism has thoughtfully brought in images, rituals, festivals and ceremonies so that the mind is constantly reminded of the Supreme Being even when engaged in the pursuit of desired material objects. There are numerous gods covering the entire sphere of human activities, representing in image or symbolic form the attributes of the one God.

Hindu scriptures do not recommend the

worship of an image as God and clearly state that idols (gods or goddesses) are not a substitute for God, but only a means of making the mind think about God. Mental worship of the formless God (see p.116) is far superior to worship of images, but all worship starts with images. Hindus have many forms of God to encompass the wide variety of pursuits and mental aptitudes of human beings. Even though God is timeless, formless (nirakar), all-pervading, all-knowing and omnipresent (and therefore difficult to comprehend) there is absolutely nothing wrong with worshipping him in a more 'human' form. So what are these various forms of God in Hinduism, which are represented by idols?

Various gods and goddesses

Trimurti

The Supreme Being controls the entire universe through the three major qualities represented in the Trimurti of Brahmaa (creator or generator), Vishnu (preserver or operator) and Shiva (destroyer). The word 'God' incorporates these three attributes. These powers coexist and operate simultaneously in an interconnected manner: they are inseparable. In addition, these forms include complementary male (creation) and female (strength) attributes.

Ganesh

is pictured as having a human form with an elephant head; he has a large stomach and there are food and a rat at his feet. This mystical form conveys a message. The elephant head indicates the gaining of knowledge through listening (ears) and reflection (large head). The two tusks, one perfectly shaped and the other broken, represent perfection and imperfection in the physical world. The trunk portrays physical and mental strength, and the intellect which is to be used between the pair of opposites (perfect and imperfect). The large stomach depicts the ability to 'digest' whatever experiences life brings; the rat and the food denote desires and wealth, both of which are under his control (at his feet). Ganesh is usually shown with one leg on the ground and the other leg folded in a meditative pose, symbolizing a balance between practical life and spiritual life. In one hand he is shown carrying a noose and in the other an 'ankusha' which is a sharp iron hook used by a rider to control an elephant. The noose symbolizes the trap of desires and the 'ankusha' is a reminder that the painful hook of stern self-control is needed to control desires.

'Ganesh' is a combination of two words – 'Gana', meaning people, and 'Isha', meaning god. All the symbols mentioned above represent the qualities of a good and strong leader. For this reason Ganesh has great spiritual significance for Hindus; he is considered to be a remover of obstacles and represents wisdom and perfection. That is why many Hindus worship Ganesh before embarking upon a new business or settling in a new home. Teachers are advised not to use the term 'elephant God' to describe Ganesh.

Trimurti – the Hindu Trinity of Brahmaa, Vishnu and Mahesh (Shiva)

Ganesh's Hunger

In Hindu mythology, Kubera, the god of wealth, invited Ganesh for dinner at his palace. Ganesh ate all the food that was prepared for the entire gathering. He was still hungry, so he started to eat the decorations. Then his father, Lord Shiva, offered Ganesh a handful of roasted rice which immediately satisfied his hunger.

This story about Ganesh illustrates the Hindu teaching that human beings cannot achieve happiness and fulfilment by being greedy and consuming material goods (represented by Kubera's feast). Fulfilment and real peace are attained by consuming one's own desires (represented by the roasted rice).

Shiva

Shiva, also known as Mahesh, is seen in many forms. The two most popular forms are Yogiraj and Nataraj. Shiva is blue in complexion, conveying infinite stature: blue is associated with immeasurable entities such as sky or ocean. He has a snake round his neck, representing 'Kundalini shakti' (evolutionary power) within the human body. As a Yogiraj (king of Yoga) he sits in a meditative pose with his eyes half-closed, indicating peace and perfect inner harmony. As Nataraj (king of dance) he stands in the pose of the endless cosmic dance.

Nataraj has four hands – one holding a drum to announce the 'big bang' at the beginning of the universe, the second holding a flame of destruction, the third raised in blessing, and the fourth pointing to the uplifted foot to show how to rise above ignorance. The diminutive figure of man under the second foot represents ignorance. The whole figure of Nataraj, with his flowing hair, represents movement within a circle of fire. The circle shows that the universe is without a beginning (anadi) and without an end (anant). He is fulfilling both roles: he is benefactor and he is destroyer. And the energy (shakti) with which he performs these functions is like fire. The fire can destroy but it is also essential for sustaining life. This flame of fire is also represented by another symbol called the 'Shivalinga' which looks like a lamp with a flame (see p.31).

Shiva as Yogiraj

Shiva as Nataraj

Saraswati

Saraswati is eternally young, tall, fair-skinned and has four arms. She sits elegantly on a lotus flower, playing a stringed instrument known as a 'veena' which some say she invented herself. In her other right hand she holds a book of palm leaves, indicating her love of learning and power of knowledge. It is believed that she is mother of the Sanskrit language and the Devanagri script in which Sanskrit, Hindi and

Lakshmi, the power of wealth

a young and beautiful goddess, decorated with jewels and garments. She is often depicted offering gold coins to indicate the power of wealth which is needed by Vishnu who pervades and maintains the universe.

Saraswati, the power of knowledge

other Indian languages are written. She is also the patroness of arts, sciences and speech. In short, Saraswati represents the power of knowledge which accompanies Brahmaa who carries out the creative function of God.

Lakshmi

According to Hindu mythology, whenever Vishnu was born as a man (see p.27), Lakshmi appeared as his human wife. When Vishnu was born as the dwarf Vaman, she was born as Kamla; when he was Parsurama, she was his wife Dharni; when he was Ram, she was Sita; when he was Krishna, she was Rukmani. In short, Vishnu is the male in everything and Lakshmi the universal female. She is shown as

Rama

In the life of Rama each facet of the human personality is projected to absolute perfection. The various roles that he played during his life were of idealistic perfection and these act as a template for millions of Hindus in their day-to-day existence. To many Hindus, Rama is a great hero whom they admire and try to emulate, whilst others believe that he was an incarnation of Vishnu (see pp.26–28) and worship him as God. He was the perfect son, an ideal king, a true husband, a real friend, a devoted brother and a brave warrior who fought against injustice. He epitomized absolute truth, humility and caring for others, all of which prevailed in his kingdom (see stories from the Ramayana on pp.134–138). His ideal kingdom is known as 'Rama Rajya'.

Krishna

Krishna is another great hero for all Hindus and many believe that he was an incarnation of Vishnu. Krishna is best known for his representation of the entire philosophy of life in the Gita (see pp.132–134). Every aspect of Krishna's life and deeds have been symbolized to indicate a sublime truth. There are many stories (see pp.143–146) which narrate how Krishna helped the poor and the oppressed by fighting for truth and justice. To Hindus, he represents the sum of all the qualities needed to live an ideal and practical life. He is usually shown standing with a flute in his hand, accompanied by his devotee, Radha. The affinity between Radha and Krishna is not a husband–wife relationship but a spiritual relationship between a devotee and God.

Durga

Durga is a female manifestation representing the power (shakti) of God behind destruction and creation. She is acknowledged as the energy and power of nature. She is also known by her other names such as Devi, Kaali, Bhawani, Ambika and Parvati. Durga is one of her terrifying forms for she rides a lion. Durga has eight arms holding eight symbols of power and might. (Many gods and goddesses have an excess of arms and heads.) The eight arms represent health, education, wealth, organization, unity, fame, courage and truth. The weapons in her hands are for the destruction of evil and the protection of good, represented by the lotus flower. This form therefore depicts the enormity of the power of God, by which the entire universe is sustained.

Hanuman

This god is shown in the form of a monkey and represents the Hindu concept that animals are also a creation of God and have a soul (Atma). Valmiki Ramayana describes Hanuman not as a monkey but as the son of the wind-god, Vaayu, belonging to the Vaanar tribe. He was a celibate Brahmin and a Yogi who had mastered the Vedas and had acquired yogic powers which he used when confronting Ravana. He was the chief minister of the Vaanar king Sugreeva and communicated in Sanskrit. Hanuman's attributes are his enormous strength, valour and complete devotion to Rama as his true disciple. Many Hindus revere Hanuman as a symbol of strength and energy. His devotees recite his prayer, called 'Hanuman Chalisa', to fight fear

and weakness. Teachers and pupils are advised not to use the term 'monkey god' to describe Hanuman since this is offensive to Hindus.

IN THE CLASSROOM

The Hindu concept is that God is one and formless, but ordinary humans cannot conceptualize this; hence God is represented in different forms. The form that is worshipped depends on the person's leanings and beliefs. The Hindu concept that worship of God in any form will lead to the one God can be introduced by using one of the following examples:

1. **The bicycle wheel** God is like the hub of a bicycle wheel, with the spokes running into the hub from all directions. In the same way, it does not matter which spoke (god or goddess) you follow or pray to since it will lead to the centre. What is necessary is to practise your faith and belief with honesty and sincerity so that it will eventually lead to the centre or hub or God.

2. **The mother** A son looks to her as his beloved mother, the husband looks on her as a partner/loving wife, whilst her parents see her as a daughter. There is only one person but they are all seeing her from different angles. All three are right in seeing her differently although there is only one person. Similarly, Hindus believe that God is one but can be worshipped in many different forms. In the Gita, Shri Krishna says: 'In whatever form you worship me you will reach me; of that there is no doubt.'

3. **Story: The Elephant and Six Blind Men** Use the story on p.14. It illustrates the Hindu view that, although possessing many names, God is only one.

4. **Electrical energy** People are at different stages of understanding the truth and God. For an ordinary person it is sometimes difficult to realize that there is only one God. The example of electrical energy can be used in this respect. Electrical energy is explained by a scientist by reference to the electron theory; a student perceives it as energy in the form of a

current that flows through a wire like water; a simple person's concept is that light is produced from a bulb when an electric switch is turned on. The electrical energy is the same but all three understand it in three different ways even though all experience the same result when they use it.

At KS3 and KS4, teachers may like to extend the discussion to consider questions which arise from the practice of worshipping many different forms of God.

(a) Superiority of one God over another
Though it is all right to worship many gods, devotees need to guard against the belief that one form of God is superior to another or that one's personal god is greater than the neighbour's god. In devotion to God, one is supposed to overcome one's ego. If ego is developed by fighting for one's god then the whole basis of Hinduism is totally lost. Everyone can have a personal god but they should try to see their personal god in all forms of God. By doing so, they will be able to establish the oneness of God as well as eradicate the ego and a lot of the inter-religious strife that exists in the world today.

(b) How do you explain the 330 million gods of Hinduism?
Many books wrongly assert that Hindus believe in 330 million gods. This has arisen from the misinterpretation of the Sanskrit word 'koti'. See the explanation on p.14.

Typical questions/discussion points
1. Why do Hindus have many gods and goddesses?
2. Is there just one God for all living creatures, including man?

Reincarnation, Avatar and Vibhuti

The doctrine that God can be incarnated in human form is found in most of the principal historic expositions of the Perennial Philosophy – in Hinduism, in Mahayana Buddhism, in Christianity and in Mohammadanism of the Sufis ... every human being can thus become an Avatar by adoption.

(ALDOUS HUXLEY, THE PERENNIAL PHILOSOPHY)

Reincarnation
Hindus believe that life does not end with death. What perishes is the body; the soul is immortal and eternal. When the body dies the soul assumes a new body in order to experience the fruits of our good and bad actions in the previous life. This doctrine is therefore an extension of the well-known principle 'As you sow, so shall you reap'. You cannot reap a sweet mango if you sow cherry, and vice versa. Everyone must experience the consequences of their actions sooner or later, but it is quite possible that one may not be able to do so in the same life. Rebirth or reincarnation of a soul is therefore quite logical. This theory of 'Karma' (i.e. action) and rebirth/reincarnation fits in well with the doctrine of the immortality of the soul (see further discussion on pp.35–37).

Under the law of Karma, the soul is said to be in bondage and the final goal of human life is the liberation of the soul from this bondage. This is possible when a person carries out his or her dutiful actions without expecting rewards. When the soul is free from bondage it goes back to its original pure state and enjoys eternal divine bliss. It has to suffer no further birth or reincarnation. This is the state of 'Moksha', meaning liberation, salvation or emancipation and is the final goal of human life.

Avatar
Many Hindus believe in the idea of a personal God. The origin of this concept is obscure but it became popular because people find it easier to love a personal God who they believe can descend to earth in human or animal form to help them. This concept of 'divine incarnation' is unique to Hinduism. God loves his devotees and whenever they are in distress or have problems, he appears in order to protect them. In other words, whenever there is a decline in 'righteousness', God manifests himself and restores the moral code or 'spiritual balance' or 'Dharma'. This is a divine dispensation and an assurance to devotees that they will never be deserted. Such divine incarnation is called an 'Avatar'.

There are two main beliefs about Avatars in Hinduism. One is that the supreme power descends to the earth in any life-form wherever and whenever necessary; the other states that Avatars do not fall from heaven but are men living on the earth, in whose hearts the urge to meet challenges is so great that they revolutionize and reform society to establish a world of new values.

There are innumerable traditional stories about Avatars in the past, and some Hindus hold the belief that there will be an avatar in the future as well. Each incarnation has a message. Teachers may find it useful to explore some of the following incarnation stories.

Incarnations of the god Vishnu

Vishnu is the name given to the protector and sustainer of the universe. There are many explanations for the ten avatars of Vishnu but broadly accepted one is that these avatars depict evolution of life on earth. Starting from the animal form of fish, the first six avatars can be compared to Darwin's theory of evolution. The later avatars of Vishnu as Rama, Krishna and Buddha can be seen as the continuous process of the mental, moral, intellectual and spiritual development of humanity. The tenth avatar, Kalki, is meant to mark the end of the present cycle of creation (see Kaliyuga p.122).

Incarnations of Buddha

Gautam, the Buddha, did not himself claim to be an innovator or the founder of a religion.

There were other teachers who are also believed to be incarnations of the Buddha. Commonly accepted numbers vary from seven (in the Mahapadana text) to twenty-five (in the Pali text). Many Hindus believe that Buddha was an incarnation of Vishnu.

Incarnations of Jain Tirthankaras

In accordance with the scriptures of Jain Darshan, Bhagwan Mahavira was the 24th Tirthankara who rejuvenated and propounded Jain tradition. Tirthankaras or Jinas were those who succeeded in going across the waters of transmigration to attain Nirvana - eternal salvation and peace. According to Jainism, a set of twenty-four Tirthankaras appear in each half of a time cycle. In the present cycle, Rishabhnath (Rishabhdev), the father of King Bharat (see p.9), was the first Tirthankara, and Mahavira was the last Tirthankara. The twenty-second Tirthanakara was Parshwanath who was related to Shri Krishna.

It is worthwhile to note that the twenty-four Jain Tirthankaras can be compared with the twenty-five incarnations of Buddha in Pali texts and the twenty-two Avatars mentioned in Bhagvata Purana.

Vibhuti

Hindus believe that God is omnipresent and the same spirit pervades everywhere. Just as

THE FIRST SIX INCARNATIONS OF VISHNU	DARWIN'S THEORY OF EVOLUTION
Matsya (Fish)	Life starts in water (600 million – 400 million years ago).
Kurma (Tortoise)	The first amphibians emerge (100 million years ago).
Varaha (Boar)	The first mammals evolve (60 million years ago).
Narasinha (half man–half lion)	Our earliest ancestors, half man–half animal appear (30 million years ago).
Vamana (short man)	Homo Erectus. Upright, yet short and weaponless (5 million – 2 million years ago).
Parashuram (Parashu = axe, Rama = name of God)	Bronze Age; the coming of Ramapithecus; development of first weapons such as the axe. Homo Sapiens (350,000 – 100,000 years ago).

thread is common to all fabric or mud is common to all earthen pots, so the same universal spirit abides in all beings. One concept is that divine glory is manifested more prominently in certain beings or objects which are called 'vibhutis'.

Electricity is energy which is invisible but whose presence can be experienced through innumerable appliances such as bulbs, fans, motors and so on. Similarly, the presence of God as universal spirit can be noticeably experienced in certain objects. Even inanimate objects may be significant bearers of the spirit. A mighty ocean, a lofty mountain, an immensely radiant star like the sun, for example, are all vibhutis. They are not Avatars for an Avatar is ever conscious of his own divine nature, whereas a vibhuti is not. The sages, saints and prophets are all examples of a greater divine presence, yet they are not considered to be Avatars.

In the tenth chapter of the Bhagavad Gita, Shri Krishna has named seventy-five examples of his vibhutis. Each one represents one of the divine attributes. A lion among the animals, an elephant named 'Airavat' among the elephants, 'Kamdhenu' (wish-fulfilling) among the cows, 'A' in the alphabets, 'thunderbolt' among the weapons – these are some of the prominent vibhutis.

IN THE CLASSROOM

The material presented in this section is not suitable for Key Stage 1 pupils. In KS2, the concept of soul can be introduced through a discussion about the difference between living and non-living things. Living (animate) things can act (move, eat, drink, etc.) as they wish, while non-living (inanimate) objects have no will of their own. The discussion can be extended to human beings. The human body is made up of bones, flesh, blood, skin and so on, and the body is alive as long as the soul is in the body. The joining of soul and body is called birth and the departure of the soul from the body is called death.

In KS3, the concept of rebirth or reincarnation can be introduced by pointing out that the soul never dies. It simply leaves one body at death and enters a new body at rebirth. The discussion can be extended to

consider who controls this cycle of birth and death. The law of Karma and the idea of God as the controller can be introduced at this stage. Pupils can then look at the idea that the results of all deeds done in this life, whether good or bad, have to be faced sooner or later.

In KS4, the manifestation of the Supreme in earthly form, whether human or any other form, can be discussed. Can God be seen? If God cannot be seen, can his presence or message be felt through other means? The stories of divine incarnation in Hindu mythology can be studied and their role as a means of explaining the mystery of God can be appreciated by relating them to known scientific theories. The explanation of the first six avatars of Vishnu can be given as an example.

Typical questions/discussion points
1. What is the difference between living and non-living things?
2. According to Hindu belief, what happens to the human body and the soul at the time of death?
3. What is reincarnation?
4. What is an Avatar? Do all Hindus believe in Avatars?
5. Why do Hindus believe in the cycle of birth and death? Who controls it?
6. What feelings do you have when you witness a thunderstorm or look at a beautiful flower/view?
7. In what way can people 'see' God in nature?

Religious Symbols

Symbolism is used extensively in Hinduism as a means of understanding and describing concepts like God (p.21), Self (p.35) and Creation (p.39). The underlying principles behind these concepts are very abstract and are not easy to grasp, which is why in Hinduism abstract ideas have been translated into more tangible and concrete symbols. For example, Hindus consider the Almighty God as the ultimate, which cannot be perceived through the sense organs, is not an emotion to be felt by the mind and is not a concept to be comprehended by the intellect. God is an unknown 'ideal', so a symbol or an 'idol' is often used to reach or appreciate that 'unknown' ideal. An idol leads the worshipper to the ideal.

There are literally hundreds of symbols portraying various religious concepts and beliefs. Sacred symbols embody the unspoken intuition of the spirit and God himself. Hindu symbols adorn India's art, architecture and iconography. In some instances symbols have emerged as objects of prayer, as in the temple where the deities and their individual parts of the body are symbolic representations of the supreme power and attributes. In the following sections, details of some of the important Hindu religious symbols are described. These can be categorized as follows:

(a) symbols representing philosophical principles, e.g. AUM and Swastika;
(b) symbols used in rituals, e.g. Shankha (conch shell);
(c) symbols as part of social tradition, e.g. Namaste.

AUM (OM)

This is a symbol of the Supreme God. It is considered to be the most powerful word-symbol for use in prayers and meditation. An idol can be solid (e.g. a stone image in a temple; see p.94) or subtle (e.g. fire; see p.86). Sound is the subtlest of all idols and of all sounds. AUM is the most potent and the most natural. Hindus believe that it was the first sound produced at the creation of the universe, the Big Bang. As such, everything emanates from this and represents the initial eternal 'energy' released at the time of the Big Bang. The sacred syllable AUM is the name of God. It is uttered at the beginning and the end of most Hindu prayers. It is considered to be the essence of the Hindu scriptures and also represents the concept of one god, 'Ek Omkar', in Sikhism. Many explanations have been given for this sacred symbol; the main facts are given below:

1. The proper way of writing Om (monosyllabic) is AUM (three syllables). The latter symbolizes the Trinity representing the three functions of God: generation, preservation and destruction. 'A' is the sound emanating from the base of the throat, 'U' is produced by the impulse rolling forward in

The sacred symbol of AUM (Om)

the mouth and 'M' is produced by closing the lips. There is no sound beyond these two extremes. So 'AUM' covers the full range of sounds and the entire phenomenon of sound.

2. AUM stands for pure consciousness or reality and pervades all states of mind: waking, dreaming and deep sleep. It is called 'pranava', which means something that pervades life or runs through 'prana' (breath).

3. AUM represents the omniscient, omnipotent and omnipresent qualities of God. It is the most revered name of God mentioned in the Vedas, believed to be the oldest scriptures of the oldest religious tradition, but is also found in other faith traditions.

4. The first sound of the word AUM is 'A' which occupies a very prominent place in all languages.

5. Hindus believe that AUM is the highest mantra. The chanting of AUM has an extraordinary effect on the human mind. It creates harmony, peace and bliss by producing vibrations which awaken dormant vital centres within the body.

6. AUM is the common religious symbol among all the sects of Hinduism and is written in many different forms in various Hindu languages. The most popular is the symbol ॐ The shape of 3 represents the Trinity; the ~ accompanying the 3 is the symbol of consciousness. On top is the half moon and the dot. The dot represents the momentary silence between two successive chants. This can be interpreted as AUM having five syllables.

Swastika

Swastika is a symbol of auspiciousness. It represents the world-wheel (life-cycle) or the eternally changing world around a fixed, unchanging centre or God. The fragmentation that occurred at the Big Bang, scattering energy in all directions, appears like the figure of Swastika. It creates an impression of perpetual motion and symbolizes welfare. The right-angled arms of this ancient sun sign denote the indirect way that divinity is apprehended. The four limbs represent:

- Four Directions – space
- Four Vedas – knowledge (see p.130)
- Four Purusharthas – objectives of life (see p.64)
- Four Ashramas – stages of life (see p.64)
- Four Varnas – social classes of society (see p.70)
- Four main seasons – symbolizing the cyclic nature of time (see p.42)

The Swastika of Hinduism is a religious symbol of auspiciousness, world peace and prosperity; it should not be confused with the Nazi swastika which has a different design and a totally different meaning.

The colour saffron

Flags on Hindu temples, as well as the robes worn by swamis and sanyasis (religious and spiritually advanced individuals), are of this colour. It denotes the sun's life-giving glow. The sun has the highest place in Vedic literature as the sustainer of all life and the source of energy. It acts as a reminder of the power of God, the act of selfless service and renunciation.

The lotus flower

The lotus flower is a symbol of vegetation and prosperity. The lotus bud is born in watery mud and unfolds itself into a beautiful flower; hence it is seen as a symbol of the universe coming out of the primeval waters. It also symbolizes the fact that it is possible to raise oneself out of evil (mud) to purity.

The conch (shankha)

A conch shell is in the form of a multiple spiral evolving from one point into ever-increasing spheres. It thus symbolizes the origin of the universe from a single source (i.e. God). Being found in water, it also symbolizes the waters from which the universe evolved and into which everything is dissolved. When blown, the conch produces a sound which represents the primeval sound (AUM) from which creation developed. A conch shell is kept in temples and places of worship and blown at times of special prayers like the Aarti (see p.113).

Tilak

Tilak is the mark of red powder or sandalwood paste that is applied on the forehead by Hindus before prayers. The forehead is the seat of memory and the 'spiritual eye or the third eye'; applying the Tilak thus symbolizes the retention of the memory of the Lord. The tilak also has other functions: it is a mark of respect to the higher centres in the brain where the thoughts are generated and it has the psychological effect of keeping away evil thoughts. Sandalwood is used as it has cooling properties and a very pleasant aroma: this signifies that one's head should remain calm and cool and should generate pleasant thoughts. Tilak is also a reminder of vows. The most popular is the red Tilak (Bindi) worn by Hindu married women to symbolize their marriage and the wedding vows.

Hindu greetings

Namaskar (Namaste)
The traditional Hindu greeting is 'Namaskar' or 'Namaste', which is said by joining the two palms in front and bowing the head. This greeting acknowledges the presence of divinity in all human beings. The person saying 'Namaskar' implies, 'with all my physical

strength (represented by folded hands) and my intellect (represented by bowed head) I pay respect to the Atma (soul) within you'.

Asheervaad (Blessing)
Respect for elders, particularly parents and grandparents, is often shown by bowing and touching their feet. The elders respond by placing a hand on the person's head; this gesture is called 'Asheervaad'.

Symbols in temples
The most important symbols to be found in a Hindu temple are: AUM, bells, Jyoti (sacred flame), coconut or fruit, water and Kalash (a container). The significance of these are explained on pp.29–30 and 112–114.

Shivalinga
Another very popular but often misunderstood icon is the symbol of Lord Shiva (see p.23) which is called 'Shivalinga'. Some Hindu sects believe that Lord Shiva fulfils two roles: he is benefactor and he is destroyer. The energy (shakti) with which he performs these functions is like fire: fire can destroy but it is also essential for sustaining life. This omnipotent power of God which creates, preserves and destroys is represented by a flame of fire. In the Vedic period, this sacred flame was kindled in a havan kund (see p.102). Later, in the Puranic period, the symbolic flame was represented by Shivalinga. The base of the Shivalinga is called Brahmabhaga, representing the creator Brahma; the octagonal middle part is called Vishnubhaga, representing the preserver Vishnu; and the projecting flame-like cylindrical part is called Rudrabhaga. Shivalinga is usually made of black stone. The pouring of milk on the Shivalinga is meant to be the same as the pouring of ghee on the sacred flames of a havan yajna. Both these acts represent selfless action.

IN THE CLASSROOM

At KS1, pupils can be taken to a local Hindu temple or introduced to symbols like Om, bell, Swastika and Jyoti (sacred flame). They may be encouraged to draw and colour the symbols and learn the greeting 'Namaste'. At KS2,

other symbols like the lotus flower, Tilak and saffron colour may be introduced. It is important to relate the lotus flower symbol to growth of vegetation (creation) and the symbol of Tilak to the process of thinking. At KS3, the temple symbols of bells, Jyoti, coconut, water and Kalash can be introduced by relating them to the five physical elements – sound, heat/light, vegetation, water and space – which are essential for supporting life (see p.40). KS4 pupils can study the Swastika and the Shivalinga symbols in detail.

The importance of symbols in general can be considered in the classroom by discussing the following topics:

1. Symbols can sometimes convey meaning more easily than words. Examples from everyday life are: road traffic signs, national flags, washing and ironing instructions on garments.

2. Symbols can explain difficult concepts: for example, the symbol of a heart for the emotion of love, and £ or $ sign for monetary value.

3. An example of symbolism can be taken from mathematics. A teacher may say, 'Let "A" be a point and "B" another point, so that "AB" is the straight line joining the points.' The points 'A', 'B' and the line 'AB' are symbolic. The science of geometry is built on the use of symbols.

4. Discuss the aids people use to feel close to those whom they cannot see: for example, photographs, keepsakes, mementos.

Typical questions/discussion points
1. Why do people use symbols? Give an example of a symbol you use in your daily life.
2. Why are symbols sometimes more useful than words?

Gurus and Disciples

The guru is the stepping stone, the guru is the boat, the guru is the raft of Hari's name. The guru is the lake, the sea, the guru is the

place to ford the stream.
Would you like to glisten in the lake that is
made of truth?
Go then and bathe in that name.
(GURU NANAK DEV, SIRI RAGU 9-3, TRANSLATION
FROM THE 'SONGS OF THE SAINTS OF INDIA')

One of the cardinal tenets of Hinduism is the belief that 'each soul is potentially divine', and the goal is to manifest this divinity. It means that everyone is destined to become perfect sooner or later. God-realization, self-realization, Nirvana or the Kingdom of Heaven – all these expressions used by different religions mean the same thing.

Sometimes, we wonder why we are here, where we are going, and what is truth. In the course of time this search becomes more serious. When the human soul becomes restless to find this truth, it seeks a guru. As mentioned earlier, Hindus believe that a book, a symbol or a person can be a guru. A person can be a spiritual guide or a teacher but only the one who has realized God can be a true guru. There are repeated warnings against false gurus: the blind leading the blind. Only a true teacher is capable of dispelling ignorance and able to lead a seeker or Shishya (disciple) to their goal.

To Hindus, scriptures are more like maps or signposts which point out the path, but inspiration and the impulse to follow the spiritual path often comes from another soul. In the words of Swami Dayatmananda, head of the Vedanata Mission in the UK: 'The person from whom such impulse comes is called the guru, the teacher. And the person to whose soul the impulse is conveyed is called the Shishya or the student. To convey such an impulse the teacher must possess the power of transmitting; and the soul to which it is transmitted must be fit to receive. The seed must be a living seed and the field must be ready; when both these conditions are fulfilled a wonderful growth of genuine religion takes place. There is a mysterious law – as soon as the field is ready the seed must and does come. As soon as the student is ready the teacher appears.'

Hence a true spiritual teacher must have certain qualifications. He must: (a) be a realized soul or at least an advanced one in the spiritual path; (b) have a special capacity for guiding the students according to their fitness; (c) be unselfish and motiveless. Once a sage was asked whether a guru is really necessary. The sage beamed and replied, 'Even to become an expert pickpocket one needs a guru. How much more one would need a guide if one wants to reach God!'

The word 'guru' is now well known in the English language. Today, guru means anyone who is a leader of a new wave of thinking.

Guru Nanak Dev, the founder of Sikhism

The Guru and Three Disciples

In a traditional ashram, deep in a jungle, lived a learned guru with his three disciples. They had attained knowledge, so before their graduation, the guru decided to give them one final test. He gave a wooden bowl to each of the disciples and asked them to fetch some water from the nearby river. The problem was that the bowls had many holes in them.

The first disciple looked at the bowl and laughed, 'I cannot fetch water in this. It will all leak out.' And he sat down. The second followed his guru's instructions precisely. He went to the river, filled the bowl and raced back, but the water leaked out. So he went back to the river and repeated the process. After many hours, as a result of the dampness, the wood swelled and closed the holes. The disciple then managed to fetch some water. The third disciple had quietly immersed the bowl in the water and patiently waited for the wood to swell and close the holes. He also then fetched water for his guru.

The first disciple failed the test because he had lost all faith in his teacher. The second disciple also failed because he used his knowledge blindly. Only the third disciple passed because he had used his knowledge with skill and ingenuity.

For example, in the West, Shakespeare is regarded as a guru of theatre, Newton of physics, and Darwin of evolutionary theory. In India, where this term originated, 'guru' literally means a spiritual guide and teacher who steers the course of the student in search of God.

To attain God-realization is a very difficult task. One can learn physics or chemistry from even an ordinary person who has sufficient knowledge. But in the field of spirituality, only one who is pure and spiritual can convey such knowledge. Moreover, a guru must have the ability to gauge the capacity of the student and show him a path which is best suited for him. There may be many pitfalls on the way. Just like an experienced mountaineering guide, a guru can warn of the dangers and make the journey of the student easier. If the student becomes despondent the teacher must inspire and enthuse him. Until the student reaches the goal there is no respite for the teacher. Like a loving father who wishes only for the good of his child, the guru remains with the shishya until he attains God and becomes liberated. It is for this reason that the guru–shishya relationship is considered in Hindu tradition as a most sacred one. The student on his part must have complete faith in the guru and must be sincere and have a real desire to realize God. He must also have great perseverance for the journey is long and arduous and full of pitfalls. According to tradition, the student offers 'guru dakshina' to his teacher at the end of his studies. The essential qualities of a guru and a disciple are summarized in the chart on p.34.

Gurus must ensure that their disciples make the right use of knowledge. This traditional story (alongside) tells what, in the opinion of a guru, is the best quality of a disciple.

IN THE CLASSROOM

There is an ancient tradition of gurus and disciples in Hinduism. Many sects and subsects in Hinduism have passed on their traditions, philosophy and scriptures through this guru–disciple relationship, one of the most famous is Guru Nanak Dev who founded Sikhism. This concept of guruship can be introduced at KS1 or KS2 by looking at how knowledge is passed on to younger generations. The total respect for and dedication to the teacher in Hindu tradition can be illustrated by using the story of Krishna and Muni Sandipani given on p.16. At KS3 and KS4, in addition, it should be explained that the teacher who passes on spiritual knowledge is called a guru.

Typical questions/discussion points
1. How has knowledge been passed from one generation to another?
2. What are the qualifications and functions of a guru?

QUALITIES OF GURUS AND DISCIPLES	
Guru	**Disciple**
Pure	Inquisitive
Sinless	Full of service and love
Compassionate	Shows reverence and devotion
Full of divine love and wisdom	Perseverance

Brahman – the Ultimate Reality

'Brahman' means that which is large and expansive, i.e. infinite. The Hindu idea of the all-pervading God is the doctrine of Brahman. For an English reader, this term can be confusing because of its similarity with two other terms – 'Brahmaa' representing one of the Hindu Trinity, and 'Brahmin' meaning the priestly caste of Hindus.

One school of philosophy, Vedanta, asserts that the world which is perceived by our senses is only an appearance: it is not what it seems to be. Scientists agree with this assertion. A table, a flower, a waterfall, a man – all these are merely different arrangements of identical units called atoms. The world is something other than its external appearance. Moreover, this outward aspect is subject to perpetual change. Vedanta goes on to assert that beneath this appearance, this flux, there is an essential, unchanging Reality which is called Brahman, the all-pervading Godhead. The universe came out of Brahman and is sustained by it, and ultimately merges in it. It is the ultimate Reality. It is unique, pure, eternal, infinite; it is beyond time, space and causation, beyond all names and forms; it is pure consciousness. It is absolute being (Sat), absolute knowledge (Chit), and absolute bliss (Ananda). It is both personal and impersonal; it is both with and beyond all qualities. If there is such a Reality called Brahman, then it must be omnipresent; it must be within each one of us, within each creature and object. Vedanta calls this 'Reality' within each of us 'Atman' (see p.35). Since it cannot be separately distinguished, mind and speech cannot comprehend Brahman. Hindus believe that humans can at best say what Brahman is not, and not what it is.

There is another school of philosophy which believes that God is by nature different from the soul. The attributes, activities and nature of God are not found in the soul, because the soul is bodied and God is not bodied. God is the pervader and the soul is the pervaded.

Looked at from the absolute point of view, Brahman is comprehended as the distinctionless, impersonal God. When looked at from the empirical point of view, it is called God, the creator. Hindus call the creator of this world 'Ishwara'. Ishwara in his three aspects of creation, maintenance and dissolution is respectively termed Brahmaa (a masculine word), Vishnu and Mahesh (Shiva). This is the Hindu Trinity. They are not three different gods but three aspects, three functions of the same God.

As we saw earlier, Hindus worship the formless God and the same one God in innumerable male and female forms. Many people, puzzled by this phenomenon, regard Hinduism as pantheism and Hindus as idol-worshippers. This is unfounded: Hindus do not worship different gods, they worship the one God, but they believe that, though beyond form, God, out of love and compassion for his devotee, can assume any form the devotee wishes. Nothing is impossible for him! Ultimately the worshipper's goal is to attain liberation through that particular form of worship. If the devotee sincerely prays to him, God reveals the truth about his true nature. This is called the theory of Chosen Deity (Ishta Devata). This theory is one of the strongest pillars of Hinduism and is what makes Hindus so liberal and tolerant. It is the reason why Hinduism has remained a non-proselytizing religion.

Here a doubt may arise. How can God be

both with form and without form? How can he be both with qualities and without qualities? It seems illogical. But one must not forget that the human mind is limited and the mystery of God cannot be fathomed by it. He can be rightly understood only by one who has realized God. Realization is the ground where all paradoxes are harmoniously synthesized. A great saint, Ramakrishna, used to say: 'Everything in this world is polluted, coming out of the mouth of man. But Brahman alone is unpolluted since nobody was ever able to say what it is.'

The story below illustrates the Hindu concept that the whole world is pervaded by God. He is both immanent and transcendent.

The Story of Shwetaketu

There was a boy called Shwetaketu who regarded his father, Uddalak, as his guru. He started a discussion about Brahman, the ultimate Reality and the following conversation took place.

Shwetaketu (still very inquisitive): 'Please, Sir, explain to me further.'

Uddalaka: 'Be it so, my child. Place some salt in this water and bring it to me tomorrow morning.' The son did as he was told.

Next morning the father said, 'Bring me the salt which you put in the water.' The son looked for it but could not find it, for the salt had dissolved.

The father said, 'Taste some of the water from the surface. How is it?'

Shwetaketu: 'It is salty.'

Uddalak: 'Taste some from the middle. How is it?'

Shwetaketu: 'Salty.'

Uddalak: 'Taste some from the bottom. How is it?'

Shwetaketu: 'Salty.'

Then the father said, 'Here likewise in this body of yours, my son, you do not perceive the Truth; but there in fact it is. In that which is the subtle essence, all that exists has its self. That is the Truth, that is the self, and you, Shwetaketu, are that self, that Brahman.'

IN THE CLASSROOM

It is important to clarify the difference between the similar-sounding words of 'Brahman' (the ultimate reality), 'Brahmaa' (one of the Trinity) and 'Brahmin' (one of the castes). It is also important that the doctrine of 'Brahman' presented in this section is understood in order to remove the misconception that Hindus worship many gods. The material on p.13 about the concept of one God should be helpful in explaining the concept of 'Brahman'. The story of Shwetaketu could be acted out by two pupils. The dialogue about the example of salt in water will help to convey the Hindu concept of the all-pervading God.

Typical questions/discussion points
1. What is Brahman?
2. Why do Hindus worship so many gods?
3. What is pantheism?
4. What is idolatry? Are Hindus idolaters?
5. In the story of Shwetaketu, what lesson does his father teach him?

Atman and the Law of Karma

> *O Rama, the result of good action is good while that of evil actions is evil. With this knowledge do as you please.*
>
> (YOGA VASHISHTHA)

Atman

Perhaps the greatest contribution of Hindu philosophy is the concept of Atman or self. In spite of many differences, all schools of Hindu philosophy are one in regard to this concept. Atman means self. Self is that which remains if we take away from a person all that is non-self, foreign and extraneous and all that which passes away. It means the changeless, inseparable essence of one's being.

According to Hinduism, man's personality consists of body, mind and spirit or soul. Everyone is considered to be potentially divine. The Atman is immortal, divine, bereft of birth and death; it is of the nature of pure being, pure consciousness and pure bliss. It is immortal and eternal.

The most primary, basic and intimate of

human experiences is the awareness of one's own existence. One can never doubt the existence of one's self, for it itself is the doubter of the doubt. Another experience which is equally self-evident is the unchanging persistence of 'I'. The 'I' is the common denominator of all thoughts, experiences and expressions. It gives continuity to human existence. 'I' was a boy, 'I' am now a young man, 'I' will soon be an old man: to have this kind of experience or thought there must be an unchanging 'I'; so these two experiences – the existence and the continuity of the self – are self-evident. True, but what is the real nature of this Atman or 'I'? Does everyone know his own real nature? 'No' is the answer given by all the Hindu seers. If everyone knew his real nature there would be no problems at all in the world; everyone would be happy forever.

Hindus believe that the real nature of the human soul cannot be known through ordinary means; it can be known only through scriptures. But to know it without the slightest doubt one has to realize it through personal experience. Spiritual disciplines are meant to lead one to this experience.

The Law of Karma
Hinduism tells us that this is not our first birth. We were born many times in the past and, depending upon whether we did good or bad, we are reaping the results. This is called the law of Karma in Hinduism. Karma means action. Everything we do or think is action: good actions bring good results; bad actions produce bad results. So, if some are happy they must have done good in the past; if others are suffering they must have done something bad. Hindus believe that this is the reason for all the differences we see in life in this world. And so our future depends on our present actions. If we want to be happy we must do only good now, then in the future we shall reap good results. This is not fatalism; the law of Karma says that we alone – not God or the Devil – are responsible for our fate. The corollary of the Karma theory is the law of reincarnation.

Hinduism believes in reincarnation (see p.26). Through pain and pleasure and through various experiences we go on improving ourselves. We have to go on experiencing birth after birth until we realize our real nature,

'Atman', which is one with Brahman or God. Once we realize that we are 'Atman' we become liberated from this cycle of birth and death, which is called 'Samsara' or transmigration. So the goal of life is to go on evolving until we realize our true nature, 'Atman'.

I died as mineral and became a plant, I died as plant and rose to animal, I died as animal and I was man. Why should I fear? When was I less by dying? Yet once more, I shall die as man, to soar with angels blessed; but even from angelhood I must pass on; all except God doth perish. To him we shall return!

(JALAL-UDIN-RUMI, A PERSIAN SUFI SAINT)

Here is another story about Shwetaketu, from the Chhandogya Upanishad. It illustrates the Hindu concept of soul (Atman): it cannot be seen but it is there in all living things.

Shwetaketu and the Seed of the Banyan Tree

Shwetaketu was a twelve-year-old boy. He wanted to know about Atman (soul) and wanted to see it. He went and asked his father, Uddalak.

Shwetaketu: 'Please teach me about Atman, Sir.'

Uddalak: 'All right. Bring me a fruit of the nyagrodha tree.' (A large tree common in India)

'Here is one, Sir.'

'Break it.'

'It is broken, Sir.'

'What do you see there?

'Some exceedingly small seeds, Sir.'

'Break one of these.'

'It is broken, Sir.'

'What do you see there?'

'Nothing at all.'

The father said, 'My son, the subtle essence which you do not see there, in that subtle essence is the being of the huge nyagrodha tree. In that which is the subtle essence, the root of all that exists has its self. That is the truth, that is the self, and you, Shwetaketu, are that self.'

IN THE CLASSROOM

The following is a suggested way of introducing this concept. Start by raising the question: 'Who am I?' 'It is not my clothes: I change them. It is not my teeth or arms or legs: if I lose them I do not feel I am any less. It is not my eyes or other sense organs, for I may lose them: I may feel uncomfortable but I can carry on. It is not my mind, for when I am in deep sleep or unconscious I stay alive; moreover, it is changing and growing all the time. So who am I? What remains if all these are taken away? Hindus believe that what remains is the soul, called "Atman", for it never changes.'

'At all times I feel I am. Never, even for a moment, can I doubt my own existence. So my real self is that which always remains even if everything else is taken away. They tell us that our real self is the only Real of all Realities; it has no birth, death or change; it is one, pure, immortal and eternal; it is the very essence of everything. Stripped of all adjuncts like the body, senses, mind, etc., the real "I" in you, in me, in everything is one and the same. Normally we are accustomed to thinking of ourselves as Jacks or Janes or whatever, so it is difficult to imagine ourselves as divine, as sparks of God. But Hindus believe that through spiritual practice gradually one can understand what one's real nature is. Then only can one become fearless and happy.'

'If we are all souls why do we find so much difference? Some are born healthy, rich, intelligent and happy; some are not. Some are good, others are downright wicked. Why? The answer given by Hinduism is that it is because of the actions we did in our past lives.'

Typical questions/discussion points
1. Who are you? Ignore your name, your clothes, parts of your body and then think about what is really inside you which keeps you alive and active.
2. Does the law of Karma explain the differences we find in the world?
3. According to Hinduism, what is the goal of life?
4. Do you think that one day we shall all be one with God?

The instrument is still,
Its strings snapped.
What can the poor thing do?
Its player no longer there.

(SAINT KABIR, SAKHI 16-1)

Maya – Illusion

The Sanskrit word 'Maya' means 'that which is not'. Something which does not exist and yet mysteriously makes its presence felt for the time being is called Maya. Hindus generally consider this world to be Maya. What they mean by this is that even though we feel that this world is very real, it does not endure and hence too much reliance should not be placed on it; it is impermanent.

Maya is a technical term used especially by that school of Hindu philosophy known as Advaita or non-dualism. A great teacher, Shankara Acharya, was the main propagator of this philosophy. According to Advaita, there is only one reality, called Brahman. It is of the nature of absolute existence, absolute consciousness and absolute bliss; it is infinite, eternal and indivisible beyond name, form, time, space and causation. There is nothing else besides Brahman.

If this is true, how is it that everyone feels aware of such a great multiplicity of experiences? The answer given by the Advaitin (a follower of this philosophy) is as follows: Brahman, the one, appears as many because of the power of Maya. Maya obscures the one reality and makes it appear as this wonderful multiplicity that we call the world. It does this by making us ignorant of the truth. Here, ignorance is not total absence of knowledge but wrong or mistaken knowledge. An illustration is given to make this clear. In insufficient light we might mistake a rope for a snake. In this case we are not totally ignorant of the rope, but we have wrong or partial knowledge of it; we know there is something, but we take it for a snake and become frightened. When light is brought we recognize it correctly as a rope and become fearless. Thus Maya means superimposition, i.e. mistaking one thing for something else.

According to Shankara, a great Hindu philosopher, what is called the world is in reality Brahman (Godhead) only, but because of this power of Maya it appears to us as a very real world. It is like dreaming: as long as we are dreaming we take it for real. But appearance is not reality. When we have right knowledge we perceive this world as Brahman. This right perception is called realization of God. For a Hindu, this realization is the goal of life. All religions point a way to this goal. As mentioned above, it is only Advaita which uses this concept of Maya in order to explain the reason why the one appears as many. The infinite can never become finite, but it can appear to be so, and that is Maya.

There was another great teacher, called Ramanuja Acharya. His school of philosophy is known as Vishishtha-Advaita or qualified non-dualism. This school also accepts that the highest reality is non-dual Brahman, but it does not consider this world as a mere appearance. The world is a real creation of God, but it is not separate from him. Our body has hands, legs, eyes, etc. but is still called one body. Though Brahman is one, this world consists of matter and souls which are integral parts of Brahman, separate and distinguishable yet entirely dependent on him. Thus for this school of philosophy, Maya is not an obscuring power but the creative power of God. It is, in fact, his glory.

IN THE CLASSROOM

The concept of Maya can be introduced using the story below, followed by discussion. 'We see all around us strange things. We see people who cannot give up drinking even though they know that it is ruining them. We see students who waste their precious time in

Narada and Krishna

A legend tells us how once Narada (a devotee) said to Krishna, 'Lord, show me Maya.' A few days passed, then Krishna asked Narada to accompany him on a trip to a desert. After walking for several miles, Krishna said, 'Narada, I am thirsty; can you fetch some water for me?' 'I will go at once, sir, and get you water.' So Narada went.

At some distance there was a village and he entered the village in search of water. He knocked at a door, which was opened by a most beautiful young girl. At the sight of her he immediately forgot that his master was waiting for water. He forgot everything and began to talk to the girl. All that day he did not return to his master. The next day he was again at the house talking to the girl. The talk ripened into love and Narada asked the father for the daughter, and they were married and lived there and had children. Thus twelve years passed. His father-in-law died and Narada inherited his property. He lived, as he thought, a very happy life with his wife and children, his fields and his cattle, and so forth. Then came a flood.

One night the river rose until it overflowed the banks and flooded the whole village. Houses fell, people and animals were swept away and drowned, and everything was floating in the rush of the stream. Narada had to escape. With one hand he held his wife, and with the other two of his children; another child was on his shoulders. He tried to ford this tremendous flood. After a few steps he found the current was too strong, and the child on his shoulders fell and was swept away. A cry of despair came from Narada. In trying to save the child, he lost his grasp of another and it also was lost. At last his wife, whom he clasped with all his might was torn away by the current, and he was thrown on the bank, weeping and wailing in bitter lamentation. Behind him there came a gentle voice, 'My child, where is the water? You went to fetch a pitcher of water, and I am waiting for you; you have been gone for quite half an hour.' 'Half an hour!' exclaimed Narada. Twelve whole years had passed through his mind and all those scenes had happened in half an hour! This is Maya. Life, which seems to us to be true, is Maya, a statement of facts.

useless activities; though they know that their future is at stake they seem unable to change their habits. Looking at ourselves, how many times have we resolved to become better and yet failed to put our intentions into practice? We are helpless in spite of knowing what to do. This mysterious something which seems to be preventing us from the right way of life is what Hinduism calls Maya. However, the case is not entirely hopeless. Through right knowledge, strong resolve and regular practice one can change one's life for the better. This is proved by countless saints and sages.'

Typical questions/discussion points
1. What is the meaning of Maya?
2. What do you understand by the word 'superimposition'?
3. What is liberation?
4. How can one overcome Maya?
5. Discuss the views about Maya given by the two Hindu philosophers: Shankara called it illusion, Ramanuja called it creative power.

Sansara – World

Human beings influence the world and the world influences human life, but it cannot be said that humans make the world or that the world makes human life; they closely depend on each other. In Hinduism, different thinkers have provided different answers to the basic question of what the world is.

The view about the nature and reality of the world is strongly related to the view about who created the world. Generally, all concepts of the creator of the world can be grouped into three categories:

(a) Theists: they believe that the creator of the world is an intelligent, living and all-powerful divine spirit who exists at all times.
(b) Atheists: they do not believe in any living non-material spirit.
(c) Neutrals: their view takes the middle path between the theistic and the atheistic view. They believe that the world is governed by a non-intelligent, purposeless existence with immutable and unchangeable laws. These laws are eternal and work automatically, and no one has the power to alter or override these laws.

Hindu scriptures based on the Vedas present the theist view, but in keeping with the tradition of allowing freedom of thought, some scriptures presenting the atheist view (e.g. Charvaka) and some following the so-called neutral view (e.g. Buddhism and Jainism) are also considered as Hindu scriptures. Some different views about the world are considered below.

The world is an illusion
One of the greatest Hindu philosophers, Shankara, wrote commentaries on the major Upanishads. He followed the non-dualistic (Advaita) philosophy which proposes that ultimate reality behind everything (animate or inanimate) is Brahman. All the variety of objects we see is simply Maya (see p.37), an illusion which is superimposed on the real Brahman. All the things we see do not really exist, they merely appear to exist.

The world is real
Another great Hindu philosopher, Ramanuja, argued against the position of Shankara. Ramanuja was influenced by the Vaishnava tradition. He believed that the world is real and, owing to Karma, embodied selves are trapped in the world. Knowledge is important but release from bondage needs devotion to a personal God. Other philosophers like Nimbaraka and Vallabha held the same view.

The world is a puppet show
Some theists believe that God created the world and only that which God wills can happen. Humans are like puppets who are made to act by the will of some moving power.

The world is a jail
Some theists believe that the world is a jail. We must have done some grievous sin in our past life and for this reason we have been placed in this painful world. They define a better place than this world as heaven.

The world is a matter of chance
As mentioned earlier, some atheist views have also been admitted into ancient scriptures. Charvaka was one of these atheists. He said, 'As long as you live, live happily. Borrow and

Coconut, water, Jyoti (lamp), bell and Kalash (container) representing the five physical elements (earth, water, fire, air and space) are found in all Hindu temples.

enjoy. When your body has been cremated there is no coming back.' Many flaws were found in the idea of 'the world coming into existence by chance and without any creator'; that is why this idea has remained buried in the books and is not believed by practising Hindus.

The world is a school to gain knowledge
This is perhaps the most popular and appealing theistic view. It regards the world neither as an illusion, nor as a jail, nor as a product of chance. It was explained by Swami Dayananda Saraswati in his book *Light of Truth*. According to him, the real Vedic view is that there is an infinite number of eternal, unborn and immortal spiritual entities (souls). These

souls are neither all-knowing nor all-powerful; they are finite. They exist at different levels and these levels change according to the work they do. They are free to act but must face the results of their acts. Their protector is the Supreme Being who gives them many things in earthly form for their use. The world is just like a school: facilities are provided and pupils are free to use them. Those who work hard and learn will advance, others will lag behind.

Building blocks of matter
The whole universe is made of matter. According to Hinduism, the matter consists of five substances which are called 'Panch Mahabhut' – earth, water, fire, air and ether. Earth is the most gross of all the substances: it is solid. Water is less gross, fire is finer than water, air is finer than fire and space (ether) is the most subtle of all the elements. The human body, called 'sharira' or 'pinda', is also made of these five physical elements. These elements are inanimate, they are subject to change according to the laws of nature, and they possess only those properties which can be sensed by sensory organs, as shown below.

Ether is the name given to the medium in which waves of sound, light, heat and energy can be transmitted. The concept of these physical elements has been accepted by Greek philosophers, such as Aristotle, and is also found to be acceptable to modern scientists.

The very first verse of the Atharva Veda defines the world (Sansara) as an interaction of twenty-one basic constituents: the five physical elements, the five senses, the five sensory organs, the five vital airs (gases) in the body (see p.115) and the soul.

IN THE CLASSROOM

The material presented in this section is mostly suitable for pupils at KS3, KS4 and above. For

ELEMENT	PROPERTY	SENSORY ORGAN
Earth	Smell	Nose
Water	Taste	Tongue
Fire	Light	Eye
Air	Touch	Skin
Space (ether)	Waves	Ear

younger pupils, at KS1 and KS2, a discussion on identifying living and non-living things can be started. The non-living things can then be related to matter. The building blocks of matter (the five basic elements – earth, water, fire, air and space) could be introduced by creating a mural representing the five elements. A group of students could work on each element. KS3 and KS4 pupils will find it easy to identify at least the first four elements given in the table opposite. Point out to pupils that the human body is nearly 80 per cent water by weight.

Typical questions/discussion points
1. Name the five physical elements which, according to the Hindu view, form all the matter in the world. What are the properties of these elements and how can we recognize them?
2. Which of the Hindu views about the world appeals to you and why?
3. Why do religious people feel that nature brings them close to God?

Three Gunas – Qualities

An important concept in Hinduism is that all animate and inanimate objects in this universe have three basic Gunas or qualities – Sattvic, Rajasic and Tamasic, which can be roughly translated as positive, neutral and negative. Each of the five physical elements, described on p.40, also possesses one of these qualities. According to the Hindu sage Kannad the relationship is as shown in the chart below.

The Hindu concept that all matter possesses three basic qualities of positive, negative and neutral is now accepted by modern science. Science has also proved that the basic building block of matter is an atom which comprises positively charged protons,

negatively charged electrons and neutral neutrons. This modern scientific discovery seems to agree with the theories of Hindu philosophers like Kapila, who viewed everything in terms of these triple attributes which they believed to be the root cause of all actions of nature.

All actions are being done by the modes or attributes (Gunas) of Prakriti (matter).
(GITA, CHAPTER 3, VERSE 27)

This concept of the three basic Gunas underlies Hindu metaphysics, psychology and sociology. The very nature of the human mind is also described by the three Gunas. The Sattvic mind is pure and calm, working to gain 'higher' knowledge of God. The Rajasic mind is involved in worldly actions and busy gaining 'lower' worldly knowledge. The Tamasic mind is an inactive mind.

These qualities are also used to describe the four types of human beings. A person of Sattvic tendencies is 'Brahmin', one with combined Sattvic and Rajasic qualities is 'Kshatriya' , those with Rajasic and Tamasic trends are 'Vaishya' and the ones with only Tamasic qualities are 'Shudra'. Satyavrata Siddantalankar, in his book *Heritage of Vedic Culture – A Pragmatic Presentation*, points out that these are not the four professions but, psychologically speaking, the four main propensities of the human mind.

IN THE CLASSROOM

The material presented in this section is related to the discussion on 'Sansara' (world) on pp.39–40. It is recommended that discussion on the three Gunas should take a scientific line of enquiry, and pupils' knowledge about matter and atoms can be a helpful starting point.

GUNA	PHYSICAL ELEMENTS	QUALITY	ACTION
Sattvic	Fire (Agni)	Positive	Uplifts
Rajasic	Water (Jal)		
	Air (Vayu)		
	Ether (Akash)	Neutral	Levels
Tamasic	Earth (Prithvi)	Negative	Pulls down (gravity)

Typical questions/discussion points
1. What are the three qualities that Hindus believe are possessed by all animate and inanimate objects?
2. Evaluate the scientific evidence for the Hindu view that all matter has three basic Gunas (qualities).

The Nature of Time

This section describes the Hindu view of Kaal (time). It provides a definition, examines the nature and explains the concept of time within the context of current scientific understanding of this complex issue. It explains how Hindus measure time in relation to the creation, evolution and annihilation of the universe.

Definition and nature of time

Time is a measure of the elapsed duration of an event; it has no meaning unless it is associated with some event. Past, present and future are all relative. The Hindu concept of time, the zodiac, the calendar and the techniques for astronomical calculations were perfected around 1200 BCE and were found to be accurate to the third decimal point when compared with modern-day computations of the same measurable concept (Sylvain Bailley et al., *Historie de l'Astronomie Ancienne*, p. 483, and the *Proceedings of the Society of Biblical Archaeology*, December 1901, Part 1).

Hindu concept of cyclic time

The Hindu concept of time is that it is a continuum and is set and reset in tune with the cyclical nature of the universe, from Big Bang to Big Crunch. This concept is based on several factors and considerations concerning the relative motion of earth with respect to other celestial objects, including:

• the daily rotation of the earth at 3200 k.p.h. around itself;
• the annual rotation of the earth at over 106,000 k.p.h. around the sun;
• the motion resulting from the gravitational pull of the star Hercules at 69,500 k.p.h.;
• the time duration between the two main conjugations of all planets with the first point of Aries at a reference point on earth.

The concept of time is discussed in one of the Hindu scriptures, the Rig Veda (first of the four Vedas), and includes a description of the creation of the universe, the motion of stellar and solar bodies and a discussion of sidereal and synodic periods. Madeleine Biardeau, in *Hinduism – The Anthropology of Civilization*, has compared the Hindu concept of cyclic time with Western thinking. Whilst cyclic time in the West is associated with the idea of cosmology governed by movements of the stars, in Hinduism it is linked to the idea of creation and reabsorption of the world, the process which is endlessly repeated. The annual cycle of seasons (referred to under Swastika on p.30), and the feasts which punctuate them, also favours a conception of time which continually repeats itself.

These ideas are elaborated in Hindu scriptures like the Surya Siddhanta (a treatise on the solar system) and in the Vedangas (branches of Vedas) such as Jyotir Shastra (Science of Light) which was compiled around 1350 BCE. The concepts are further explained in Srimad Bhagavatam.

Origin of time

It is remarkable that the Hindu concept and explanations of the origin of time agree with modern scientific theories. The phrase 'in the beginning', often used in religious literature such as the Bible, has a profound consequence upon science as well as religion. The phrase presupposes the existence of 'energy and matter' bounded by the dimension of 'time and space'. To a mathematician, 'in the beginning' equates to a singularity, where 'time and space' has no meaning and all the laws of physics break down. Professor Stephen Hawking, in *A Brief History of Time*, has described the state of the universe at the beginning of time. He concludes that at the beginning of time, a singularity existed with all energy stored at a point with infinitely dense mass. This concept of the entire energy and matter stored at a point at the beginning of the universe exists in the Hindu scriptures. The state of each universe at the beginning is described in Rig Veda (10-121-1) and Atharva Veda (4-2-7) by the words 'Hiranya Garbha', literally meaning 'the seed or womb of all energy'.

The Hindu scriptures offer many ideas

about creation, but they all agree that each universe is ultimately dissolved and transformed into another one. This transformation point is the 'Big Bang' (known as Bindu Visphot) which happens periodically and thus sets the process of endless rhythmic cycles of expansions and contractions ('Big Crunch') of the universe. In this process, time is also initiated as part of that continuum.

> *The universe turns into minute (subtle) form at the time of dissolution and takes gross form at the time of creation.*
> (GITA, 9-7)

> *There was a universe before this one and there will be a universe after this one.*
> (RIG VEDA, 10-190-3)

Time within the context of creation

For Hindus, time is a continuum because the process of creation and annihilation cycles is 'anaadi' (has no beginning) and 'ananta' (endless). There is no reference to the date when creation first took place. This rhythmic, cyclical expression of Sristi (creation), Stiti (sustenance) and Laya (destruction) is metaphorically expressed in the Tandava Nritya (cosmic dance) of Lord Shiva (see p.23).

Units of time

At each 'Big Bang' time and space dimensions are initiated and they end when the 'Big Crunch' occurs. Hindus picture the universe as periodically expanding and contracting and give the name 'Kalpa' to the time-span between the beginning and the end of such periods or the cycle of one creation. In Hindu scriptures, time is calculated in terms of divine days and nights. One universal cycle is called a Kalpa. The current one is called Swetavaraha

Kalpa. Each Kalpa is further divided into Mahayuga and Yuga (see pp.104–106).

At present we are at the start of the Kali Yuga, with 425,151 years left in the current Yuga. The current scientific estimation of the last Big Bang at about 18+ billion years ago can be matched to certain multiples of the Kalpa.

> *WHEEL OF TIME*
> *With its twelve spokes, this wheel of eternal time*
> *Knows no decay and revolves round the heavens high.*
> (ATHARVA VEDA, 9-9-13)

IN THE CLASSROOM

Teachers could introduce the idea of the measurement of time by discussing the concept behind the terms BCE and CE. It is important to let pupils wonder about the length of time (compared to an average human lifespan, for instance) it takes for a universe to evolve. The evolution concept of Darwin can also be considered. Pupils could be asked to give their ideas about how old this universe is and how long it will last. During the discussion, the Hindu concept of cyclic creation and destruction of the universe can be introduced.

The Hindu concept of cyclic time could also be introduced by looking at cycles in nature, e.g. cycles of plants/animals, the rain cycle, the cycle of the food chain, and so on.

The following experiment can be conducted to demonstrate the scientific theory of an expanding and contracting universe:

1. Take a balloon with geometric patterns marked on it.
2. Blow up the balloon and as the size increases

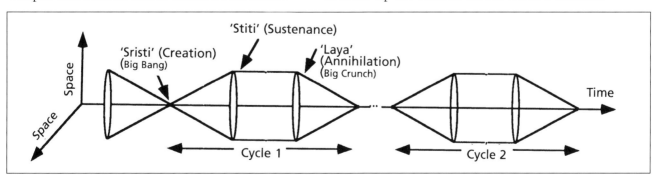

The cyclic nature of time and space

draw attention to the way the patterns move further from the opening of the balloon.
3. Finally, blow the balloon until it bursts. This stage is 'Big Crunch' and the starting stage is 'Big Bang'.

Typical questions/discussion points
1. What is the definition of time and the nature of time according to Hinduism?
2. Do Hindu concepts provide the arguments for the origin of time?
3. What is the scientific relevance of Hindu concepts?
4. How long is a day of 'Brahma'?
5. What is the term used by Hindus for 'time, creation, sustenance, destruction'?
6. What is the apparent relation between 'Big Bang', 'Big Crunch' and the Hindu concept of time?

Yoga

The words 'meditation' and 'Yoga' are becoming more and more widely known throughout the world and are often used synonymously. Meditation can be defined as contemplation of religious matters as part of a religious act. Today meditation and/or yoga are practised for a number of reasons, such as relieving stress/tension, relaxation, enjoyment of peace and solitude, control of the physical senses and the mind.

The word 'Yoga' means to unite, to connect or to establish a relationship with God, the Supreme Being. Yoga is communication with God in which one consciously directs one's thoughts towards him and establishes a silent conversation: it is not just twisting and turning the body in awkward postures. Yoga is designed to bring mental peace and calmness.

The difference between meditation and Yoga is that meditation is the thought process – the process of turning within and tuning – while Yoga is the result – the connection, union or link with God, the Supreme Being.

Krishna, who gave the sermon in the Gita, tells Arjuna that it was he who taught Yoga originally to the progenitors of the human race. Besides the four main types of Yoga which are widely practised today and

discussed in the following paragraphs, there are other forms of Yoga explained in the Gita, including Buddhi Yoga (Yoga of intellect), Sanyasa Yoga (Yoga through renunciation), Hatha or Laya Yoga (Yoga through determination and discipline), Samatwa Yoga (Yoga through equanimity), Brahma Yoga and Moksha Yoga (Yoga of liberation).

Bhakti Yoga (Yoga through love and devotion)

Bhakti Yoga is based on the worship of a personal God. The path of Bhakti is the easiest of all the paths. In this path the aspirant worships a God, the Supreme Being and develops a loving relationship with him, adores him, remembers him and praises him by chanting and singing. The love of the Supreme Being is experienced and there is also great humility developed within oneself. The devotee who surrenders completely to God attains peace and tranquillity of mind. A true devotee dedicates his/her actions to God and takes complete refuge in him.

Jnana Yoga (Yoga through knowledge and understanding)

Jnana means knowledge. This form of yoga is based on worship of an impersonal God. The seeker on the path of Jnana Yoga seeks God through self-realization. To attain divine wisdom one must have complete faith in God. Shankara Acharya, one of the great Hindu philosophers, suggested that ignorance is the cause of all pain and misery in life. It is only in ignorance that one regards temporary as permanent, and unreal as real. When one achieves complete self-mastery and self-control and has intense faith and devotion, then true knowledge dawns within and one attains liberation and freedom from all bondage.

Karma Yoga (Yoga through action)

This Yoga is based on worship of a God of action. Following the path of Karma (action) one can attain perfection by performing all actions as a divine offering, imbued with a spirit of detachment and devotion. When actions are performed out of love for the Supreme Being, one is not caught in the bondage of actions.

Nobody can ever remain for even a

moment without committing an action. One has to perform actions through the force of nature, i.e. Prakriti. Engagement in walking, talking, eating, sitting quietly, sleeping, working, etc., means the performance of one action or another. Action is superior to inaction and even the maintenance of the body would not be possible without action.

Raj Yoga (Yoga of self-control)
This form of Yoga is called Raj Yoga for several reasons:

1. The word 'Raj' means sovereign or king. By practising Raj Yoga one becomes king over one's own physical senses and mind.

2. 'Raj' also means secrets. Raj Yoga opens up all secrets: Who am I? Where do I come from? Who is God? What does he do? What do I attain from him?

3. Raj Yoga works on the soul. This yoga (union of soul and Supreme Soul) is the method by which there is a transformation in the very personality, the very nature of the soul itself.

Raj Yoga is more than a technique for the control of stress and relaxation. It is a tool which enables one to create new attitudes and responses to life through a clear spiritual understanding of oneself. The Hindu sage Patanjali laid down the eightfold spiritual path also known as the Ashtanga Yoga or Ashtanga Marga. These eight constituents of Raj Yoga are:

(a) Yama (five abstentions)
(b) Niyama (five observances)
(c) Asanas (eighty-four balanced postures)
(d) Pranayama (regulation of breath or the life force)
(e) Pratyahara (withdrawal of senses)
(f) Dharana (concentration)
(g) Dhyana (meditation or deliberation)
(h) Samadhi (contemplation)

This eightfold path proposed by Patanjali has also influenced Buddhists. Further details are given in the section on personal worship in Chapter 4 (pp.114–118).

The benefits of Yoga
Yoga can be practised by anyone irrespective of their age, faith, creed, colour, etc. It helps one not only to relax and relieve stress but it also brings about a transformation within oneself,

Salutation to the sun (Suryanamaskar Yoga)

for instance by developing positive values and reforming habits. The mind becomes quieter, calmer and more stable. This ultimately brings contentment within. It improves will power and the power of concentration, helps to improve the power of intuition and makes one active and alert. It enables the aspirant to look at himself or herself and others as souls or spiritual brothers and sisters and helps in the realization that 'the whole world is one large family under the One Incorporeal and Universal God' (Vasudhaiva Kutumbakam). This develops the qualities of love, mercy, kindness, humility, honesty towards others and helps in bringing peace, happiness and harmony all around.

Finally, it should be noted that while many systems of Yoga are found in Hinduism and they may differ in their approach, all of them are aimed at achieving the same objective.

Whatever path men travel is my path, no matter where they walk, it leads to me.
(GITA, CHAPTER 4, VERSE 11)

IN THE CLASSROOM

Meditation posture

The concept that the four main systems of Yoga are related and have a common objective can be introduced in the classroom by using the example of an athlete trying to win a gold medal in Olympics. The objective is to win a gold medal. The athlete must first of all decide which race he wants to run. Knowledge (Jnana) in the form of a trainer or a coach is required to find out the techniques. But knowledge alone will not win the race. The athlete has to devote himself to the sport and keep the aim in mind (Bhakti) all the time. Also, action (Karma) is needed; no race can be won without running. And above all, self-control and self-discipline (Raj Yoga) are required to turn the hard training into winning the race.

Pupils could be asked to sit quietly, preferably in a cross-legged meditation posture (as shown in the illustration above). Ask them to close their eyes and imagine a picture of a calm sea with the sun setting on the horizon. Let them concentrate for a few minutes, feeling only the inhaling and exhaling of their breath. Then ask them to discuss their feelings.

More energetic pupils could try the Yoga postures of the 'Salutation to the sun' shown on p.45.

Typical questions/discussion points
1. Why do you think Yoga is becoming popular in the West?
2. What is the meaning of the word 'Yoga'? Does Yoga involve only postures and physical exercises?
3. Briefly describe the four main systems of Yoga. Is there any relationship between them? Are they mutually exclusive or are they complementary?

God, Soul and Matter

The cosmos is controlled by the Divine
The Divine is governed by the Truth
Truth is governed by noble beings
The noble beings are the Divine itself.
(A SANSKRIT SHLOKA)

The concept of God in Hinduism has been discussed earlier (pp.13, 21 and 26). In summary, it consists of the idea of one all-pervading Supreme Being or God, free from all material needs, requiring matter neither for his existence nor for his sustenance. The concept of soul has been clarified on pp.35–37 and the Hindu view about the world has been presented on pp.37–42. Hindus believe that there are an infinite number of souls which never die but need matter for their growth and development; they are imperfect but are progressing towards perfection, i.e. God. All the dead, inert and non-spirit is identified as matter.

In this section, the relationship between the three eternal entities – God, soul and matter – is discussed. Hindu scriptures set out many principles dealing with the three entities and they consider the question 'Are they all different entities or are they different manifestations of the same?'. The three main principles explaining the inter-relationship are:

1. Advaitavada (non-dualism or monism):
Some philosophers have proposed that there is
only one ultimate reality behind everything.
The prefix 'a-' denotes 'not', so 'Advaitavada'
means that there are not two but just one
eternal entity. A school of thought known as
Vedanta believes in this idea and was made
popular in the West by a Hindu monk, Swami
Vivekananda.

2. Dvaitavada (dualism): The word 'dvi' means
'two'. Some philosophers have proposed that
there are two separate entities – God (Brahma)
and matter (Prakriti). They believe that soul is
part of God.

3. Traitavada (pluralism or trinity): This is the
doctrine of three eternals (God, soul and
matter) existing independently and separately
from each other. The Hindu philosopher
Swami Dayananda propagated this idea as the
true teaching of the Vedas.

IN THE CLASSROOM

This section should be tackled only after
completing the previous sections describing
the concepts of God, soul and matter. It is
important for students to understand that
Hinduism does not enforce one view on this
subject.

Typical questions/discussion points
1. What are the different views found in
Hinduism regarding the relationship between
God, soul and matter?
2. How do Hindu philosophers differentiate
between God, soul and matter?

Hinduism as the Foundation of Many Religious and Reformist Movements

In the UK, Hinduism, Buddhism and Sikhism
are taught as separate topics within the
Religious Education (RE) syllabus. Buddhism
and Sikhism may be taught as separate
religions but both of them should be treated
as branches of Hinduism. There are many
religions and faith traditions within
Hinduism, out of which the Buddhist and the

Sikh faith traditions have become very
popular and deserve to be taught as separate
topics. In some other countries where RE is
taught in schools, Buddhism, Sikhism and
Jainism are included in the Hindu Religious
Education syllabus; in Kenya, for example,
this is prepared jointly by the Kenya Institute
of Education and the Hindu Council of
Kenya.

The aim of this section is to provide
material which will help RE teachers to
establish the link between various branches of
Hinduism. Information is also included about
well-known reformist movements and
organizations which have influenced the
Hindu way of life.

Buddhism
Some Western Buddhist Orders often attempt
to prove that Buddhism is not linked to
Hinduism; on the contrary, however, the
historical and philosophical links between the
two are well established and unquestionable.
It is a fact that the founder of Buddhism was
born as prince Siddhartha to a Hindu king of
a state in India called Kapilvastu. Also, it was
a Hindu king, Ashoka, who became a follower
of the Buddhist faith and spread it beyond
the boundaries of ancient India. At the
International Workshop on Hinduism and
Buddhism held at Sarnath in India during
March 1994, the following consensus was
reached:

1. Karma and rebirth: the cycle of birth-death-
rebirth and the belief that Karmas (see p.36)
keep accumulating and cause rebirth are
shared by Hindus and Buddhists.

2. Soul and consciousness: the concept of
Atman (see p.35) as the true and endless
consciousness is the same as the concept of
Chetna or consciousness believed by
Buddhists.

3. Moksha and Nirvana: the ultimate goal of
human consciousness, according to Hindus
and Buddhists, is enlightenment. This is the
state of liberation (Moksha or Nirvana) from
the bondage of Karma, resulting in final
release from the cycle of birth and death and is
equally true for Hindus and Buddhists.

4. Par-Brahman and Sunyata: the concept of ultimate reality in Hindu and Buddhist philosophies, denoted by the terms Par-Brahman and Sunyata respectively, conveys the same meaning. For Hindus, the Par-Brahman is devoid of all attributes or Nirgun and beyond expression in words or gestures, i.e. it is indescribable (see p.34). The Sunyata propounded by Buddhists conveys exactly the same meaning. The Sunyata is Nirgun (attributeless) and indescribable. Thus, both terms – Par-Brahman and Sunyata – are synonymous.

5. Incarnation and Lord Buddha: Buddha is God according to the Buddhist creed, and the same belief is held by many Hindus when they say that Lord Sakya Muni, the enlightened one, is the incarnation of Vishnu in the present age (see p.27).

Dalai Lama

In Sanskrit grammar it is pointed out that a child may pronounce 'r' as 'l'; for example, 'rail' may be pronounced as 'lail'. In some of the Indo-Sanskrit languages, 'r' is freely replaced by 'l'. One such word is 'Lama', which is a distorted form of the word 'Rama'. The name 'Dalai Lama' (known as the spiritual leader of the Tibetan Buddhists) comes from the words 'Darayee Rama', meaning 'Rama of the caves'. Many Hindus believe the Dalai Lama to be a reincarnation of Rama living in the Himalayan mountains.

H.T. Coolebrooke, in *Essays on the Religion and Philosophy of the Hindus*, says that Buddhist theology has been borrowed from the ideas of the Hindu sage Kapila (see p.159). In *Heritage of Vedic Culture*, S. Siddhantalankar has compared the eightfold path with Ashtanga Yoga, proposed by the Hindu sage Patanjali (see p.45). In his book *Indian Religions*, Dr Radhakrishna writes, 'Buddhism did not start as a new and independent religion. It was an offshoot of the more ancient faith of the Hindus, perhaps a schism or a heresy.' Most probably the impression of total independence of Buddhism from Hinduism comes from the misconception that Buddha rejected the authoritativeness of the Vedas. In fact, Buddha rejected rituals, particularly those involving animal sacrifices, which were being carried out in the name of the Vedas. It should be noted that animal sacrifice is not sanctioned in the Vedas; this misleading idea was put forward by some commentators, particularly those known as 'Vam Margi', who attempted to defame the Vedas. In the words of P. T. Raju in *The Philosophical Traditions of India*, 'Buddhism like Jainism was mainly a reform movement in India's spiritual life'.

Sikhism

Guru Nanak, the founder of Sikhism, was the son of Kaluram Mehta, a member of the 'Kshatriya' caste of Hindus. His teachings and philosophy were based on the Vedas. The concept of 'Omkar' in Sikhism is the Vedic concept of 'AUM' (see p.29). Guru Nanak also believed that the Vedas were revealed by God. His own words recorded in the Sikh holy book, Guru Granth Sahib, state:

> *Sama Veda, Rig Veda, Yajur Veda and Atharva Veda have been revealed by God. No one can evaluate their importance. They are priceless and eternal.*
>
> (MAHLA 1, SHABAD 17)

Guru Nanak saw the presence of God in the beauty of nature and preached the idea of a universal God – the same as the Hindu Vedic concepts. Not only Hindus but many Muslims also came under the influence of his teachings. After Guru Nanak, Sikhism was spread by successive Gurus who also came from Hindu families. There is a long history of sacrifices made by the Sikh Gurus to protect the Hindu Dharma against the onslaught of Mogul invaders like Aurengazeb. The Ninth Guru, Tegh Bahadur, went to see the Mogul ruler, Aurengazeb, to protest against the forcible conversion of Kashmiri Hindus to Islam. He was arrested and beheaded. At the place of his execution, in Delhi, stands Gurdwara Sheesh Ganj where many Hindus go to pray.

The Tenth Guru, Gobind Singh, is hailed by Hindus as the protector of Hindu Dharma. Guru Gobind Singh's two sons were buried alive in a wall by Moguls when the young boys refused to convert to Islam. Gobind Singh sent his followers to Varanasi to study Sanskrit and Hindu scriptures and later translated them for the benefit of ordinary people. He wrote the holy book called the Dasham Granth. The great Sikh ruler of Punjab, Maharaja Ranjit Singh, banned cow slaughter in his kingdom. It is clear that there is a close link between Hinduism and Sikhism. A prominent Sikh leader, Master Tara Singh, was also one of the founding members of the Vishwa Hindu Parishad (World Council of Hindus). Many Hindu families in Punjab still follow the tradition in which the eldest son of the family follows the Sikh faith. The word Sikh is derived from the Sanskrit word 'Shishya', meaning disciple. The Kara (metal bracelet) worn by Sikhs symbolizes the Hindu philosophy of an unending circle of continuity.

Jainism

Jainism, like Buddhism, developed Hindu ideals of renunciation and love. It also believes, like Hinduism, that during each cycle of time, divine personages appear to assist mankind in evolution. It is believed to be a very old tradition, but modern Jainism was established by Vardhaman Mahavir whose father was Siddhartha and who was born in the holy city of Vaishali in India. Mahavir is believed to be the last of the twenty-four Tirthankaras (see p.27). He started the movement to oppose the meaningless rituals which had taken root in India as a result of illiteracy. He developed Jainism as an ethical doctrine with rigorous self-discipline at its core. Their moral principles are the same as the Yamas and Niyamas laid down by the Hindu sage Patanjali (see p.52). The concept of soul, the law of Karma and the cyclic nature of time are the key Jain beliefs and these are the same as Hindu beliefs. Their main symbols of AUM and Swastika are also identical to the Hindu symbols described on pp.29–30. Today, the followers of Jainism are known for their strong beliefs in non-violence and vegetarianism, both of which are recognized as hallmarks of the Hindu way of life.

Modern Reformist Movements in Hinduism

A student of Hinduism would very quickly appreciate that in the long history of the faith there has been remarkable flexibility and tolerance of a variety of religious ideas. Whilst this flexibility allowed Hinduism to survive the political upheavals caused by foreign rulers like the Moguls and the British, it nevertheless had some drawbacks; for instance, it permitted the growth of certain meaningless and useless rituals and practices. That is why, in Hinduism, one will find numerous reformist movements which were started to bring society back on to the right path. Some of the reformist movements, mostly from the nineteenth century, which have left an enduring mark on the Hindu way of life are briefly described in this section. These movements contributed towards the revival of Hinduism.

Ramakrishna Mission

This movement was started by Swami Vivekananda under the inspiration of Sri Ramakrishna, who was born in Bengal in 1836. With intense renunciation and yearning Sri Ramakrishna practised many spiritual disciplines and realized God in many ways. He encouraged his followers to cultivate renunciation and devotion. Swami Vivekananda, his chief monastic disciple, preached the Vedanta philosophy (see p.159) throughout the world. He established the Ramakrishna Mission in 1897 and started a programme of social service through its branches.

Arya Samaj

Swami Dayananda was born in 1825 in a village of Tankara in Gujarat. He wrote commentaries on the Vedas after mastering the old Vedic Sanskrit language. He founded Arya Samaj in 1875 at Bombay. This movement has brought reforms in five areas:

(a) Religious: re-established the monotheistic (One God) philosophy; provided scientific and logical interpretation of the Vedic texts and countered propaganda of others who had misunderstood the Vedas; removed meaningless and superstitious rituals from religious ceremonies.

(b) Social: campaigned to break the barrier of the caste system and worked to eradicate untouchability. The most notable contribution has been to re-establish the equal status for women which existed in the Vedic period. It opposed the 'purdah' system, established educational institutions for women, campaigned against child marriages and allowed re-marriages of widows.

(c) Political: Arya Samaj was recognized as a strong nationalist movement. Its followers opposed British rule in India and fought for independence.

(d) Educational: Arya Samaj was the first to raise its voice for national education during the British Raj. It established many educational institutes where science and English were combined with the study of Hindi and Sanskrit.

(e) International: in the twentieth century, thousands of Indians were sent to other countries as workers. As immigrants arrived in countries like Fiji, Mauritius, Surinam, East Africa and South Africa, the first missionaries to visit them were sent by Arya Samaj.

Aurobindo Ashram
Aurobindo Ghosh was born in Calcutta in 1872. He spent fourteen years in England to complete his education, including two years at King's College, Cambridge. After returning to India, he studied Sanskrit and Hindu scriptures and began to write articles in newspapers. He became a prominent leader of the Nationalist Party and believed in dynamic leadership based on self-help and fearlessness.In 1914 he met a French lady, Mirra Alfassa, who is now known as the Mother. Together they started the Ashram. They believed that each one must find his own way of doing Yoga and realizing God and made no distinction between castes or nationalities or sexes. They have done much work to bring together the philosophies of East and West.

Brahmo Samaj
Raja Ram Mohan Roy was born in 1774 in Bengal. He was a scholar of many languages and worked relentlessly for social reform. He condemned the caste system and opposed child marriages and polygamy. He formed Brahmo Samaj in 1828 and appealed to the educated to join him in removing malpractices and blind beliefs. His most notable achievement was his vehement protest against the 'suttee' custom in which widows immolated themselves on the funeral pyre of their husbands. He finally succeeded in convincing the British Government, and a law was passed in 1829 to ban the 'suttee' custom.

Contemporary Religious Movements
There are many religious sects and movements in Hinduism. New organizations aimed at promoting one or other idea from Hinduism are formed almost every year. In this section, a brief introduction is given to the main sects or movements started in the twentieth century.

The Brahmakumaris
The Brahamakumari movement, now known as the World Spiritual University, was started by Dada Lekh Raj in 1937. It has over 3000 branches in sixty-two countries and operates as an educational organization. It encourages individuals to develop spiritual understanding through meditation. The University is now affiliated to the United Nations as a non-governmental organization and in consultative status with UNICEF. Its headquarters is at Mount Abu in the state of Rajasthan in India.

ISKCON (Hare Krishnas)
The International Society for Krishna Consciousness (ISKCON), generally known as the Hare Krishna sect, was founded by Swami Prabhupada who, at the age of seventy, travelled from Bombay to New York by ship to preach the message of Bhakti Yoga centred on the deity of Krishna. This sect follows Vaishnavite tradition started by Chaitanya. Initially, in America it attracted the hippies and flower-children of 1960s, but now it has a worldwide following from all walks of life with centres in many major cities.

Satya Sai Baba
The Satya Sai Baba is a sect headed by a charismatic founder and leader, Satya Sai Baba, who is claimed to be the reincarnation of an

Indo-Muslim saint called Sai Baba of Shirdi. The movement's headquarters is based in Puttaparthi, a village in the state of Andhra Pradesh in India. It is a highly structured organization with many followers around the world who believe that Satya Sai Baba is the divine source of all authority. The Community of the Many Names of God is a Shaivite ashram in rural Wales which at one time was linked with the Sai Baba sect.

Swaminarayana

The Swaminarayana movement was started by Sahjanand Swami, a high-caste Brahmin who was born in 1780 in the state of Uttar Pradesh in India. His followers mostly came from Gujarat and belong to the Vaishnavism school of Hinduism. He introduced a clear dichotomy between lay householders and renouncers and strictly prohibited contact between renouncers and women. These strict rules were imposed to remove any accusation of moral or sexual corruption. Unlike other Vaishnav sects, such as the Pushtimargs, he welcomed lower-castes into his movement. This religious movement is still very active in the form of many separate and autonomous organizations, some of which are based in Britain.

Transcendental Meditation (TM) Movement

The TM Movement, started by Maharishi Mahesh Yogi (born Mahesh Verma in 1917), focuses on the teachings which come from the Vedic tradition of Hinduism that can be traced back more than five thousand years. Around 1941, Maharishi became a disciple of Swami Brahmananda Saraswati who was the head, or Shankaracharya, of one of the most ancient monasteries of India – Jyotir Math in the Himalayas. Maharishi spent thirteen years there as a disciple. After his guru's death, Maharishi began to teach Transcendental Meditation, which is a simple form of meditation requiring no renunciation or control of mind. He started the TM Movement in southern India and then undertook five world tours between 1958 and 1964 and established meditation centres in over a hundred cities. TM has been learnt by about 4 million people of all cultural, religious and educational backgrounds in the last thirty-five years. Studies on anxiety and depression show positive effects achieved by patients who practise TM. It has been shown to reduce high blood pressure and cholesterol levels, improve sleep patterns and reduce asthma symptoms. Some doctors in the UK have started to recommend TM to their patients because it has no harmful side effects.

Vishwa Hindu Parishad

Vishwa Hindu Parishad (VHP) is the World Council of Hindus. This is perhaps the major twentieth-century organization of Hindus, formed by heads of various religious faiths in India in 1966 with the main aim of uniting all the sects and sub-sects of Hindus under one global name of Hindutva.

In Religions of Immigrants from India and Pakistan, Raymond Brady Williams presents an in-depth analysis and understanding of the VHP. He describes the primary function of this organization as an umbrella group that on both national and local levels maintains informal associations among Hindu groups, temples and religious leaders to advance the concept of ecumenical Hinduism. It includes other religions of Indian origin – Jains, Sikhs, Lingayats and Buddhists. The VHP has held many International Conferences in the USA, the UK, Germany, South Africa and Denmark. These conferences are aimed at bringing together lay leaders of many Hindu temples and organizations and some of the leading religious leaders and teachers from India to address the problems faced by Hindu individuals, families and organizations. For example, in 1985, the conference in Copenhagen addressed the two major challenges faced by Hindus living outside India: identity (How can Hindus outside of India maintain their identity without enclosing themselves in ghettos?) and mission (Now that the opportunity is open for Hindus to tell people in Western countries directly about their religion, how can they best present it?). The preparation of this book is one example of VHP's work in the UK.

IN THE CLASSROOM

It is important to clarify the fact that Hinduism is the oldest religious faith and that it started in India. The information given in this section can be used to demonstrate that many different sects and faiths come within the fold of Hinduism. Students can be set the task of visiting and interviewing two or three different Hindu (including Sikh) families; this will give them an insight into how many different religious traditions exist within Hinduism.

Typical questions/discussion points
1. Discuss the relationship between various faiths and sects which originated in India.
2. Do people need the freedom to believe in any faith they want to? Is it right to impose just one book or one faith on everyone?

Self-discipline

The Hindu code of conduct or ethics lays great stress on self-discipline in all areas of personal and social behaviour. Hindu sages recognized that human beings cannot live without nature. They need air, water, sun and materials from the earth to sustain life. Both the human race and nature are part of God or God's creation. So what should be the relation between the human race, nature and God? How should humans behave towards nature and God? Surely there must be some rules to follow? If we have to use natural resources to survive, then there must be some limits because the world cannot sustain unlimited consumption of limited resources.

Hinduism was the first religion to realize this problem and a code of conduct or ethics was developed for human beings to follow. These ethics were designed to limit selfishness which, if left unchecked, can destroy the whole balance of nature. In the Vedas, codes of personal, social and spiritual conduct were written down. Over the centuries, many more different faiths and sects within the fold of Hinduism came into existence and they also specified their codes of conduct. The most common Hindu ethics are known as 'Yamas' (abstentions) and 'Niyamas' (observances) which form part of Ashtanga (the eightfold path) Yoga or Raj Yoga, introduced earlier on p.45. There are five Yamas and five Niyamas, which were recorded by sage Patanjali almost 2200 years ago. These spell out the moral dos and don'ts.

Yamas (The Five Abstentions)
Yama means to control and discipline the animal instinct in humans. The five Yamas are:

1. **Ahimsa**: restrain arrogance and anger. Hindus quote examples from Mahabharat and Ramayana in which the heroes Krishna and Rama are always described as calm and non-violent; they used their strength only against unjust and wicked people.

2. **Satya**: refrain from lying. Do not break promises and don't betray confidence. Character and integrity lead to success and are respected by all.

3. **Asteya**: do not steal. Crime never pays. Involvement in crime destroys one's career.

4. **Brahmacharya**: control lust and all wrongdoing. Give up evil company and don't consume alcoholic drinks or use tobacco. Drugs can destroy life.

5. **Aparigraha**: discipline desire and greed. Ambition to achieve good targets is not wrong but greed to acquire useless things is bad.

Niyamas (The Five Observances)
These help to develop a cultured and civilized person. The five Niyamas are:

1. **Shaucha**: be pure in body, mind and speech. Impurity leads to stress; stress and unhygienic conditions lead to physical and mental diseases.

2. **Santosh**: seek contentment. Be satisfied; don't enter the rat race.

3. **Tapa**: be prepared to make sacrifices. Be patient; learn to be calm even under stress and difficult circumstances.

4. **Svadhyaya**: study the scriptures. Learn and don't become a blind follower.

5. **Ishwarapranidhan**: cultivate devotion through daily worship and meditation. Remember God and thank him.

Teachers might wish to start a discussion about the need to have ethics. If all members of society are to follow certain ethics then who is going to set them? It is important to convey the fact that no rigid dogmas or strict rules are imposed in Hinduism because it has evolved and changed over time. However, basic human nature has not changed, so the need for there to be personal and social discipline still remains.

Typical questions/discussion points
1. Describe the five Yamas and the five Niyamas set by sage Patanjali. Are they still relevant?
2. Compare the eightfold path of Raj Yoga with the eightfold path in Buddhism. What similarities do you see?
3. Discuss your own ideas about discipline. Do you think we need to have rules to follow?

Ahimsa – Non-violence

The word 'Ahimsa' is often understood to mean non-killing. However, the concept of 'ahimsa' in Hinduism is not restricted to physical violence but is more to do with mental attitude. It is not merely a religious principle of non-killing or non-harming which has to be observed at certain times of the day or week; rather this principle is considered as an essential part of the Dharma of individuals, society and nations. It is regarded as one of the moral laws of Hinduism (see Yamas on p.52).

The concept of Ahimsa is related to the message of human survival – survival with dignity, conveyed by the teaching of Hinduism, including Buddhism and Jainism. Mahavira, who preached Jainism, said that all species on this globe are interdependent and one's welfare depends on the welfare of another. How do different sections of human society and species of plants and animals survive whilst competing for the same resources? The answer to this ethical question was provided by Hindu sages in the concept of 'Ahimsa'. They believed that lack of animosity will generate peace, hence Ahimsa is equivalent to Universal Brotherhood which should be practised at all levels, including the lowest living entity on the planet. In this context, Ahimsa links the philosophies of matter and soul, and links science with religion, because both sides are seeking ways to end suffering for all.

Mahavira, whose childhood name was Vardhaman, is considered to be the greatest teacher of non-violence. He was born in 539 BCE. At that time there was a decline in the study of the Vedic scriptures and in this period of illiteracy and ignorance some strange customs involving animal sacrifice had begun. These cruel practices had no sanction in the Vedic scriptures. Mahavira strongly condemned animal sacrifice and influenced people to give up meat-eating. He preached that there must not be any harm done to anyone in thought, word or deed. Thus, Jainism gave a great boost to the spread of vegetarianism which many Hindus practise as an ethic for ecology and physical and mental health. More detailed discussion on vegetarianism can be found on pp.77–79.

Non-violence does not mean that one should allow injustice or permit evil doings. Hindus have a great tradition, called Kshatriya (see p.70), of bravery, courage and fearlessness in protecting truth and justice. According to the Rig Veda, defence of oneself when attacked is the right conduct (see p.177). According to Mahatma Gandhi, one must resist evil but one must not hold any ill will towards the evil-doer.

The concept of Ahimsa can be introduced in the class by starting a discussion on feelings such as jealousy, hatred and ill will. Why do humans have these feelings? Do these feelings lead to peace and happiness or do they cause malice and quarrels? If they are harmful, what can be done to overcome them? The idea of non-jealousy, non-hatred and good will is the concept of Ahimsa. If appropriate, a teacher may extend the discussion to relate Ahimsa to vegetarianism.

Typical questions/discussion points
1. Name two people who made famous the concept of non-violence.
2. Is vegetarianism related to non-violence?
3. How can non-violence resist evil and injustice?

CHAPTER THREE
FAMILY, COMMUNITY AND TRADITION

Hindus around the World

*T*here are over 800 million Hindus spread throughout 160 or more countries around the world. Hinduism started in India, so how has Hinduism spread to other countries?

There are normally three main ways in which a particular religious faith might be carried from one country to another:

(a) by force, involving war and persecution;
(b) by missionaries going out to convert people from other faiths;
(c) by the migration of people seeking a better life in other countries.

Out of these three, Hinduism has spread only as a result of the migration of Hindus from India to other countries. In Hindu history no example of imposing Hinduism by coercion or conversion can be found.

Large-scale migration of Hindus from India started in the early nineteenth century when they were sent as indentured labourers to work in various colonies around the world under the British Raj. People were sent to colonies in East Africa, South Africa, Burma, Malaysia, Singapore, Fiji, Mauritius, Jamaica and Guyana. In East Africa most of the Indians worked on building railways, whilst in the Caribbean islands they worked mainly on sugar plantations. In spite of cultural differences and physical hardships, they managed to keep their Hindu traditions alive. The majority of Hindus in the industrialized countries arrived after the Second World War. By sincere and dedicated work, Hindus in

WORLD HINDU POPULATION

Africa & Middle East

Kenya	65,000
Malawi	4,000
Mauritius	700,000
Middle East	60,000
Nigeria	20,000
Others	20,000
South Africa	800,000
Tanzania	65,000
Uganda	20,000
Zambia	20,000
Zimbabwe	5,000
TOTAL	**1,779,000**

America

Canada	380,000
Carribbean	700,000
Mexico	500
Surinam	160,000
USA	800,000
TOTAL	**2,040,500**

Europe

Austria	5,000
Belgium	5,000
Denmark	5,000
Eastern Europe	5,000
France	30,000
Germany	36,000
Italy	1,000
Netherland	160,000
Norway	1,000
Portugal	10,000
Spain	12,000
Sweden	1,000
Switzerland	5,000
UK	1,200,000
TOTAL	**1,476,000**

One in every sixth person in the world is a Hindu

Asia & Australia

Afghanistan (was over 120,000 in 1989)	12,000
Australia	60,000
Bali & Indonesia	600,000
Bangladesh (was over 20 million in 1947)	10,000,000
Bharat	900,000,000
Bhutan	65,000
Burma	7,000,000
Fiji (over 700,000 before Col Robuka took power)	400,000
Hong Kong	90,000
Japan	5,000
Kashmir (was over 600,000 in 1989)	50,000
Malaysia	1,170,000
Nepal	20,000,000
New Zealand	50,000
Pakistan (was over 7,000,000 in 1947)	1,100,000
Singapore	150,000
Sri Lanka	2,000,000
Thailand	10,000
Vietnam	5,000
TOTAL	**942,767,000**

54

these countries have established themselves and made a notable contribution to the economic, cultural and religious life of their adopted nations. In Western society they are regarded as a disciplined, friendly and successful community.

According to an extensive study of multi-racial Britain published in 1996 by the Office of National Statistics, the Indian community (almost all of it is Hindu) had the highest levels of academic achievement and home ownership and the lowest unemployment level compared to the other Asian and Afro-Caribbean ethnic minorities. The map opposite shows the approximate distribution of the Hindu population around the world. Nepal is the only Hindu Kingdom in the world, its official calendar is the Hindu Vikram Samvat.

IN THE CLASSROOM

Typical questions/discussion points
1. How did Hinduism spread around the world?
2. Do the Hindus living in Britain come only from India?

British Hindus

Seekers of Truth and Pilgrims of Love

Mother India's children have been abroad in search of knowledge, and wisdom, as seekers of Truth and as pilgrims of Love, wandering over the world's surface, greeting every part of mother earth as their own.

They carry with them their vision of Oneness, of the One in All, and of the All in One, the compassionate one, who creates, dissolves and recreates, who is all forms and yet formless, who is all names and without name, ever has been, and will ever be, who dwells in the whole Human Family, which is one, as on the river banks and the forests, as on the mountain tops, in the East or in the West, in the North or in the South, in the Tropics or in the wild region of the Arctic Pole. He is the Unity in all the colourful, rich diversity of the universe, the divine spark in everyone that makes everyone our kith and kin, be it man or woman, bird or animal, all creatures in the animal and vegetable world.

(PROF. K.L. VASWANI)

Hindus have been living in Britain since the beginning of the British Empire. Early in the seventeenth century some Hindus, particularly from Bengal, came to Britain for further studies or to represent the Princely States that existed in India. The large-scale migration of Hindus began after 1950.

Population of Hindus in the UK

It is estimated that the number of people of Indian origin settled in different parts of the world is about five million. Hindus in the UK are estimated to number about a million. They have come from various countries: India, Pakistan, Bangladesh, Sri Lanka, Indonesia, Guyana, West Indies, Singapore, Hong Kong, Malaysia, Kenya, Uganda, Southern Africa, Sudan, Ethiopia, Trinidad and Tobago and other countries in the West Indies.

Integration of Hindus into British society

Hindus have by and large maintained their cultural and religious identity in the UK and at the same time have fulfilled their role as British citizens by making contributions in economic, educational, cultural and religious fields. They have established themselves in many areas including business, medicine, accountancy, engineering, pharmacy, law, and many other sectors. Hindus have also entered into wholesale and retail enterprises of all kinds. By their perseverance and hard work, they have prospered by running small businesses like corner shops and post offices. Their strong sense of community and close family relations have helped them in these achievements.

Jawaharlal Nehru, the first Prime Minister of India, once remarked that every Indian abroad carries with him a bit of India. By this he was citing a specific instance of the general truth that emigrants carry with them a bit of their own countries wherever they go. The adaptability and flexibility in the Hindu character has helped Hindus to integrate into British society without losing their identity in the process. Generally, Hindus are law-abiding, peace-loving, honest and hard-working people and this reflects upon their cultural heritage.

Hindus have brought with them to the UK social customs and traditions which are new to the indigenous population of this country. Throughout their history Hindus have preferred a joint family system and it is a new experience for the local community to see the Hindus' way of living. The respect that the parents and elders of the family receive from their children, and the love and care that children are given by their parents is particularly notable. A Hindu always respects his mother, father, teacher and guest (*Matru Devo Bhava, Pitru Devo Bhava, Acharya Devo Bhava, Atithi Devo Bhava*). He sees in them divinity; as he knows that through them he will achieve success in the future. Social workers and various organizations have appreciated the value of the way of life followed by Hindus and have advised them to adhere to their culture and identity.

The keynote of Hindu culture is 'unity in diversity', allowing people with all their differences in custom, creed, language and tradition to live together in one society. This ideal is expressed in the beautiful words of the Bard of Humanity, the Poet of Man, Ravindranath Tagore, who was awarded the Nobel Prize for Literature. In his talks in China, Tagore read from his poem 'Gitanjalee':

> *Let all human races keep their personalities*
> *And yet come together*
> *Not in a uniformity that is dead*
> *But in unity that is living.*

Hindus have introduced Indian classical dance, Indian music, Indian languages and Yoga to the UK. Many singers and dancers of good repute come to this country to perform and some of them have settled here and founded dance and music schools where people of all denominations learn the classical arts.

Hindus in British politics

In the past British Hindus have been apathetic towards politics, preferring not to be involved. In recent years, however, they have started taking part in political life. There are now many Hindu councillors in the larger towns and cities, and in some of these areas and in borough councils they have served as mayors. More and more Hindus have come to realize the need to participate in politics.

Hindus' attitudes towards their religion

Though Hindus have settled in this country they want to preserve their religion and culture. Hindu leaders and social workers from the Hindu community have started to work along these lines. There are now more than 200 Hindu temples in the UK. Hindus who have settled here come from different parts of India and have different customs, traditions and beliefs. There are Shaivas, Vaishnavas, Sikhs, Buddhists, Swaminarayanis, Jains, and others. All these sects want their children to know about their religion. Today there are many religious, social and cultural organizations with temples or places of worship, offices and buildings from where they administer the activities necessary for their children and community.

Hindu organizations in the UK

There are several hundred Hindu organizations in the UK. Some of the more well-established ones are described below.

Vishwa Hindu Parishad (VHP)

Vishwa Hindu Parishad (World Council of Hindus) is active in consolidating Hindu society all over the world. Its UK chapter was established in 1966. It is a registered charity in the UK and has fourteen branches; those in Bolton, Newham and Ilford have their own temple-cum-community-centres. VHP strives to promote and project Hindu Dharma and culture amongst the Hindu community. The organization has always played a prominent role in addressing the problems facing Hindu society in this country. It celebrates festivals to help Hindus learn about their Dharma and organizes large religious gatherings where Hindus from different sects come together.

Virat Hindu Sammelan was the largest religious gathering of Hindus in Europe. It was held at Milton Keynes over two days in 1989 and approximately 100,000 Hindus participated. They had come from all parts of the world and included many saints and religious leaders from India and Nepal who had come to take part. Local MPs, councillors, the High Commissioner of India and many other dignitaries attended the conference. It was a unique occasion, the first time that Hindus had gathered in such a vast number in the UK.

Hindu Swayamsevak Sangh (HSS)
The HSS has over fifty branches throughout the UK. It is a registered charity which caters particularly for the young people in this country. At its weekly meetings, through discussions and lectures and physical activities like games and exercises, it instils leadership qualities, self-confidence and self-discipline in the youngsters. The aim is to unite the Hindu community. It holds youth leadership training camps for its members (who are called swayamsevaks) every year. It also runs service projects like Hindu Sahitya Kendra (Hindu Literature Centre) and an aid organization called Sewa International. Through another project called the Hindu Marathon, it aims to promote sporting activities among young people. HSS is known for its efficiency, team work and well-disciplined programmes.

Swaminarayana Hindu Mission
Under the guidance of Shri Pramukh Swami Maharaj, this mission holds weekly prayer meetings in twenty-six centres. Activities for young people and children are organized on a regular basis. Dedication and service are the hallmark of the youth movement members. The mission started an independent Hindu School in London for the 3–18 age group in 1992. It covers the National Curriculum and also provides cultural and religious education based on Hinduism. It is the only school of this type in the Western world. The mission organized a Cultural Festival of India at Alexandra Palace during a month in 1985 and this attracted over half a million visitors. It has temples or places of worship in many towns and cities in the UK. In August 1995, a temple was opened in Neasden, London, in the style of a traditional Hindu temple; it is the largest marble temple outside India. Over 1500 craftsmen produced 26,300 carved pieces using 2828 tonnes of limestone and 2000 tonnes of marble and it took three years to assemble. Its dome is the only layered segmental dome in the UK that does not use steel or lead. There is a permanent exhibition, 'Understanding Hinduism', on display at the temple.

Arya Samaj
There are two Arya Samaj centres, one in London and the other in Birmingham. They regularly hold Satsang (congregational singing and discourses) and perform Havan. They also celebrate the birthday of the great people of India who have sacrificed their lives for the propagation of Hindu Dharma. They hold language classes for children to learn Hindi and Sanskrit. The Arya Samaj in Birmingham runs a very successful charitable matrimonial service for the Hindu community.

International Krishna Consciousness Society (ISKCON)
This organization has attracted members from the host community as well as from Hindu families. It has its own temples in many cities in the UK. The main temple is Bhaktivedant Manor near Watford, donated to the Society in 1973 by George Harrison of the Beatles. The local council made several attempts to curtail public worship at the temple, but British Hindus campaigned to keep the temple open for the celebration of festivals like Janmashtami. In May 1996, the government finally recognized the importance of this shrine and allowed ISKCON to worship and celebrate festivals there. This victory demonstrated the unity and commitment of Hindus in preserving their religious traditions and their ability to resolve conflict through peaceful and lawful means.

Ramakrishna Mission
The order has more than 130 branches in India. It has numerous publication centres which publish magazines and books on religion and philosophy in many languages. The publications of the order are highly respected and sold all over the world. The order's only affiliated branch is in Bourne End, 40 kilometres from London. The centre holds regular discourses both at its premises and at Bharatiya Vidya Bhavan in London. The head of the centre gives talks on religion and philosophy both here and abroad.

Shri Satya Sai Centre
The followers of this movement hold regular congregations every week in a number of cities.

The Brahma Kumaris
This organization has forty-five centres in the UK. Each centre offers courses and lectures on positive thinking and meditation.

National Council of Hindu Temples
A number of Hindu temples in the UK are affiliated to this organization. It actively participates in inter-faith activities.

IN THE CLASSROOM

At KS1 and KS2 pupils should be made aware of the fact that nearly one million Hindus now live in Britain and that they have come from different countries. You could talk about the importance of belonging to a group or a community. Start with a discussion on the signs of belonging, e.g. name, appearance, dress, rituals, family history and faith.

At KS3 and KS4 pupils can investigate how Hindus in Britain maintain their allegiance as British citizens and at the same time manage to retain their cultural identity. Discuss the role of religious organizations like the Vishwa Hindu Parishad and the Hindu temples.

Interview a young member of an organization like the Hindu Swayamsevak Sangh in order to find out about the issues facing young Hindus in the UK and how Hindu organizations help them.

Typical questions/discussion points
1. Hindus living in Britain have come from all over the world and have brought with them their traditions and culture. How are Hindus maintaining their cultural identity in Britain?
2. Describe a Hindu custom which you have observed in the UK.
3. What role do Hindu organizations play in Britain?
4. What problems does a Hindu face when trying to live as a Hindu in the UK?

Hindu Family Life

In Hinduism great importance is placed on family life. The family is considered as the building block of society and the entire nation. Starting and maintaining a family is considered a religious duty. According to Hindu scriptures, this is the most productive and active stage of life and is called 'Grihastha Ashram' (see p.65). During this stage, the key concept is that by maintaining a family, the householder fulfils his or her obligations towards ancestors, society and God. This is based on the idea of sharing; the Hindu concept of family life, therefore, is not founded on an individualistic life-style which has become the hallmark of modern living.

Changes in social and economic conditions have had their effect on the Hindu tradition of extended families. Whilst an extended family, in some sections of Hindu society, may have become divided into separate smaller units, they still maintain strong emotional, financial and social bonds.

A family life is where one shares one's joys and sorrows, successes and failures, ups and downs with one's parents, brothers, sisters and other relations. Hindu families still benefit from this tradition even when some members live in different parts of the world. Such links help to maintain cultural identity in countries where Hindus are a minority, particularly when compatible partners are sought for children of marriageable age.

Hindu sages recognized the importance of a happy stable family for the all-round development of a child. A recent survey of GCSE and A-level school results showed that Hindu children do much better in their studies. The number of Hindu professionals working in universities, hospitals and various industries is increasing. The reason for such success is that young Hindu students are encouraged and supported by their families.

Another unique feature of Hindu family life is the role of grandparents. V.P. Kanitkar in *What we believe: We are Hindus* explains: 'Hinduism is absorbed through observation and participation, and the grandparent's role is important; elders pass on traditions by involving members of their family in the prescribed rituals of religious festivals and sacraments, thus ensuring continuity.' The grandparents pass knowledge and family customs on to the younger generations.

IN THE CLASSROOM

At KS1, a general discussion could be started on names used to define relations, e.g. brother, sister, grandad, grandma. It can then be widened to introduce the idea of the extended family by pointing out that Hindus have specific names for all relations. For example, some of these names in Hindi are:

Maternal grandfather – Nana
Maternal grandmother – Nani
Paternal grandfather – Dada
Paternal grandmother – Dadi
Mother's brother – Mama (and his wife is called Mami)
Mother's sister – Mausi (and her husband is called Mausa)
Father's younger brother – Chacha (and his wife is called Chachee)
Father's elder brother – Taya (and his wife is called Tayee)
Father's sister – Bhua (and her husband is called Fufaa)

There are many more example of such names. The use of specific names to describe family relations indicates the importance of family unity and respect for elders.

Reflect on issues like: What makes a house a home? What makes my home special? Why do we need families? Relate the responses to the need for caring and sharing.

At KS2, the role of grandparents in teaching traditions and family history can be discussed. Pupils can be encouraged to bring in old family photographs and/or they can find out how the older generation has moulded their thoughts.

Typical questions/discussion points
1. Why do Hindus have extended families?
2. What makes a family happy and stable?
3. Why is it important for Hindus in Britain to keep in close contact with their relations in India?
4. What are your responsibilities as a member of your family?

Unity in Diversity

Hinduism originated from India which, in spite of several partitions, remains one of the largest countries in the world. India is a land full of contrasts. Geographically, in the north are the high mountains of the Himalaya and in the south are the tropical beaches. There is a huge desert in the west and lush green rolling plains

in the east. The weather also ranges from severe cold to tropical heat. These variations in geographical and climatic conditions, combined with the inherently flexible nature of Hindus, has resulted in a rich diversity. Hindus in different parts of India wear different clothes, eat different types of food, speak different languages, play different music and have contrasting social traditions. The migration of Hindus to other countries has added further variety of tastes and traditions. In this section, the rich diversity of traditions in Hinduism is described, along with some basic common features which identify all Hindus.

Variety of tastes and traditions

Languages
Hindi is the national language of India but there are thirty-three other languages and many more local dialects. Hindi, Gujarati, Punjabi, Bengali, Marathi, Kannada and Tamil are some of the languages which are common among British Hindus.

Clothes
Traditional Hindu clothes vary from region to region. Hindu women usually wear a sari. It may be a simple, patterned or richly decorated piece of cloth which is elegantly wrapped around the body with hand-folded pleats. Hindu brides wear red or pink coloured saris with sparkling silver or golden embroidery. Hindu women from the north of India, particularly Sikh women, often wear a trouser-like garment called a salwar with a long tunic called a kameez.

Traditional attire for Hindu men is a long-sleeved shirt called a kurta. Some men wear a lungi, which looks like a Scottish kilt, whilst others may wear a dhoti which is a loose piece of cloth wrapped around the legs and the waist. Some also wear a turban. The wearing of a turban is considered a religious duty by Sikh men.

Food
The taste and flavour of food eaten by Hindus also varies according to region and religious faith. Most Hindus are vegetarian and even non-vegetarian Hindus will most certainly not eat beef. A typical Hindu vegetarian meal

consists of several dishes including spicy vegetables, lentil soup (dhal), rice or chapatti. Hindus from the south of India mainly eat rice, whereas those from the north prefer chapattis or naans. This is because rice is the main crop in the south, while wheat is mostly grown in the north. Further details about traditions related to food can be found on pp.77–79.

Festivals
The style of celebration of some Hindu festivals varies from region to region. This is explained in more detail in Chapter 4 (see pp.97–101).

Common features
An important point to note here is that all the differences mentioned above are only outward differences. In spite of this external diversity, there is an inner unity among all Hindus. This unity is based on the following five main commonalities:

Common race
All Hindus, whether they be Buddhists, Sikhs, Jains or adherents of other sects, belong to the same race. They all have common forefathers and ancestors who lived in India (Bharat).

Common Dharma
Hindu Dharma may appear to be divided into many sects and sub-sects but they all share the same basic principles and concepts, explained in Chapter 2. The founders of various sects or '-isms' did not intend to disunite Hindus, they were simply explaining Hinduism according to the need of the time.

Common motherland
The founder of every Hindu sect was born in India (Bharat). They all share the history of the same land and in their holy books recognize Bharat as their motherland.

Common language
All Hindu scriptures are written in Sanskrit or in a language derived from Sanskrit.

Common philosophy
The main philosophical ideas of all branches of Hinduism are based on the Vedic literature.

The information presented here may help the teacher to explain that there are many outward differences in Hindus' lives but fundamentally they are all one. At KS1, pupils may be introduced to the idea of diversity by talking about the variety of food that people eat or the different clothes people wear.

At KS2, pupils may be asked to consider the questions: Do people have to wear the same type of clothes to belong to a religion? Can people speaking different languages belong to the same faith? Show them an Indian currency note (rupees) and count the number of languages in which the value of the note is printed. If possible, show a film about India and let the diversity and colourful variety of life in India capture the children's imagination. At KS3 and KS4, pupils should be able to grasp the idea of 'unity in diversity' found in Hinduism.

Typical questions/discussion points
1. What is the traditional dress of a Hindu woman?
2. Name some of the languages that Hindus speak.
3. Why is there so much diversity in Hinduism?
4. Describe the main common features which unite all Hindus, including Buddhists, Sikhs and Jains.

Music, Dance, Drama and Poetry

These art forms play an important part in Hindu religious and cultural tradition. In this section some of their main features are introduced and their role in Hindu religious traditions explained.

Bhajans and Keertan
Bhajans are songs of praise and expressions of devotion to God. In Hindu temples prayers are followed by Bhajans. Music accompanied by devotional songs sung in public is called Keertan. This particular activity is very joyful, often the whole congregation joins in the singing and some clap hands in rhythm with the music. Hindus believe that music is a

divine gift. Shri Krishna is always shown standing with his flute. Bhajans sung by Mira, a famous poetess and devotee of Krishna, are very popular among Hindus. One of the Hindu goddesses, Saraswati, is usually shown with a sitar-like musical instrument in her hand. Music was studied very carefully by ancient Hindu sages who wrote down the rules in the Vedas. One of the scriptures, called 'Gandharva Veda' (see Upa-Vedas in the family tree of Hindu scriptures on p.126), is considered to be the source of Indian classical music.

Poet-saints

There have been many poet-saints in Hindu history. In fact, all the Vedas and the epics 'Ramayana' and 'Mahabharata' are written in poetic language and are meant to be sung. The 'Mahabharata' is the longest poem in the world. Rig Veda says: 'A poet becomes a seer and a scholar by poetic compositions' (8-79-1).

In *Songs of the Saints of India*, J.S. Hawley and M. Juergensmeyer have translated selected poems written by six famous poet-saints: Ravidas, Kabir, Guru Nanak, Surdas, Tulsidas and Meera Bai. They comment that the poems, though religious in context, are universal in theme. They speak of the trials of life in society, the hollow shell of the body,

friendship, betrayal, beauty, birth, death, pain and exaltation of love.

Another literary masterpiece of poetry is the 'Tirukural' written in the Tamil language by the weaver Saint Tiruvalluvar around 200 BCE near the present-day Madras in southern India. In an extraordinarily compact verse form of fourteen syllables, the poet-saint presents 133 subjects in ten verses each on human relationships, human strengths, statecraft and other subjects. Many Hindus consider the Tirukural as the 'bible' on virtue for the human race. In fact, it is sworn on in courts of law in southern India.

Nataraja

One of the Hindu Trinity, Shiva, is also known as the 'Nataraja', the King of Dance. See the description of Shiva (Mahesh) on p.23. The image of Shiva as Nataraja, standing in a circle of fire performing the cosmic dance, with flowing hair, four arms and the posture of one uplifted leg, is a very popular one.

Bharatnatayam

Dance and Yoga were viewed as the same and gave rise to the tradition of ritual dancing in Hindu temples. The most ancient dance form is the 'Bharatnatayam' which originated in the temples. In this dance form, every hand gesture (Mudras) and body movement is

The poet-saint Tiruvalluvar

Wealth's Goddess dwells
In the hospitable home
Of those who welcome
Guests with a smiling face.

To utter harsh words when
Sweet ones would serve
Is like eating unripe fruit
When ripe ones are at hand.

'Sweet are the sounds of the
Flute and the lute,' say those
Who have not heard the
Prattle of their own children.

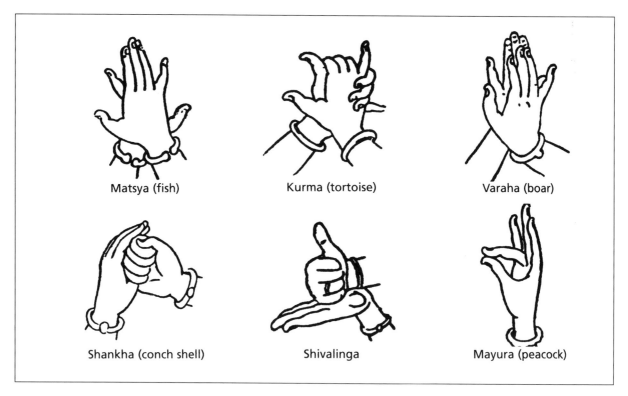

Matsya (fish)   Kurma (tortoise)   Varaha (boar)

Shankha (conch shell)   Shivalinga   Mayura (peacock)

Hand gestures (Mudras) of Bharatnatayam

imbued with meaning to create a language of motion by which stories from religious scriptures are choreographed. There was a time when young girls were dedicated to this art form and were raised in temple environs with years of rigorous training in classical singing and dancing. They were called 'Devdasis', meaning servants of God. Some Western scholars have tarnished the image of Devdasis by wrongly classifying them as 'public women'. During the British Raj, temple dancing was banned and this art form was consequently relegated to a secular art. It was restyled and nurtured mainly by married women of the Brahmin caste; now it has been revived again and has become very popular. Bharatnatayam dance is taught in nearly all the big cities in the UK.

Raas Garba

Dance is also associated with the worship of the goddess Durga. The most popular event among British Hindus is the Raas Garba. These dances are performed every night during the festival of Navaratri (nine nights) in honour of the three Hindu goddesses and are organised by Hindu community groups throughout the country. These events offer a

spectacular combination of dance and worship. If you ever happen to look in, you will find women wearing the best of their glittering saris and men all smartly dressed dancing around in circles to melodious devotional songs accompanied by the rhythmic beats of Indian drums called 'dholaks'. Each dancer carries small decorated wooden sticks which are struck in rhythm. As armies of dancers

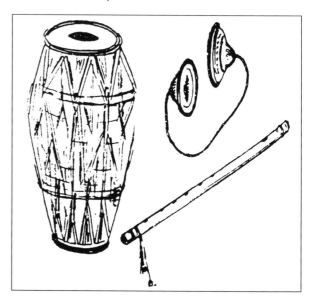

Traditional musical instruments in Hindu temples: drum, cymbal and flute

swirl around in circles and their sticks collide in mid-air like swords, it gives the impression of a mock war. But with all the singing, dancing and festivities, it is certainly not a war dance; it is a celebration of victory, the victory of good over evil.

This dancing and worshipping over the nine consecutive nights commemorates the nine-day-long war which was waged between Shri Rama and Ravana. Rama represents good and Ravana represents evil because, in spite of his intelligence and wealth, he had allowed the evil forces of jealousy, anger and arrogance to influence him (see the 'Ramayana' story on pp.134–138).

This strength to fight the bad, and power to protect the weak, is believed to be a feminine quality. Hindu philosophers have always advocated that one should be morally and physically strong, so that good can be protected. Hence, the goddess of strength is worshipped in these nine days in the name of Durga, Kaali, Amba and Mahishasura Mardini.The tigress-like strength of Durga, the ferocity of Kaali, the pure white embodiment of Amba and the slayer of demons Mahishasura are all represented through dance and drama which manifest this feminine power to eradicate suffering caused by injustice.

Ramalila

There has been a long tradition of enacting the story of 'Ramayana' known as 'Ramalila' before the festival of Dussera during the month of October or November (see p.99). Hindus gather in large numbers to see the 'Ramalila' in which local artists enact the whole story of Shri Rama. During this festive season, drama plays an important role in portraying the idealism personified by Shri Rama.

IN THE CLASSROOM

This topic will be enjoyed by pupils of KS1 and KS2 levels. The music and dance can be introduced by using audio-visual aids. Let pupils listen to the ringing of bells, the blowing of a conch or the rhythms of drums (dholaks) being played in temples. If possible, show them a video of Bharatnatayam dance.

Make sure that the dance postures and steps used to convey the story are explained. The story of 'Ramayana' or Ganesha expressed in this dance form is very enchanting. Show pupils the hand gestures (mudras) depicted in this book and relate them to the incarnations of Vishnu (see p.27).

Typical questions/discussion points
1. Draw a sketch of Nataraja.
2. Why do Hindus think that dancing and singing can be part of worship?
3. What is 'Ramalila'? What role does it play in passing on the tradition?
4. What is the significance of the 'Ras Garba' dancing?

The Journey of Life

Your chance of human birth, does not come time and again
Once the ripe fruit falls, you can not stick it back again.

(KABIR, SAKHI 15-5)

What is the purpose of life? And how should life should be lived? These are questions which have perplexed thinkers of all generations. Often answers are given based either on a materialistic view or on a spiritualistic view. The Hindu view which has evolved over thousands of years presents an outlook on life which synthesizes both spiritualism and materialism. This view is practical because it is based on an understanding of the desires of human nature, but at the same time it acknowledges the ultimate reality that the physical body is only transient. We must enjoy because we are here, we should renounce because we shall go: this is the basic thought. Based on this principle of 'enjoyment and renunciation', a scheme of life has been evolved.

If life is a journey then the Hindu view is that it must have a purpose and a plan. For such a journey to reach its successful conclusion, it must have its destination specified, one should know the stages it will go through and of course one must have the directions. In the following sections we cover these three topics.

Destination: the four objectives (Purusharthas) of life

Have you ever wondered why we are all here, living as humans on this earth? Are we just born to eat and drink, sleep and wake up again to eat and drink? Is there any useful purpose in life? All these are very difficult questions to answer, but Hindu sages have provided an answer in four simple words: Dharma (duties), Artha (material prosperity), Kama (enjoyment) and Moksha (salvation). According to Hinduism, these are the four Purusharthas (efforts or actions) which every person should perform. They are the objectives of all actions. Brief meanings of the four are as follows:

1. Dharma (Duties)

There are many meanings of the word 'Dharma' (see p.7). In this context, the most pertinent meaning is 'duties'. This is the path to reach God by means of a disciplined life. Rather than being selfish, all actions should be aimed at fulfilling one's Dharma. For example, a doctor must treat a patient irrespective of who the patient is; similarly, a policeman must catch the criminal even if the criminal happens to be his friend. Honesty, truth, love and justice are the virtues which should be practised in life.

2. Artha (Material prosperity)

This is the means of obtaining the necessities of life. Human beings cannot be expected to live like wild animals in the forests. Everyone needs a home, food and clean conditions to live in. There are many material things which are required to lead a worldly life. In modern society, it means that one needs money to live. In Hinduism, the need to earn money and gain material goods is recognized, but these should be earned by fair and honest means. It also reminds us that gaining wealth is not the only objective, other duties must also be carried out.

3. Kama (Enjoyment)

Kama deals with the natural desire of man to obtain and enjoy worldly happiness. God has created this beautiful world and given everyone the five sense organs: a tongue to taste delicacies; eyes to see beauty; ears to hear music; a nose to smell fragrances; and skin to

touch and feel. Through these senses man is meant to enjoy the world, but is also warned that it is difficult to satisfy all desires, therefore there is a need to discipline one's life (see Self-discipline on p.52). Hinduism teaches that there is a time and a place for enjoyment and one's actions should be self-controlled. One should not always expect immediate satisfaction of desires because that may cause unhappiness. In particular, young people need to understand that the desire for sexual happiness is a natural desire. In the Hindu way of life, fulfilment of such desires is not forbidden, but a special stage in life (called 'Grihastha ashram') has been set aside for it. That is why Hindu youngsters are expected to follow much stricter codes of conduct in sexual matters than those in the more permissive Western society.

4. Moksha (Salvation)

This is the final and ultimate objective of life – to gain freedom from worldly suffering. Everyone knows that life is not always full of happiness. Humans have to face disease, old age and death. There are natural disasters, wars and many social problems which cause pain and suffering. Birth follows death, and death follows rebirth; this cycle goes on. The ultimate aim is to be free from this continuous cycle of birth and death. This is Moksha, and Hindus believe that it can be achieved only by following the path of Dharma and by leading a disciplined and virtuous life.

Finally, it should be noted that these objectives of life are not just for Hindus but can be applicable to all human beings. To achieve these objectives we need to have a plan, just like a school which plans for pupils' study and examinations by setting timetables. So what is the plan for life?

Stages: the four Ashramas

How does one go through life? The tenets of Hinduism have identified four basic stages through which a life passes. In a way, it is a plan to achieve the four objectives. In our complex modern society we have to do so many things and it becomes almost essential to plan for them. Schools have timetables, governments have schemes, businesses and industries, big and small, all plan out the work they have to do in order to achieve their targets or objectives. The section above presented the four objectives of life; so what does one have to do to achieve these objectives?

According to Hindu thought, life is simply divided into four logical stages (called Ashrams). Even though the names of these stages may sound rather strange, the idea of planning life by going through these four stages is still very relevant in our modern society. The four stages are:

1. Brahmacharya (Student life)

No one is born with knowledge, so obviously the first stage has to be the stage of learning. As a child grows, the first priority is to be educated and learn about duties (Dharma) which have to be performed. At this stage, a celibate student is known as a 'Brahamchari' who has to keep away from distractions and therefore has to practise self-control. During this stage the foundation of life is laid; things one does now will determine what one will become later in life. Therefore, the emphasis is on self-discipline to make oneself physically and mentally strong for the future.

2. Grihastha (Family life)

Having received education and after reaching maturity, the second stage of life, called Grihastha Ashram, begins. This is when, as a householder, one has to carry out one's duties towards family, society and the nation. The objectives of Kama (enjoyment) and Artha (material prosperity) are to be achieved during this stage. Parents bring up children and they have to earn money to pay for all their needs. There is also the need to help others by paying taxes and making donations. This Ashram is based on the feelings of mutual love and sharing and depends on respect for family life. If family life breaks down, people stop sharing and become selfish, and ultimately society and the nation will suffer. Therefore, Grihastha Ashram is thought to be very important and the most demanding of all the four Ashramas.

3. Vanaprastha (Retirement)

As children grow up and retirement from work takes place, most of the family and financial responsibilities are over. The body will also begin to show signs of tiredness and aging. That is the time to slow down the pace and spend life in a calm, serene way. This is the third stage of life, in which a person should start to detach from worldly life and practise meditation. One should develop an attitude of friendliness towards all and learn to live a simpler and less complicated life.

4. Sanyasa (Preparation for salvation)

In this final stage of life, one prepares for the ultimate objective of attaining Moksha (salvation) from this cycle of life and death. Birth and death are a reality every human being has to face. Hindu scriptures advise that in this final stage of life, one should have no bonds of relationships and attachments. The mind should be free of all desires, there should be no more yearning for wealth, children and fame. Such a desire-free mind, full of spiritual knowledge, is the perfect state of mind for the last stage of life.

Directions: the sixteen sacraments (Sanskaras)

Hinduism contains the concept of Sanskaras, which are acts of purifying, refining and developing the body, the mind and the intellect. These Sanskaras are performed at important stages of life by means of religious ceremonies which include a certain amount of ritual. It would be wrong to call the Sanskaras rituals, the better word in English is sacraments. There are many sacraments defined in the scriptures, but the most widely accepted number is sixteen. Each one provides directions for the journey of life, starting from the time of conception until death. In *The Science of Making a Better Man* by Dr Satyavrat Siddhantalankar, the psychological and medical significance of the sacraments is described. A brief outline of the sixteen Sanskaras is given below:

1. Garbhadhana

Performed after the wedding ceremony for the fulfilment of one's parental obligations and the continuation of the human race. It involves prayer for the impregnation of the foetus with a life-giving soul.

2. Punasavana

Performed during the second or third month of pregnancy. It creates the atmosphere for the strong physical growth of the unborn child.

3. Simantonnayana

Performed in the sixth or eighth month of pregnancy, with special emphasis on the healthy mental growth of the unborn child. Manu's views are accepted by modern science: 'Mental state of pregnant woman affects the unborn child, therefore the woman should stay in an environment which is beneficial for producing a healthy child.'
(Manu Smruti, Chapter 9, verse 9)

4. Jatakarma

Performed at birth. The newborn child is welcomed into the world by putting a small amount of honey in the mouth and whispering the name of God in the ear of the child.

5. Namakaran

Naming ceremony performed about eleven days after birth. Hindu tradition is to use a name which is meaningful and is intended to be a source of inspiration throughout the life of the individual. Names are often associated with the date of birth (see p.122) and with Sanskrit words.

6. Nishkramana

Introduction of the child to mother nature. Normally performed about four months after birth. The child is taken outside and exposed to the rays of the sun.

7. Annaprashana

First solid food for the baby when teething commences.

8. Choodakarma (Mundan)

Performed at the age of either one or three years. This has become one of the most popular Sanskars for children, often done in the presence of many friends and relations. There is a misconception that this Sanskar is similar to 'Confirmation' or 'Christening' ceremonies. Such ceremonies do not exist in Hinduism because it is believed that a child is born as a Hindu and this does not need confirmation. The Choodakarma or Mundan sacrament is related to the development of the brain. All the hair from the child's head is shaved for the first time. Head shaving signifies the removal of bad thoughts but also has medical significance because it enables the scalp to be checked and the proper joining of the skull bones to be seen. Modern science confirms that the skull is fully formed after three years.

9. Karnavedha

Performed between three to five years of age, when the lower lobes of the ears are pierced. It is still popular among girls. According to Hindu scripture, Sushrut (Chapters 19, 21), it is a medical process that prevents occurrence of diseases and should be performed by a specialist. It is similar to what is known as acupuncture.

10. Upanayana (Yajnopaveet or the sacred thread ceremony)

This is the well-known sacred thread ceremony performed when a child reaches school-going age. 'Upanayana' means getting closer to someone. With this Sanskara, the child is introduced to the guru (teacher) and given the sacred thread (Yajnopaveet) which consists of three strands. The three strands symbolize the three obligations (Rishi Rin, Pitri Rin and Dev Rin) which the child vows to fulfil. Rishi Rin is the obligation to promote knowledge gained from all the sages, thinkers and scientists. Pitri Rin is the obligation to look after and respect one's parents and ancestors. Dev Rin is the obligation towards the society and nation in which one lives. The ceremony lays stress on a life of moral rectitude and sexual purity for students being initiated into 'Brahamcharya' (see p.65). Because the thread symbolizes these vows, those who wear it ensure that the thread is never broken or taken off. Teachers should note that the ideas of sexual purity, moral rectitude and respect for teachers which are conveyed by this Sanskara are still held in high esteem by Hindu parents.

11. Vedarambha

Whilst the earlier Upanayana Sanskar meant introduction, Vedarambha means the start of education. 'Veda' means knowledge and 'Arambha' means start. This was normally performed at the Gurukul (school) before the first lesson. It starts with the explanation of the meaning of the famous 'Gayatri Mantra' (see p.123), a Hindu prayer which is aimed at the attainment of sound intellect.

12. Samavartana

Graduation ceremony performed at completion of studies. The individual is ready to participate fully in the social and economic life of the community.

13. Vivaha (marriage)

This Sanskar marks the start of the second and the most important stage of life, called the 'Grihastha Ashrama' described earlier on p.65. Two individuals who are considered to be compatible form a lifelong partnership at this ceremony in which the responsibilities and duties of a householder are explained. The precise details and rituals performed in a wedding ceremony vary from region to region and often take several hours to complete. The main stages of a Hindu wedding are as follows:

(a) Varmaala: First, the bride's parents welcome the bridegroom and his family at the boundary of the house where the wedding is taking place. A red kum-kum (a kind of powder) mark is applied to their foreheads (see Tilak on p.30). Members of both families are formally introduced, marking the start of the relationship between the two families. The bride and the bridegroom then exchange garlands (Varmaala) and declare: 'Let all the learned persons present here know, we are accepting each other willingly, voluntarily and pleasantly. Our hearts are concordant and united like waters.'

(b) Madhu-Parka: The bridegroom is brought to a specially decorated altar called 'Mandap' and offered a seat and a welcoming drink – a mixture of milk, ghee, yoghurt, honey and sugar.

(c) Gau Daan and Kanya Pratigrahan: 'Gau' means 'cow' and 'Daan' means 'donation'. Nowadays, the symbolic exchange of gifts, particularly clothes and ornaments takes place. The groom's mother gives an auspicious necklace (Mangala sootra) to the bride. Mangala sootra is the emblem of marital status for a Hindu woman. 'Kanya' means 'the daughter' and ' Pratigrahan' is an exchange with responsiveness on both sides. The bride's father declares that their daughter has accepted the bridegroom and requests them to accept her.

(d) Vivaha-homa: A sacred fire is lit and the Purohit (priest) recites the sacred mantras in Sanskrit. Oblations are offered to the fire while the prayers are said. The words 'Id na mama', meaning 'It is not for me' are repeated after the offerings. This symbolizes the selflessness required to run a family.

(e) Paanigrahan: This is the ceremony of vows. The husband, holding his wife's hand, says, 'I hold your hand in the spirit of Dharma, we are both husband and wife'.

(f) Shilarohan and Laaja Homa: 'Shilarohan' is the climbing over a stone or rock by the bride to symbolize her willingness and strength to overcome difficulties in pursuit of her duties. Both gently walk around the sacred fire four times, the bride leading three times and the groom leading the fourth time. He is reminded of his responsibilities. The couple join their hands and then the bride's brothers pour some barley into them which is then offered to the fire to symbolize that they will all jointly work for the welfare of society. The husband marks the parting in his wife's hair with red kum-kum powder for the first time. This is called 'Sindoor' and is the distinctive mark of a married Hindu woman.

(g) Sapta-Padi: This is the main part of the ceremony. The couple walk seven steps, reciting a prayer at each step: the first for food, the second for strength, the third for prosperity, the fourth for wisdom, the fifth for progeny, the sixth for health and the seventh for friendship. A marriage is considered to be complete after the seventh step and a symbolic matrimonial knot is tied.

(h) Surya Darshan and Dhruva Darshan: The couple look at the sun in order to be blessed with creative life. They look in the direction of the Dhruva (polar star) and resolve to remain unshaken and steadfast like the star.

(i) Ashirvada (blessings): The couple are blessed by the elders and the priest for a long and prosperous married life.

It is important to clarify two misconceptions about Hindu marriages: arranged marriages and child marriages. Hindu scriptures prohibit the use of force or coercion in marriage (further details are given on p.167), so arranged marriages are not forced marriages. In the Vedic period, child marriages were strictly prohibited. Later, owing to political and economic changes, some new social traditions started which deviated from the Vedic teachings. Child marriages and the associated tradition of dowry were some of the deviations, which reformist movements in modern times have attempted to correct. Child marriages are now extinct. Hindus accept the minimum age of marriage set by the law of the country they live in.

14. Vanaprastha
This Sanskar marks the start of the third stage of life, at the age of fifty, called the 'Vanaprastha Ashram' described earlier on p.65. An individual begins to withdraw from worldly life and prepares for the spiritual life.

15. Sanyasa
At the age of seventy-five years, the fourth and final stage of life 'Sanyasa Ashram' begins with this Sanskara. At this ceremony, an individual becomes a 'Sanyasi' and renounces all desires and all worldly connections with relatives and wealth. True Sanyasis roam from place to place. Householders have a duty to offer them food and shelter if required.

16. Antyeshti (Death rites)
This is the last sacrament, performed at death. Hindus believe that the Atman (soul) is immortal, only the physical body dies (see p.170). The body is believed to be made of the five physical elements: earth, air, fire,

water and space. Cremation returns it to these elements. The objectives of the Cremation Society of England are identical to the directions given in the Hindu Vedic texts. In Britain, the Cremation Act legalized cremation in 1902. There are now many crematoria in Britain, but owing to time constraints and other restrictions, Hindus have to perform many of the death rites at home. Some Hindus believe in keeping the body on the ground to signify its return to the lap of mother earth.

Before cremation the male body is washed by males and the female body by females. It is wrapped in white cloth as this colour signifies peace and purity. During the mourning period, Hindu women wear white saris. This tradition may vary; in some states in southern India women wear red saris during the mourning period. At the cremation ground, traditionally mourners bathed in cold water; this was not practical for women so they did not accompany the funeral procession. Normally, the eldest son or the husband or the nearest male relative lights the funeral pyre. Prayers for peace are recited and offerings are made to the fire. After three days, the ashes are collected and dispersed according to the family tradition. Some Hindus go to India to immerse the ashes in the River Ganges. There are many death rites which vary from region to region and from family to family. Some of them are mere superstitions. Normally, after the last sacrament of 'Antyeshti', a mourning period lasting thirteen days is observed and no more rituals are performed, but one ritual worth mentioning is the 'Shradha' ceremony.

'Shradha' and 'Tarpan' are two aspects of 'Pitri Yajna' specified as one of the five great duties of Hinduism (see p.76). 'Shradha' means devotion and respect; 'Tarpan' means to please. Hindu scriptures specify that learned men, sages and ancestors should be respected and pleased. Acts performed to show respect are called 'Shradha'. Ideally, these acts are to be performed whilst the parents and grandparents are alive, but some families continue to perform symbolic acts on the anniversary of their ancestor's death. They recite prayers and offer food and gifts to learned priests in memory of their ancestors.

It should be noted that Hindus nowadays do not formally follow all the sixteen Sanskaras listed above. However, close observation of their daily lives reveals that they have not totally forgotten the basic ideas. In one way or another, they do cover all sixteen Sanskaras. For example, the Samavartan Sanskar is not formally performed but many Hindu families will hold a quick ceremony on the day before the wedding to carry out this sacrament. Such Samavartan ceremonies are also known as 'Saints'. Similarly, the sacred thread ceremony (Upanayana) may be overlooked, but at the wedding ceremony, extra time is found to put on the sacred thread.

IN THE CLASSROOM

The material presented in this section is meant to cover all key stages. At KS1, teachers can start by talking about an ordinary journey. Pupils' experience of travelling can be useful. Where did they go? How did they get there? Which areas did they pass through? Answers to these questions can then lead to an introduction to the concept of the journey through life. Explain that Hinduism has a destination, stages and directions for the journey of life. The destination is the achievement of the four Purusharthas, the stages are the four Ashramas, and the direction signs are the sixteen Sanskaras. Talk about Hindu weddings. One of the most fascinating aspects of a wedding is the way a Hindu bride is decorated with mehendi patterns (see p.80) and brightly coloured saris.

At KS2, extend the discussion into defining the four stages, presenting it simply as student life, work life, retirement and death. Pupils can be asked to think about growing older. They can try to predict the future by guessing the stages they have to go through. KS3 pupils can be introduced to the detailed meanings of the four objectives and some of the Sanskars. Pupils at KS4 and above can study the relevance of the sixteen sacraments, the four objectives and the four Ashramas in modern life. Do they see any similarities? Are the four stages of life natural ones?

Typical questions/discussion points
1. Do we need a reason to live? Explain the four objectives of life defined by Hinduism.
2. Define the four stages (Ashramas) of life which are mentioned in the Hindu scriptures and relate them to modern life.
3. Comment on the sequence of the sixteen sacraments. Does the sequence follow the natural development of a human being?
4. According to Hinduism, what is the purpose of life? In what way is it different from those of other religions you have studied?

Social Structure: the Hindu Caste System

The caste system in Hinduism has attracted a lot of attention. No book on Hinduism seems to be complete without some discussion on this social structure, also known as the 'Varna Vyavastha'. The view of Hindus on this subject in modern times has changed. Their view has been articulated by the famous writer and social reformer, S.S. Apte, alias Dada Apte, the first General Secretary of Vishwa Hindu Parishad, when he said:

'The Hindu caste system was the consummation in the process of evolution of a scientific structure of human society achieved by our forefathers. It was accomplished millennia before a western philosopher like Plato vaguely conceived of organising human society on the basis of talents, virtues, capacities and needs of the constituents. Having eulogised the system as a perfect one, I do not in the least propose to plead for its restoration and continuance.'

Caste

It is important to understand the meanings of the terms 'Varna', 'Jati' and 'Upajati' and the hybrid word 'caste' and indeed how they arose. As is well known, caste or 'casta' is a Portuguese word which these people applied to different sections, cross-sections and classes in Hindu society when they first arrived in India. They had never seen such a classification and structuring of society and, in total ignorance of the distinct features of the evolution of the system, they called it 'casta' which has come to be popularly known as caste. 'Casta' in fact means breed or race in Portuguese.

If you look at the astounding fact that there are about 3000 castes and 25,000 sub-castes in Hindu society today, it is clearly wrong to imply that there are so many breeds and races in one country. The word 'caste' therefore is not an appropriate way to describe the 'Jatis' and 'Upajatis' which all belong to one race now called 'Hindu'.

Varna

This concept of Varna is supposed to have arisen in the bygone past of our Vedic times. In the Vedas it is said, 'There was only one Varna in the beginning' ('eka eva varna asid agre'). As the Vedic people began to evolve a civilized and progressive life, they became aware of varying needs to maintain society. In stages they developed divisions of society based upon talents, virtues and functions. It was in the classic Vedic song, called 'Purusha-sukta', that the four Varnas were described as being created. 'Purusha-sukta' is an allegory upon a 'Nation-Person' or a 'Society-Person' – 'Samaja-Purusha'. The whole of society is conceived to be one composite entity, with head, hands, stomach and belly, and feet – from the top of the head to the tips of the toes. All these organs make one complete person. According to this concept the teaching, preaching and guiding section of society was called the 'head' – the Brahmin. When there was danger of attack on the Society-Person from outside, the hands defended and protected the person; those who performed this work were called the Kshatriya. But the body cannot live only by head and hands. There must be food in the belly in order to sustain life. The third class was enjoined to produce food, which was considered to be the most inestimable wealth of a nation; this class was called 'Vaishya'. Finally, the feet which have to carry the whole burden of this Society-Person were called 'Shudra'. They were assigned the hard job of serving, attending upon, cleaning, washing and fulfilling all the needs and functions to keep the body – Society – in perfect order. Thus came the four Varnas – Brahmin, Kshatriya, Vaishya and Shudra –

none superior, none inferior, each one indispensable and equal in its obligation to keep the body – Society – living and moving. This is the correct original meaning of the classic song 'Purusha Sukta'. And this too is what Plato in the first millennium BCE vaguely thought of evolving but could not achieve.

PURUSHA SUKTA
The entire human race is visualised as one
   human being – a Society-Person.
Into how many parts was this Society-Person
   divided?
What was his mouth? And what were his
   arms?
What represented his thighs and what were
   his feet?
(RIG VEDA, 10-90-11)

The Brahmins (the intellectuals) were
   regarded as the mouth;
the Kshatriyas (administrators and
   warriors) were the two arms;
the Vaishyas, the producers of wealth like the
   traders, artisans
and agriculturists, represented the abdomen
   and the thighs
and the Shudras (labourers) carried the
   weight of society as the two feet.
(RIG VEDA, 10-90-12)

Jati and Upajati

Initially all the four Varnas were equal. There was no touchability or untouchability. There was common mixing in all the functions and behaviours of life – eating, drinking, marrying and so on. In fact history tells us that the four Varnas were never watertight, but had exits and entries according to demerits and merits. A Shudra could rise to the Brahmin's status and a Brahmin could fall down to the Shudra's stage. A Kshatriya like Vishvamitra became a Brahmin.

This continued for thousands of years. But as often happens, a good system becomes spoiled by bad conventions, customs and practices. This happened in Hindu society. Over the course of time the Varna came to be determined by birth and not according to qualities. Slowly communities became segregated according to differences and divisions in the practice of their professions and their habits and inhibitions. That is how so many Jatis and Upajatis arose in the last 5000 years. There are many Jatis and Upajatis but only four Varnas.

Modern life and Jatis

This division of Hindu society into different castes – or indeed the whole caste system – has no relevance to actual life, even in India, the land of its origin, and much less abroad, where many Hindus have now settled. There is hardly any functional discrimination or different types of behaviour between different castes. It remains merely the notion inherited by birth.

Attempts at reformation

There are many examples in Hindu scriptures of inequality being treated as a sin. Hindu society has produced many reformers who have never shirked their obligations to remove wrongs. It may be that after the days of Manu, the divisions became objectionable; and later on the law-givers saw the inequality, partiality and cruelty that existed on account of birth and tried to mend matters. In the days when the four Varnas arose, the Shudra had the privilege to cook and feed the Brahmin. It was a Shudra who carried out all the service of the whole of society. Hindu reformers now question that if 'labour' is not a bad word, why the term 'Shudra' should be sinful. Old words have come to be understood in the wrong sense.

Centuries back Hindu law-givers prescribed that no discrimination, touchability, untouchability, etc. should be observed in the mixing of society: 'tirthayatrotsaveshu sprishtasprishtir na vidyate' – which means that there is no idea of touchability and untouchability in holy places, on the banks of the holy rivers, in pilgrimages, in ceremonies and so on. Another law-giver, when he saw that the whole of society was overtaken by a common calamity, 'Viplava', gave a dictum that 'when there is a common danger like flood, fire, famine, no discrimination of Shudra, Vaishya, etc. should be observed. Later on another law-giver saw that in battlefields, wars, partitions of countries, when all have to flee for their life, it was not possible to observe these rules, so he added 'desha-bhangeshu cha', i.e. 'do not practise untouchability during partition of the country'. The following story illustrates how

Shankara Meets a Chandala

Shankara travelled from place to place, meeting learned people, religious leaders, kings and chieftans, teaching all those who came to him. One day, on the banks of the River Ganga in Varanasi, a Chandala (an outcast) was passing.

Shankara: Who is this man coming our way?

First Brahmin: He is a Chandala. Teacher, ask him to go away.

Second Brahmin: Ask him to move away from our path. He is coming nearer. He is a Chandala, an untouchable.

Shankara: Go! Go! Move away!

Disciples and Brahmins also joined in: Move away. Go.

Chandala: I just want to meet your Acharya. I want to seek his blessings.

O Master, When you say, 'Move away, move away', what do you wish to move? The physical body is only elements or matter. Matter cannot move away from matter, nor can awareness move away from awareness.

Is the sun reflected in the Ganges any different from the sun reflected in the gutter water? Just as neither the reflection nor the sun is affected by the reflecting medium, so too, awareness reflected in my mind or your mind is pure and untouched. Is the space in the golden pot different from the space in the mud pot? I am untouched by any caste or creed. Tell me, O revered Master, why are you silent?

(Having said this to Shankara, the Chandala fell on his knees with hands folded.)

Shankara helped him up, saying: The one who knows himself to be awareness, the one who knows himself, the one who is a witness to the whole creation, he is my guru, be he a Brahmin or an outcaste. Unto my guru, my salutations!

(And Shankara bowed his head to the Chandala. All the disciples and Brahmins also bowed to the Chandala.)

the famous Hindu Acharya Shankra broke the tradition of untouchability.

The modern view

Today it has become fashionable to call the caste system a curse and a crime, a blot on Hindu society. Without looking to the noble origin and evolution of the system some are abusing their Hindu forefathers and cursing future generations. This should not happen, however. Historical imperative produced a system which may today have become harmful and anachronistic. The most famous Hindu of the twentieth century, Mahatma Gandhi, has categorically asserted that the spirit behind caste was never of arrogant superiority. Many admit that it was the caste system which saved Hindu society and helped it survive long periods of foreign rule.

Attitudes in the last century have changed dramatically. The founder of Arya Samaj (see p.49) started a reform movement in which so-called untouchables were accepted back into the mainstream of society. Mahatma Gandhi used the name 'Harijan' meaning 'people of God' for the untouchables.

In his book *No Full Stops in India*, Mark Tully has astutely observed the caste system and concluded: 'It would lead to greater respect for India's culture, and indeed a better understanding of it, if it were recognised that the caste system has never been totally static, that it is adapting itself to today's changing circumstances and that it has positive as well as negative aspects. The caste system provides security and a community for millions of Indians. It gives them an identity that neither Western science nor Western thought has yet provided, because the caste is not just a matter of being a Brahmin or a Harijan: it is also a kinship system. The system provides a wider support group than a family.'

Hindus now accept the fact of the abolition of the caste system. It does not exist any more; only some notional distinctions of caste may exist and these are fast disappearing.

United your resolve, United your hearts;
United be your mind, Thus you live long
together.

(RIG VEDA, 10-191-4)

The Role of Women

Status of women

There is a great Hindu saying 'where women are worshipped there the gods dwell'. Indeed, in a home where peace, prosperity and harmony prevail there the woman is considered to be Lakshmi, the goddess of fortune and wealth. When she imparts knowledge and wisdom, especially to her young children, she is considered to be the goddess of learning, Saraswati. In the way she runs the household she is considered the goddess of power, Parvati. These three are also consorts to Brahma, Vishnu and Shiva. The mother God, Shakti, comes before this Trinity, so in mythological literature women are held in very high esteem. She is half of man, Ardhangini, as described in Hindu scriptures. Man's moral and psychological personality is imperfect without her. She is his constant companion and consort, sharing with him his joys and sorrows and assisting him in his life's mission of attaining the final bliss of emancipation.

Whilst this was the traditionally held view in the Vedic times, there has been a downgrading of women's status in the modern 'post-Vedic' era. This has been due to a misinterpretation of religious texts, especially the Law Books of Manu (Manu Smriti) which quite clearly state that 'men and women are equal as sons and daughters' (Manu Smriti 9-131). Friedrich Nietzsche, a Western philosopher and spiritualist, says: 'I know of no book in which so many tender and kind remarks are addressed to woman as in the Law Book of Manu; these old grey-bearded saints have a way of being polite to women which has perhaps never been surpassed.'

We know that in Vedic times scholarly women existed and were respected by society, were equal in their rights, privileges and duties. Maitreyi, Gargi, Anasuya and Arundhati are household names from this period. The relegation of women to a lower order has been a universal phenomenon; in India the oppression of women increased during the Moghul rule. Women were put on a pedestal in Hinduism but at the same time their 'freedom' was curtailed for the sake of protection.

Woman's role as wife
Traditionally the Hindu woman accepts marriage as her natural destiny. So important is this stage in her life that she believes that with marriage her womanhood is fulfilled. The marriage ceremony itself is considered to be a sacrament (see p.67), a spiritual union, with God as its constant overseer. Hence it is indissoluble. Marital infidelity is rare in rural India. A man may withstand ignominy through being unfaithful but for the wife to lose face for this reason is a disgrace sometimes worse than death. At the marriage ceremony she takes the vow of undying fidelity to her husband, whom she promises to serve, protect and care for . She is capable of undergoing severe privations in maintaining those vows. Because of the spiritual nature of this union, separation and divorce amongst Hindus are rare.

The Hindu wife's dedication and selfless service to her husband and his family (which she adopts on marriage) are sometimes misinterpreted by non-Hindus as perpetual bondage. This is far from the truth. She regards her husband as master of the household, akin to a partnership. She creates a religious aura at home, makes small altars for worship and sits with her spouse in all religious ceremonies. In this partnership she shares adversities and joys through her faith and devotion. Even if misfortune should befall her early in marriage, thrusting upon the wife the burden of chief breadwinner, the vows of fidelity, service and devotion to the man whose hand she took in marriage remain with her. She respects and honours him as spouse and on his death she never insults his memory.

Sita, the ideal Hindu wife
This role of a wife is most truly exemplified by Sita, wife of Rama in the epic Ramayana. 'Whatever one may feel about the nature of this epic, Sita epitomises all that is good in womanhood – to be emulated in real life.' (Swami Vivekananda, in his Letters from San Francisco 1900).

Sita, the princess of Ayodhya, is looked upon today by all Hindu women as virtue incarnate and the ideal of Indian womanhood. She shines in this respect, principally as the obedient wife of Shri Rama, sharing his joys

for a short time and thereafter following him in exile for fourteen years. In so doing she cast aside the pleas and warnings of her elders, resolving to stand beside Shri Rama at all times, bearing the rigours of forest life cheerfully. At one time in the forest she was abducted by Ravan, the King of Sri Lanka, and suffered intense humiliation by him and his attendants. She defied Ravan, who was intent on making her his queen, rejecting his offers and in his presence extolling the virtues of her own husband, Rama. In the end she was rescued by Shri Rama in the Battle of Lanka. Her speeches from Ramayan prior to her departure with Shri Rama in exile are regularly quoted both in homes and temples. Strength of character, fidelity and willingness to undergo dire hardship for Shri Rama have not only earned her the accolade of the ideal wife but also the status of a goddess.

Woman's role as mother
The Hindu mother is an object of reverence. The saying 'Matri devo bhava' ('mother is divine') is apt. According to Hinduism, God creates, maintains and destroys the universe but the power with which he performs these functions is called Shakti (universal energy) and this takes a female form. This Shakti or power is worshipped alongside God as the Divine Mother. This is the origin of mother worship and thus the idea that the human mother is worthy of reverence and worship just as the Divine Mother or Shakti.

The Hindu child grows up in a religious atmosphere; from birth to marriage, a number of religious ceremonies must be performed for the child. The mother supervises each of these with great care. She considers her household and herself blessed with the arrival of children. The true purpose of marriage is thus fulfilled. A strong attachment is built up between the mother and child and this bond is eternal and persists into old age. The mother's blessings are regarded as a necessity for progress by her children in all walks of life. For example, when a child leaves the house he or she touches their mother's feet and on return does the same. At congregational worship, the Mother God is garlanded, earthen lamps (divas) are waved over her and sandalwood paste is placed on her forehead. In the same way that a Hindu worships his God, he also pays reverence to his mother. In her old age she is protected and cared for by her own children. The idea of placing her in a home to be cared for by others is abhorrent to Hindus. Caring for one's mother (and father) until their departure from the world is considered a duty resulting in copious blessing.

Women in other roles

Though marriage and the rearing of children are the principal roles of women, there are women who have distinguished themselves in other spheres and have earned the admiration of the world. Examples of these are:

1. Gargi – A great intellectual in the time of the Upanishads who astonished her male counterparts by the depth of her learning and debating power.

2. Maitreyi – Also of Upanishads fame who renounced the pleasures of the world and followed her husband Yajnavalkya into the forest in search of God.

3. Savitri, the Indian Alcestis – A woman of great courage who gladly faced dangers from which a man might shrink in terror (see the story opposite).

4. Rani Rasmani – A great administrator in the nineteenth century and one of the pillars of the Ramakrishna Mission.

5. Rani Lakshmi Bai of Jhansi– A queen who defied the British in India and is now deified.

IN THE CLASSROOM

Read the famous speech of Sita, in The Holy Ramayan of Tulsidas, in defence of her going with Shri Rama to the forest in exile for fourteen years. You might wish to record this speech for a critical examination by a group of students.

Typical questions/discussion points
1. Describe briefly the role of the Hindu wife. Who is considered to be the ideal wife and why?
2. Research the goddesses Lakshmi and Saraswati and prepare a paper on them to present to your group.
3. Find out more about Rani Lakshmi Bai of Jhansi and consider whether she can be compared with any of the queens in English history.
4. Do you consider the statement 'Hindu women are in perpetual bondage' to be justifiable? Give full reasons for your answer.
5. There are Islamic schools for girls in the UK. Do you think that Hindus in the UK should have separate schools for their girls?

The Five Great Duties (Panch Mahayajna)

The Sanskrit word 'Yajna' is derived from the root 'yaj' which has three meanings: (a) prayer to God; (b) collective action; (c) selfless service. Deeds performed with this triple attitude are called 'Yajna'. The word 'Panch' means five and 'Maha' means great. Hindu scriptures, such as the Vedas, Shatpath Brahmana, Laghu Vishnu Smruti (5-9), Manu Smruti (4-21), Mahabharata and many more, identify five great duties (Panch Mahayajna) to be performed in daily life. These were designed to remind people of their obligations towards religion, environment/nature, ancestors/elders, society/nation and all animals (domestic and wild). They are not merely obligations to perform religious rituals but are social and moral obligations which have become deeply ingrained into the Hindu way of life over many centuries. The idea of 'Panch Mahayajna' has influenced many Hindu traditions. Its principles are still followed, knowingly or unknowingly, by Hindus in their daily life, even by those Hindus who do not strictly adhere to religious practice. In the paragraphs below, a brief description of each of the five great duties and their relevance to daily life is given.

Brahmayajna (Towards knowledge)

Brahmayajna has two main aspects: prayer and study. Brahmaa is a name given to the creative function of God and creative power (Shakti) is identified as knowledge. Therefore, prayer to God and gaining

Savitri,
the Indian Alcestis

Sister Nivedita, formerly known as Margaret Elizabeth Noble, in her book *Cradle Tales of Hinduism*, has compared Savitri with Alcestis from Greek mythology who bravely faced death to save her husband's life. In the Greek story, it is shown that woman, though weaker than man, can perform heroic deeds which man may not be able to do. The story of Savitri in the Hindu scriptures illustrates the physical and moral strength of Hindu women.

Savitri was the daughter of King Ashwapati. She was born after the king and the queen had prayed for a child by chanting the prayer 'Savitri'. Thus through the devotion of two royal lives, the Princess Savitri was born. When she was seventeen years old, her parents wanted her to get married, but she made a request to go on a pilgrimage and see the world beyond the palace. She set off on an adventure, travelling through villages, towns and forests.

One day she met a tall strong man who was evidently a forester. He was strong but gentle and courteous. He was Prince Satyavan who was forced to live in the forest because his blind father had been driven away from his throne. When she returned to the palace, Savitri informed her parents about the young prince and expressed her desire to marry him. Elders were consulted immediately. One of them found out that Satyavan, the chosen husband for Savitri, was under a curse and was due to die within a year. The king urged his daughter to seek someone else, but Savitri replied, 'One gives one's faith but once. I cannot name anyone else as my husband. I must face whatever is the result of my choice.'

The marriage took place and Savitri started to prepare herself for the secret date when her husband was due to die. She prayed to build her courage. She was getting ready to face Yama, the Lord of Death. Because Yama is as true as death and never breaks his word, Hindus call him the God of Truth and Faith.

On the appointed day, she took Satyavan to a remote place. There he suddenly felt ill and went into a deep sleep with his head in her lap. At that moment, Savitri saw a terrible dark figure advancing towards her. It was Yama. He spoke in a calm cold voice: 'Dear child, I have come to take the soul of Satyavan, his time has come to an end.' As he looped a rope to drag Satyavan's soul away, Savitri also stood up. She was not trembling with fear. With her head bowed, she said, 'I will accompany my husband.' Yama said firmly, 'No. I cannot take two souls with me. My duty is to take only Satyavan's soul.'

As he marched away, Savitri followed him. Yama tried to persuade Savitri by offering her gifts. She asked for sight to be restored to her blind father-in-law. It was granted. She asked for the lost kingdom to be returned to her father-in-law, and that too was granted. Yama was getting very impatient with Savitri because she still continued to follow him. He pleaded, 'Please go back and this time ask for something for yourself and go.' Savitri quickly requested, 'May I have sons?' 'Yes,' replied Yama. 'Now please go back.' But Savitri, still standing there, slowly raised her head and said with a smile, 'My Lord, how can I have sons without my husband? Wouldn't it be untrue to have sons without Satyavan?' Yama stopped for a moment and thought. As Lord of Death how could he neglect death? But as God of Truth and Faith, how could he ask Savitri to be untruthful and unfaithful? 'You are peerless amongst women', and with these words Yama disappeared.

Satyavan woke up from his deep sleep and said, 'I had a strange dream, I thought I was dead.' Savitri looked at him lovingly and said, 'It is getting late, let's go home.' That was the day when even the gods accepted defeat in face of the love and faith in a woman's heart.

knowledge are both considered as a daily duty. Hindu scriptures state: 'Self-study is Brahmayajna.' (Shatpath Brahma Granth, 11-3-8-2); 'Study is Brahmayajna.' (Manu Smruti, 3-70)

In modern life, different types of knowledge are gained from different sources for specific purposes. In this context, the Hindu view of Brahmayajna can be summarized as follows:

<table>
<tr><td colspan="3" align="center">**MODERN HINDU VIEW OF THE BRAHMAYAJNA**</td></tr>
<tr><td align="center">**TYPE OF KNOWLEDGE**</td><td align="center">**SOURCE**</td><td align="center">**PURPOSE**</td></tr>
<tr><td align="center">Formal/professional education</td><td align="center">School/university</td><td align="center">To earn a livelihood</td></tr>
<tr><td align="center">General knowledge</td><td align="center">Media (press, TV, radio)</td><td align="center">To understand the world</td></tr>
<tr><td align="center">Spiritual knowledge</td><td align="center">Scriptures</td><td align="center">For a balanced view of life</td></tr>
<tr><td align="center">True knowledge</td><td align="center">Meditation/prayers</td><td align="center">To realize God</td></tr>
</table>

Studying at an educational institute, gaining knowledge about the created world, individual study of the scriptures, and finally praying and meditation are all aspects of Brahmayajna in the daily life of a Hindu.

Dev Yajna (Towards nature)

Dev Yajna specifies the protection of the environment as a religious duty. The word 'Dev' here means the one who gives or the one on whom we depend. The givers (Devas) are all considered to be elements of nature. In order to maintain purity of atmosphere, Hindus perform Agnihotra or Havan. Some people wrongly interpret Agnihotra as worship of fire. In fact it is very similar to a scientific process of fumigation, chemical disinfection and sterilization in which camphor and aromatic substances are burnt to produce aldehydes and ketones. Further details about Havan are given on p.102. Hindu scriptures emphasize this religious duty.

Pitri Yajna (Towards ancestors)

Pitri Yajna are deeds performed to fulfil one's obligations towards one's forefathers. Three categories of ancestors are recognized: those with direct hereditary/ancestral links (blood relations); mentors with educational/moral links (gurus, writers of scriptures, Rishis); and those with national/cultural links (kings and other national leaders who have protected Dharma). Pitri Yajna has two aspects: Shradha and Tarpana. The word 'Shradha' means to offer respect. Respect is of course offered to living parents (see pp.15–16) but traditionally some Hindu families give to charities on the anniversary of the death of a forefather. Others show respect to their departed mentors or gurus by inviting learned scholars to their home and by offering them food. 'Tarpan' means to please.

Atithi Yajna or Nar/Manushya Yajna (Towards society)

An Atithi is a person who can arrive at any time without giving notice of their date (tithi) of arrival. As mentioned earlier on p.65, under the Ashram system it was the duty of householders to help others, particularly those who were still in student life or those who had renounced the world. Traditionally, the holy men, Sadhus and Sanyasis, roamed around preaching. Their arrival was usually unexpected and householders were required to provide shelter and food for them. Hindu scriptures state: 'He who eats before serving the guests loses his family's fame and glory.' (Atharva Veda, 9-6-35)

This tradition of hospitality and service to learned people and visitors is still very strong in Hindu families. It is highlighted in a traditional story about King Ranti Dev who gives up everything in an effort to save the lives of hungry people.

Bhoot Yajna (Towards animals)

The word 'Bhoot' means 'one that has life'. Bhoot Yajna, also known as Balivaishvadev Yajna, is the name given to all charitable deeds done for poor and sick fellow human beings and animals. Traditionally, Hindus remind themselves of this duty by setting aside five small portions of their food before eating. The scriptures specify the five beneficiaries as:

(a) Domestic animals, such as cows and dogs; wild animals, such as snakes and rats.
(b) The poor, homeless and destitute.
(c) The sick.
(d) Birds.
(e) Insects, such as ants and bees.

The Hindu view is that humans are the greatest of all living beings and their greatness should be reflected in doing good to all other living beings. Hindus believe that animals have a soul in the same way as humans do, and that is why vegetarianism is popular among Hindus. The protection of animals is an old Hindu tradition. Jains in India operate many large hospitals for sick animals.

IN THE CLASSROOM

Teachers may wish to cover the topic of the Five Great Duties when discussing the influence of religious scriptures on Hindu traditions and daily life. If possible, pupils may interview members of a Hindu family to find out how they remember their ancestors, how they treat a holy man visiting their home and how much importance they attach to the value of education. Pupils could be asked to evaluate these Hindu traditions in the light of modern ways of life.

When visiting a Hindu temple or when looking at pictures of various forms of God, encourage pupils to observe the presence of animals. For example, a cow can be seen with Krishna, a rat with Ganesha and a snake with Shiva. Discuss the importance of animal life.

Typical questions/discussion points
1. Describe the five great duties specified in Hindu scriptures.
2. Are there any similarities between Bhoot Yajna of Hinduism and the modern campaign for animal rights and organizations like the RSPB and the RSPCA?
3. Will an environmentalist agree with the objectives of Dev Yajna?

> *Can the world's darkness be dispelled*
> *by talking about the glory of light?*
> *Can a diseased man's afflictions be relieved*
> *by praising panaceas?*
> *Can a destitute's poverty be relieved*
> *by listening to the greatness of wealth?*
> *Can a starving man's hunger be appeased*
> *by description of delicacies?*

(A TELUGU POEM)

Food

It is now a well-established fact that food is eaten to provide energy for sustenance. This was recognized thousands of years ago by Hindu sages and is recorded in the first verse of the Yajurveda: 'the food in the body burns in the body to give energy which sustains life'. In addition, the text clarifies that 'the solar energy through which plants synthesize food and the cycle between food and energy goes on – a cycle of mass and energy'. Food, energy and consciousness are the elements through which life is manifested and this triple function has reached a climax in the human system.

The belief that food was part of a cosmic moral cycle arose from the earliest experiences and thoughts of the sages and Rishis and over the centuries this link has developed into a belief that the basis of the behaviour of all living beings is the food they eat. The amount and type of energy supplied by food determines their physical, mental, emotional and intellectual activity. This has culminated in the Hindu ethos that a lacto-vegetarian diet is probably best for spiritual development. The rationale for arriving at this view is complex and based on historical, social and health reasons.

Religious reasons for vegetarianism
Historically, meat eating has been recognized in Hindu literature as a means of sustenance. Meat eating by Rakshasas (savage tribes) has been noted in the Ramayana (an epic story of Shri Rama, see p.134) and the Mahabharata (an epic story of the victory of righteousness over evil, involving Shri Krishna, see p.138).

However, the sages and Rishis (see p.162), over thousands of years, questioned taking life for food. The idea that every living creature has a right to live, and that there should be respect and compassion for other forms of life, is a cornerstone of Hindu philosophy. Every living being, from the largest beast to the smallest insect, has a soul. Like man, other creatures also suffer pain, hence the principle of compassion and non-violence to all. This principle is expressed in the Hindu's special reverence for the cow (see below); to kill it or eat its flesh is forbidden.

If all animal life is sacred, what about plant life? Plants are alive and may also experience pain but they are regarded as a lower form of life without consciousness. The

Manu Smruti (see p.152) expounds the view that one has to survive and eat but that this should be done by causing 'least harm or evil'; survival based on plant life fell into this category. Plant life is part of God's creation (Prakriti) and is intended to sustain other life forms possessing a soul. The eating of fruits, cereals and pulses does not involve killing the plant.

The Rishis studied the qualities of all foods and the effects they produced on man; they developed a technique of food consumption which would promote growth and keep the individual healthy and disease-free. This gave rise to the Yogic diet based on lacto-vegetarianism (fruits, vegetables, cereals, pulses, nuts, sugar, honey, milk and milk products). This diet maintains a perfect balance between alimentation and elimination of waste from the body, which is vital in sustaining the natural health of the body.

There are three qualities or Gunas (see p.41) present in nature. All living and non-living (animate and inanimate) things possess these in different proportions and combinations. These three qualities are:

1. Sattvic – purity (milk, fruit, vegetables and grains);
2. Rajasic – activity (meat, alcohol, eggs, spicy food);
3. Tamasic – inertia (putrefied, over-ripe, rotten).

Since foods possess these qualities as well, the eating of different types of food will transmit the relevant quality to the individual and will almost certainly mould his body, mind and intellect accordingly. The Rishis advocated a pure, wholesome (lacto-vegetarian) diet as part of their students' spiritual development. The early programme in yogic life is linked inseparably with purity of diet. Both the Gita (see p.132) and the Upanishads (see p.146) expound this philosophy: 'By eating sattvic food, the inherent nature of a person also becomes sattvic.' For an individual who has reached higher yogic states, diet does not play such an important part since spiritual attainment is well advanced and beyond the influences of the body, mind and intellect.

The sacred cow

The cow was perhaps the first animal that Hindus in India domesticated. In the Vedic age the cow was a real blessing to the rural community. It provided them with milk and milk products. Its dung was used for fuel and mixed with mud as a plastering for walls and floors. On the farm the bull ploughed the fields and was also a means for travel and the carriage of goods. It was hardly surprising that soon the cow occupied in the life of man the same position as a mother in the life of a child. How could one even think of killing and eating the flesh of one? In Vedic literature the cow is a symbol of the divine bounty of the earth. Vishnu Purana (Chapter 13) states that the earth took the form of a cow. The scriptures prohibit cow slaughter. In some states in India there is now a legal ban on cow slaughter.

Reverence for the cow also encourages us to refrain from harming or killing any creature.

Medical reasons for vegetarianism

It was known in Vedic times that whilst the intestines could handle and digest meat, meat-eating lead to sluggishness, decreased the power of concentration and increased 'unhealthiness' from bacteria in the colon (large bowel). In addition, the sages and Rishis recognized that health depended on a slightly alkaline state of the blood (in modern terms, a pH of 7.3–7.4). Sattvic foods (some fruits, vegetables, cereals and nuts) are alkali forming, whereas foods like meat, eggs, some starches and sugars are acid forming.

In more modern times, meat-eating – and in particular the high fat content of red meats – is associated with heart disease, some cancers (particularly of the stomach and colon), high blood pressure (related to the associated higher salt intake) and diabetes. The British Government Guidelines on 'Healthier Eating' advocate an increased consumption of bread, cereals, vegetables, potatoes and fruit. In 1996, the government admitted that at least ten people in Britain had died from a new form of Creutzfeldt-Jakob disease and it was believed that this may have been related to eating infected beef.

Social reasons for vegetarianism

In ancient times, the Rishis realized that for

ecological reasons, it was sensible to preserve the wildlife in the forests to prevent it being destroyed, which would be much to the detriment of the natural balance between flora and fauna. Hindus regard the earth as mother, the provider of food (see p.15). In modern times there is a growing concern about eating meat on ecological grounds. There are several reasons for this:

• 90 per cent of productive land in the Western world grows crops fed to animals.
• It takes on average 8 kg of grain protein fed to animals to produce 1 kg of meat protein.
• A 10 per cent reduction in the production of meat could release enough grain to feed 10 million people.
• The devastated Amazon forests (cleared for cattle ranching and cash crops like sugar) have made dramatic climatic changes around the world.

Special food and thanksgiving

There are strong religious traditions among Hindus involving the preparation and distribution of special food and thanksgiving. On festivals like Diwali and Holi (see pp. 98 and 100) a symbolic gesture of offering grains to the sacred fire called Yajna is made to give thanks. On Makar Sankranti festival, which falls on 14th January every year, a mixture of sweet jaggery, a kind of brown sugar (gud), and sesame seeds (til) is distributed. As a sign of respect and recognition of the fact that food is part of God's creation, Hindu devotees offer food to the images of their gods as part of their prayers (see Puja on p.85). After prayers the food is shared as 'Prasad' among the devotees.

Hindu individuals and temples regularly arrange for the free distribution of food as part of their service towards society (Atithi Yajna) and the animal kingdom (Bhoot Yajna, see p.76). As a sign of self-discipline and devotion, some Hindus go without food on certain days.

Ayurveda and Food

The ancient Hindu scripture, Ayurveda, classifies food according to the effect it has on body. A good diet is meant to balance three types of bio-energies: Vata, Pitta and Kapha. An imbalance in them causes a disorder in the body or the mind. These energies correspond to the five physical elements: earth, air, fire, water and space. Research by the Institute of Food Research in the UK has concluded that different personalities benefitted from personally tailored diets. The Ayurveda has advocated this for thousands of years.

IN THE CLASSROOM

Discuss how food affects behaviour. The amount and type of energy supplied by food determines our physical, mental and emotional capabilities. An example might be the dangers of driving after drinking alcohol because of the alcohol's effects on the brain.

Some of the greatest personalities the world has known shared an extraordinary ideal: they were all vegetarians. It is extraordinary because these individuals, who are regarded as some of the most brilliant philosophers and original thinkers, came from diverse cultural, religious and racial backgrounds. They include: Lord Buddha, Charles Darwin, St Francis of Assisi, Benjamin Franklin, Mahatma Gandhi, Sir Isaac Newton, Plato, Alexander Pope, Pythagoras, George Bernard Shaw, Socrates, Leo Tolstoy, Leonardo da Vinci, Voltaire and William Wordsworth. Talk about the reasons for vegetarianism and the changes in diet in the Western world.

Discuss the ways in which crops are grown and how living things need care and attention. Look at the way we use the world's resources and talk about the need to guard against waste and misuse of resources.

My stomach and body are not a crematorium or cemetery for killed or dead animals. While we ourselves are the living graves of murdered beasts, how can we expect any ideal condition on this earth?

(GEORGE BERNARD SHAW)

Typical questions/discussion points
1. Why are the majority of Hindus vegetarians?
2. Why do Hindus regard the cow as sacred?
3. Do you think that food affects the mind and the behaviour?

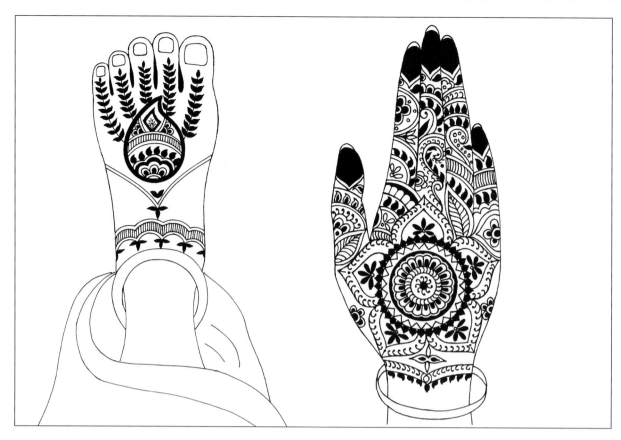

Mehendi patterns for hands and feet

Art in Hindu Customs

Hindu religious traditions and customs are full of rich art. Temples are adorned with many sculpted images and icons (see p.109). But art is not confined to temples; artistic expressions of religious and philosophical ideas are found in everyday life.

Kolamas

In southern India, householders draw patterns known as Kolamas on their doorsteps. These patterns are made with white or coloured powders and are placed within a circle representing the cosmos. These patterns are drawn ritually by some people every day. They represent one of the Hindu deities and often include images of birds and animals which usually accompany the deity: for example, a cow with Krishna, a tiger with Durga and a rat with Ganesh.

Mehendi

Mehendi (Henna or Rajani) is made from powdered leaves mixed into a paste with water. If applied to the skin it leaves a golden-brown tinge for a few days. The tradition of painting decorative patterns on ladies' hands and feet was made popular in the north of India by the Rajputs of Rajasthan. It has now become a tradition to use Mehendi on auspicious days. In particular, for a wedding the bride's hands and feet are decorated with Mehendi patterns. The mystical designs combining geometrical and floral patterns often focus on a central dot (Bindhu) which is meant to attract and destroy the 'evil eye'.

IN THE CLASSROOM

Younger pupils at KS1 and KS2 will enjoy making Kolama or Rangoli patterns with dry powder. Mehendi can be obtained from many Indian food shops or health food shops. The paste can be applied with a small stick or it may be obtainable in a tube with a nozzle. The patterns shown here and on p.98 can be copied for pupils' use.

At KS3 and KS4, pupils can discuss the significance of art in conveying Hindu religious traditions and customs.

Ganesh

Saraswati, the power of knowledge

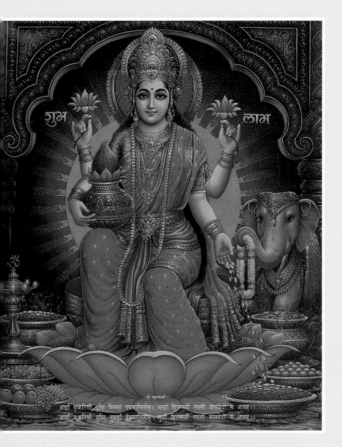

Rama with his brother (Lakshman), his wife (Sita)
and his devotee (Hanuman)

Lakshmi, the power of wealth

Krishna with his devotee, Radha

Kaali, a frightening force to punish evil

Durga, the power of protection

Vishnu's Ten Avatars

Swastika – the symbol of auspiciousness

Abhishek (Cleansing and adornment) of Shivalinga

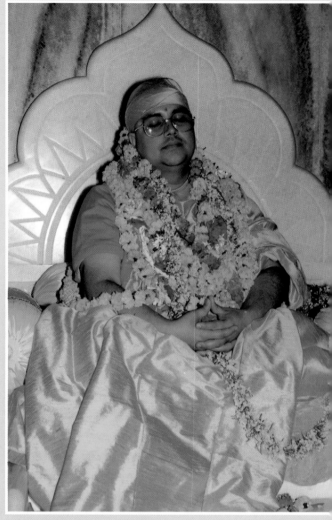

A holy man in saffron robes

Conch shell (Shankha)

Lotus flower

Saffron flag flying from a Hindu temple

Hindu greeting: Namaste

Hindu greeting: Asheervad

Priest with a tilak

Married Hindu woman with a red bindi and sindhoor

Hindus gather in large numbers to listen to Holy Men from India.

Left: Bindu Visphot – the concept of 'Big Bang' in Hindu scriptures

Hindus from different faith groups and sects come together at the Virat Hindu Sammelan (Milton Keynes, 1989) – the largest gathering of Hindus in Europe.

Events like the Hindu Marathon bring all the community together.

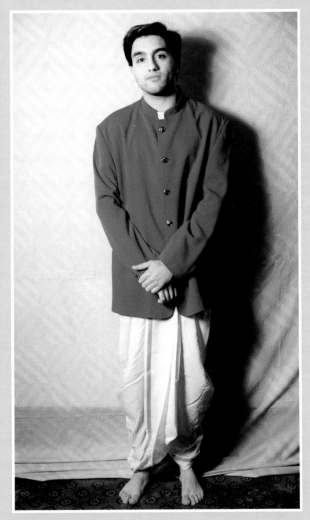

A Hindu wearing a dhoti

The sari is the most popular traditional dress for Hindu women. The cloth is about 6 metres long and is worn in many different styles.

Kurta (long-sleeved shirt) for boys and lehanga (long skirt decorated with patterns and embroidery) for girls are popular forms of traditional dress.

Bharatnatyam dancers

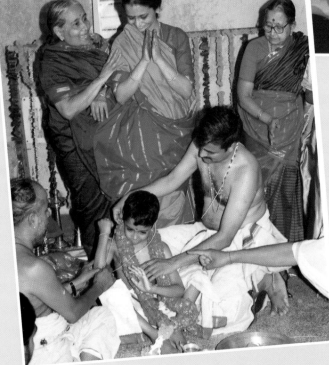

A young boy wearing the sacred thread

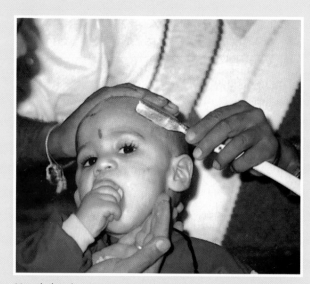

Head-shaving ceremony during Mundan Sanskar

A Hindu bride adorned with jewellery and a brightly coloured sari

A Hindu wedding around the sacred fire of Yajna

A Sadhu who has renounced the world

Bride and bridegroom exchanging garlands (Jayamaala)

A typical vegetarian meal on a thali (the large metal plate that holds all the dishes for one person)

A pattern drawn with dry powder on the ground

यशोदा-कृष्ण

Baby Krishna – adored by millions of Hindus

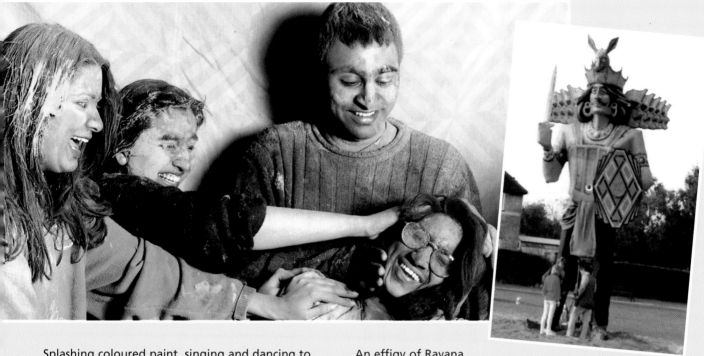

Splashing coloured paint, singing and dancing to celebrate the festival of Holi

An effigy of Ravana placed in a London park during the festival of Dussera

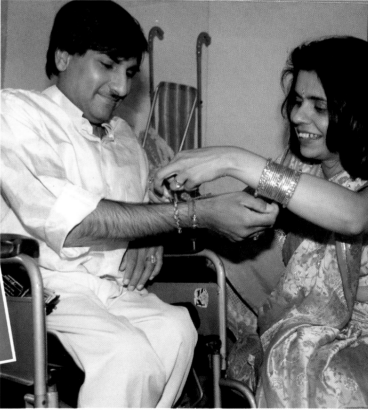

Diwali cards feature the traditional lamps used at this festival.

A Hindu woman tying a rakhi on her brother's wrist

A priest and a devotee performing a Puja

The famous march of the Jagannatha, from which the word 'jugggernaut' is derived

Hindu men and women performing Havan Yajna

Aarti – an important part of Puja is the offering of a tray containing flowers, fruits, incense and a lamp.

Temples serve as a focus of community.

Chariot wheel symbolizing the cyclic motion of the sun at Konarak temple

Madurai temple

Tirupati temple

Flower, sweet and coconut stall outside a Hindu temple in India

The Bhaktivedanta Manor at Watford attracts thousands of devotees at the Janmashtami festival celebration.

Reciting Arti at a temple

Bharat, having failed to convince Rama to come back, accepts Rama's sandals to be placed on the throne.

Jatayu, the bird, trying to stop the demon Ravana from abducting Sita

Rama's meeting with Shabri in the forest

Hanuman carrying the whole mountain to bring herbs to cure the injured Lakshman

Rama, with the help of Hanuman's army, built a bridge across the sea.

CHAPTER FOUR
WORSHIP

Festivals

*H*indu festivals are much more than celebrations. They are windows into the history of rich Hindu legends. They reveal the mind and philosophy of a nation through the different ages. Hindus take great pride in maintaining and preserving their festivals because through these events they pass their religious values from one generation to another.

The importance of festivals

If festivals were to be removed from people's lives, life would become dull. People get tired as a result of hard work alone or on account of performing the same mundane actions day in and day out. They want some change, some variety. They want relaxation and something to cheer them up. Festivals give them an opportunity to enjoy excitement and happiness.

All Hindu festivals have a cultural significance and a very deep spiritual meaning behind them. They have a number of useful purposes also: they bring people together in friendship and love, and thus help to mend broken relations between people; the whole house is thoroughly cleansed and purified. Hindus observe all their festivals with great enthusiasm, joy and cheerfulness: festivals remind them of God.

It is necessary to understand the Hindu calendar in order to understand the dates of Hindu festivals. The calendar is called the Panchang and the calculation of months and years is based on the movement of the moon around the earth (see pp.120–122 for further details).

Hindu festivals can be divided into three categories:

• Religious festivals
Diwali, Shivaratri and Sharavani are religious festivals. On these occasions vows are made and fasting is observed. Prayers, Yajna and Puja are performed, and reading of scriptures and religious discourses are conducted. The whole day has a religious atmosphere.

• Historical festivals
Hindu history is intrinsically Indian history. Therefore, the birth and death anniversaries of great men and women of India are remembered and observed. Also, some great historical events are celebrated annually by Hindus around the world. Such festivals play an important role in maintaining cultural and religious links between India and Hindus living outside India. They also help to preserve Hindu history in the minds of millions of Hindus scattered around the world. Ramnavami (birth of Rama), Krishna Janmashtami (birth of Krishna), Vijayadashami, Diwali, Guru Govind Jayanti, Shivaji Jayanti, Gandhi Jayanti, Buddha Jayanti and Mahavir Jayanti are some of the historical festivals which are celebrated by Hindus in Britain.

• Seasonal festivals
Hinduism has very close links with nature. Since early Hinduism thrived in the predominantly agricultural land of India, many of its festivals are associated with nature and farming activity. The arrival of all the seasons, particularly spring and the rainy season, is welcomed with great joy. To enable people to enjoy the influence of natural changes, many festivals linked with nature were introduced. Among them Makar Sankranti, Vasant Panchami, Sharad Purnima and Holi are famous.

Religious festivals

Diwali (Festival of Lights)

Diwali, also known as Deepavali, literally means 'row of lamps'. It is now recognized as the festival of lights. It is the most popular Hindu festival and it is unique because it has combined religious, historical and seasonal significance. It falls on the night of the new moon in the month of Kartika (October/November). No one knows exactly when Diwali started.

The festival signifies the victory of divine forces over those of evil. It is a joyous celebration of the homecoming of Rama. On this day, he returned to his birthplace, Ayodhya, after spending fourteen years in exile during which time he defeated many demons, including Ravana. The people of Ayodhya lit thousands of clay lamps, known as 'deepa', to welcome Rama, Sita and Lakshman (see Stories from the Ramayana on pp.134–138).

In the UK, Hindus decorate homes and public buildings with brightly coloured lights. The houses are thoroughly cleaned and new clothes are worn. Gifts and greetings cards are exchanged. In many cities firework displays are held and sweets distributed among the public.

In some parts of India Diwali is also a new year day for Hindus. Traditionally, Hindus regard this as an auspicious day to start a new business year. They close their old accounts and start the new ones. Some pray to Lakshmi, the goddess of wealth, for prosperity and well-being. Some even indulge in gambling under the false impression that they will gain wealth quickly. Hindu scriptures forbid gambling; there are many exemplary stories which show compulsive gambling as a harmful habit.

Diwali is a reminder that justice brings victory. On the day that precedes Diwali, Shri Krishna killed the demon Narakaasura who had enslaved many women. Shri Krishna came to the rescue of the innocents and gave freedom and equality to women.

On this day Lord Mahavira (founder of Jainism) attained 'Moksha'. As the light of wisdom had gone, the Jains produce light by illuminating lamps and this is the Jain origin of the festival of lights. Swami Dayananda (founder of Arya Samaj) also left for the heavenly abode on this day.

The seasonal aspect of the festival is that in India the harvest after the rainy season is marked by Diwali. Thanks are given to Almighty God by reciting prayers and making a symbolic gesture of offering (Ahuti) grains to the sacred fire called Yajna (see p.102). It is just like the thanksgiving of a harvest festival.

Diwali signifies the victory of light over darkness, knowledge over ignorance and goodness over evil. Its spiritual message is conveyed by the famous Hindu prayer 'Tamaso ma jyotir gamaya', meaning 'Lead me from darkness to light'.

Shivaratri

The festival of Shivaratri falls on the fourteenth day of the dark fortnight of the month of Magh (around February). It is commonly known as the Maha Shivaratri - the great Shiva night. Shiva (see p.23) means the auspicious one and is one of the Trimurti (see p.22). On this day, the devotees of Shiva observe fast and go to temples to perform puja of the Shivalinga (see p.31) with special items like the pious Ganga water, bel-patra (leave of wood-apple tree), milk, ghee, honey, fruit and flowers. The significance of offering the prayers in the tranquillity of midnight is to sit in silence, meditate, introspect and make resolve to get rid of evil tendencies and laziness and awaken the faculties of cognition like a Yogi. Devotion to God and acquiring spiritual knowledge are the main aspects of Shivaratri. Devotees sing in praise of Shiva and chant Vedic mantra "AUM Namah Shivaya, Namah Shankaraya, Namah Shambhavaya..." meaning we offer our salutation to the Almighty, the giver of peace, happiness and good fortune to all. Historically, the name of Swami Dayananda (see p.49) came to be linked with the night of Shivaratri when he took a vow to stay awake hungry all night with a determination to seek the real Shiva. After many years' study of Vedas and Yoga, he was enlightened and brought about many reforms in the Hindu society.

May there be auspicious thoughts in the mind so that we may perform noble deeds

- Yajur Veda 34-1

Raksha Bandhan or Shravani

This festival falls in the month of Shravana (August) on the day of the full moon (Purnima). It is therefore sometimes referred to as Shravani. It is celebrated in two ways:

Shravani: When a child went to his guru to acquire knowledge he or she was given a Sacred Thread of Yajnopaveet (Janeu) and initiated as a Brahmachari (a celibate student). See further details about the sacred thread on p.66. The thread is renewed every year on this day. The old Yajnopaveet is discarded and the solemn promises are renewed.

Raksha Bandhan: In ancient times, when a guru initiated his disciple he tied a red or orange thread round the right wrist. Likewise a Brahmin ties the thread round the wrist of a householder when renewing the sacred thread (Yajnopaveet). This multicoloured thread tied around the wrist started the tradition of Raksha Bandhan or Rakhi, meaning 'promise to protect'. It signified the bond of mutual love and trust between the teacher and the pupil.

In later times women began to tie Rakhi to their brothers. This meant that it was the duty of the brother to protect his sister from troubles and danger. Sometimes women without brothers tied the Rakhi on men who then considered the women as sisters. In this way Rakhi became a symbol of affection between brothers and sisters and thus also became a means of showing respect to women. Hindus use it to promote the message of universal brotherhood.

There was also a tradition of members of the public tying a Rakhi to their king. It symbolized their allegiance to the civic authority and the king's promise to look after his subjects. This tradition has been kept alive in Britain by Hindus who every year tie a Rakhi to the Lord Mayor or Mayor of the city.

Historical festivals

Ramnavami (Birth of Rama)

This festival is associated with the celebration of the birth of Rama. Rama was born on the ninth day of the bright fortnight in the month of Chaitra (March/April) in a town called Ayodhya in the state of Uttar Pradesh in India. Rama's story is described on pp.134–138.

His birth is celebrated at noon. Many Hindus fast on this day.

Krishna Janmashtami (Birth of Krishna)

This festival celebrates the birth of Shri Krishna and usually falls around the middle or the later part of August. The story of Krishna's birth in a prison cell and his dramatic escape on a stormy night is recounted on pp.144–146. Janmashtami is celebrated with love and devotion. The temples are decorated and thousands of devotees sing the glory of Shri Krishna and keep awake until midnight, the time of Krishna's birth.

Navaratri

This festival is known as the festival of nine nights. It is based on the belief that the strength to fight evil and the power to protect the weak is a feminine entity represented by Hindu goddesses. The nine nights' worship are divided into three days' worship for each of the goddesses – Durga, the goddess of Shakti (strength), Lakshmi, the goddess of wealth, and Saraswati, the goddess of knowledge. The tigress-like strength of Durga, the ferocity of Kaali, the pure white embodiment of Amba and the slayer of demons Mahishasura all feature in many traditional stories which manifest this feminine power to eradicate suffering caused by injustice.

The last day of this festival, known as 'Vijay Dashmi', the victory day, has a very special significance. It is celebrated as 'Seemollanghan', meaning 'crossing the barrier'. The message for an individual is that one should always try to progress, try to excel beyond current limitations, break new records. For society, this festival brings people together to create feelings of goodwill so that no ill feelings or evil can take root.

During these nine days, Hindus fast and pray. Some dance at night around the image of Devi Durga (see p.25). These dances are called Garbas. They are very popular in the Hindu community in Britain (see p.62).

Dussera or Vijaydashmi

Dussera follows the nine-day Navratri celebrations. This is because on the tenth day of the battle Rama killed Ravana and rescued Sita. It was a day of victory and therefore it is known as Vijaydashmi ('Vijay' means victory and 'Dashmi' is the tenth day). On this day huge effigies of the demon Ravana are burnt with firecrackers.

Varsh Pratipada or Yugadi

To record events in history all nations need to have a calendar or system of dates, and this is usually based on an important event. Varsh Pratipada or Yugadi is the first day of the year according to the traditional calendar of Bharat called Vikram Samvat (vs) and Shalivan Shaka (ss). Vikram Samvat is named after King Vikramaditya who defeated foreign tribes invading India in 57 BCE. The year 1995 was vs 2052. The Shalivana Shaka started in 78 CE, so the year 1995 was ss 1917. This festival has historical importance and also has a seasonal flavour. It falls in the beginning of spring (Vasant ritu) when mother nature is fresh and makes a new start. It brings hope and joy for the future to all. It is the time to start a new epoch, Yuga, in life, hence it is also called 'Yugadi'.

The founding of new eras in the names of the kings Vikramaditya and Shalivahana signified the supreme importance accorded in Hindu history and tradition for safeguarding the nation's freedom and sovereignty. As such, the continuing tradition of the two eras has helped to keep awake the spirit of national freedom in the nation's mind.

The founder of the Rashtriya Swayamsevak Sangh (RSS), Dr Keshav Baliram Hedgewar, was also born on the day of Yugadi, in 1889. He was born of poor parents in Nagpur, qualified as a medical doctor but became famous as a nationalist leader in India. He formulated the ways and means of achieving national awareness. As a result, in 1925, on the auspicious Vijayadashmi day, he started RSS which has now become the largest uniformed organization of volunteers working for social reform. The aim of RSS is to serve society through organized team-work, and that is the message which is given to millions of Hindus on this day.

Seasonal festivals

From ancient times, seasonal festivals have been celebrated by Hindus in order to bring man close to nature. Amongst such festivals are Diwali, Holi, Vasant Panchami, Makar Sankranti and Sharad Purnima. Diwali and Holi have connections with farming. Hindus considered the harvest as a bounty of God and all grain produced was accepted as a gift from God. When the crops were ready for harvesting, a Yajna was performed. There are two harvesting seasons in a year. The first is at the rainy season when rice, moong, maize and millet are ripe. The second harvest comes at the end of the cold season when wheat, gram, urad and sugar-cane are ripe. Diwali is celebrated at the end of the rainy season and Holi marks the end of the cold season. During both festivals, Yajnas are performed and the newly harvested grain is offered as oblation.

Holi (Festival of Colours)

Holi is celebrated on Purnima (the full moon) in Phalguna (February). When gram, wheat and other grains are roasted they are called Holuk, hence the name Holi. Even today there is a custom of lighting a bonfire (Holi) and roasting grains, corn and so on as offerings for eating and this promotes a feeling of brotherhood among the Hindu community. The story of a female demon called Holika is also linked with Holi.

Story of Holika and Prahalada

Holika was a sister of the demon king Hiranyakashipu. The king's son Prahalada was a great devotee of God. Hiranyakashipu was not in favour of this because he considered himself to be the lord of the universe. He tried to kill Prahalada and he persuaded his sister Holika to assist in this killing. It is said that Holika had a boon that she would not be burnt by fire, so she entered into a fire with Prahalada with the intention of burning him to death. Instead, Prahalada was saved but Holika was burnt to death as she was misusing her powers.

The festival of Holi reminds Hindus of the devotee Prahalada. Hence this festival is taken as an inspiration to destroy the evil that dwells within oneself.

This festival is also known as the 'festival of colour' and it is literally celebrated with colours. Men and women of all ages offer prayers, sing and dance, and splash washable colours on each other. They smear each other's faces with powder paints and laugh and hug each other in a joyous mood.

When mother nature ushers in the spring season, there is more light and more colour. For centuries, mankind has known that light and colour bring joy and happiness to daily life. The Sama Veda contains a number of verses on the splendour of nature; this is one of them:

> *Rejoice in all the moods of Nature,*
> *Experience the unseen divine stature*
> *In its various glorious forms.*
> *Spring is the season of flowers and scented*
> *   breezes*
> *Which gladden the hearts and it pleases.*
>
> (SAMA VEDA, 616)

This feeling is expressed in many Hindu religious and social traditions. Hindu temples are decorated with bright colours and if you go in you will see pictures and statues with glittering jewels and garments. Seeing is important: the visual impact of colours is to create a sensation of delight. The idea of Holi is to convert this outward sensation into an inner feeling of happiness. Enemies become friends on this day; old quarrels and personal differences are forgotten. The playful activity of throwing coloured paint and singing and dancing together is designed to remove the barriers which sometimes people tend to build around themselves. Holi renews the spirit of unity and brotherhood among families and in the community.

Makar Sankranti or Pongol

This is also connected with agriculture and the seasons. The festival is celebrated in January when the sun leaves the south (Capricorn) and moves towards the north (Cancer). This is the only Hindu festival of which the date is determined by the Gregorian (solar) calendar; it always falls on 14 January. Until 1752 CE, Makar Sankranti fell on the Western New Year's day, 1 January. However, in that year, when Britain adopted the Gregorian calendar, eleven days were dropped. Moreover, a rule

was introduced that a century year will not be a leap year unless it is divisible by 400. Consequently, from 1753 until 1799, Makar Sankranti came eleven days later, i.e. on 12 January. Since 1800 was not a leap year, the festival fell on 13 January. During the twentieth century another day was added, so now it falls on 14 January. The main significance of this festival is to encourage self-improvement and change to a better life.

Vasant Panchami

When the cold season is over, Hindus celebrate this festival to welcome the spring.

Sharad Purnima

Hindus celebrate this festival at the end of the rainy season, when the waters of the rivers become clear and the mud dries up. On the night of the full moon (Purnima) in the month of October people celebrate the festival in the moonlight.

IN THE CLASSROOM

Reflect on the seasons and the symbolism associated with them: e.g. spring – hope, new life, etc. Discuss the need to remember the past and the way in which festivals (seasonal and historical) help to fulfil this role.

Look at the symbols associated with festivals, like Diwali lamps, Rangoli patterns, Rakhis. The story of Rama and Sita could be acted out or perhaps dance could be used to share the experience of celebrating Hindu festivals.

Typical questions/discussion points

1. Describe one of the Hindu festivals and explain how it is celebrated.
2. Is there any difference between the way Hindu festivals are celebrated in India and elsewhere?

Puja

Puja is a worshipful means of direct personal communion with God. Puja can be performed in private in one's own home or in public in a temple. Hindus generally offer daily Puja at home in front of a chosen deity or a shrine.

There are many rituals associated with the offering of Puja. The rituals performed in a temple are described on pp.112–114. In this section we explain the significance of the rituals associated with Puja.

One of the Hindu scriptures says: 'Offering of perfumed substances, flowers, incense, lamps and fresh fruits are the five elements of the traditional puja which culminates with offering of the lamps.' (Kamika Agama)

Many Hindus offer Puja to Devas, which are manifestations of different powers of God. The following are the main rituals and symbolic meanings of such Pujas.

Rituals of Deva Puja

1. Avahana: invoking the presence of God in the form of an image or symbol.
2. Aasana: offering a seat.
3. Padya and Arghya: offering water to wash hands and feet.
4. Snana or Abhisheka: ceremonial bath.
5. Vastra: offering clothes, usually the sacred thread (Yajnopaveet).
6. Chandan: smearing sandalwood paste which has a very soothing effect.
7. Pushpa and gandha: offering flowers, garlands and perfume.
8. Dhupa: burning incense.
9. Deepa or Aarti: lighting lamp and waving it gently.
10. Naivedya: offering food.
11. Visarjana: bringing to a close.

Symbolic meaning of Deva Puja

These rituals have the following meanings:
1. Use of an image or a symbol as an aid to concentration.
2. Recognition of the omnipresence of God; believing that God's seat is in the devotee's heart.
3. Devotee offering service to God.
4. Cleaning off the layer of ignorance.
5. See significance of the sacred thread (Yajnopaveet) on p.66.
6. Removal of anxiety and stress; helps to achieve a calm and relaxed state.
7. Need for pure and loving thoughts. Expression of love and devotion.
8. Reminder to burn/destroy the desires.
9. Desire to seek enlightenment: knowledge is light which destroys darkness or ignorance.

10. Devotee acknowledges that food is obtained by grace of God.

The best way to introduce this form of worship in Hinduism is to take the pupils to a temple or to someone's home where Puja is being performed and let them observe the rituals. The purpose and sequence of these rituals are similar to the welcoming of a guest by offering a seat, refreshments and kind words to make the guest feel at home. Some of the common prayers recited during the Puja are described on pp.123–125; see particularly the Aarti, when a tray of lamps is gently moved in a circular motion.

Typical questions/discussion points
1. How is Puja different from other forms of worship?
2. What similarities do you see between the rituals of a Puja and the way a guest is welcomed?

Havan Yajna

The most ancient form of Hindu prayer is known as the Havan Yajna. It is a religious ceremony in which a sacred fire is lit in a square shaped container called 'havan kund' and Sanskrit mantras are recited. Some scholars wrongly think that it is worship of fire, which it is not. It is based on the principle of sacrificing for the sake of others. These are the main purposes of Havan Yajna:

- Lighting a fire and offering wood, ghee and herbs is a symbolic act of giving and teaches one not to be selfish.
- Recitation of prayers in a group teaches one to live happily by sharing with others.
- It represents the protection of the environment we all have to live in.

A step-by-step explanation of Havan

1. Sipping of water (Achman)
Great importance is attached to water in Hindu religious traditions. It is one of the five physical elements (see p.40). Without water there cannot be any life. Water is considered as a gift given to humanity by God. At the start

of a Yajna, water is sipped three times: first for the water received from the sky (rain), second for underground water (wells) and third for surface water (lakes and rivers). This signifies that God gives shelter from above and provides the ground (base) to stand on.

2. Prayer for physical health (Ang Saparsh)
These mantras recognize the five senses and the parts of the body which are needed to carry out work. Different parts of the body are touched with water to pray for physical health and strength.

3. Communion prayer (Ishwar Upasana)
God's powers and qualities are remembered in these mantras. Eight mantras selected from the Vedas are recited; they state that God created everything and that he controls everything through the physical laws he made. For example, reference is made to the planets and the earth staying in orbit owing to the force called 'gravity'. Scientists have discovered the law of gravity, but they have not found out who made this law. The Vedas say that there are eternal laws which were used by God to create the universe.

4. Benedictory prayer (Swasti Vachan)
These mantras mention various branches of science which can be of benefit to mankind. These Vedic prayers refer to the combination of different materials to make new materials (chemistry) and the making of machines (technology) and pray that they should be of benefit to society. The importance of weather and the rain cycle is described. It is also prayed that scientists, rulers (kings), soldiers, and all intelligent people should do good for others. Finally, the mantras mention the twenty-one things which make up this world: the five physical elements (fire, air, earth, water and space) which have the qualities of light (heat), sound, smell, taste and touch sensed by the five senses through the five parts of the body (eyes, ears, nose, mouth and skin) which contains the soul.

5. Prayer for peace (Shanti Prakarna)
In these mantras the prayer is for the forces of nature to be peaceful. For example, in the first mantra it is prayed that the presence of electricity in the air (lightning) should not harm; this is called 'Indra Varuna' in the mantra. Another prayer is for the chemicals in plants to be peaceful, i.e. they should work as medicine, not poison. Even psychology is mentioned: prayer is made for people to have sound and balanced minds in order to live in harmony. Finally, in the last mantra God is requested to grant fearlessness and bravery so that humans can fight bad influences and stay on the side of good.

6. Lighting the fire (Agnya Dhan)
As the sacred fire is lit, the prayer reminds us that we cannot live without consuming and wasting the things offered by nature. In this mantra the role of nature is acknowledged for giving things to sustain all life.

7. Placing the firewood (Samidha Dhan)
By placing the wood, the fire is started. It signifies that work has to be done to achieve one's goal. Without work one cannot meet one's objectives.

8. Offering of ghee (Ghrit Ahuti)
The main thought behind this offering is that just as fuel (ghee) is needed to keep the fire burning, so God is needed to keep us alive and working. The offerings are made with the words that the fuel is for the fire, not for ourselves. It also conveys the message that one should work for God, not for oneself.

9. Sprinkling of water (Jal Sinchan)
Water is sprinkled around the sacred fire and prayers are made for obtaining unbeatable strength, tolerance and intelligence. The importance of strength with tolerance and intelligence with a sweet tongue is the message given by this ritual.

10. Special prayers for both morning and evening
These mantras teach selflessness. Offerings are made to the air, sun and fire. These are gifts from God without which no one can live. Worshippers are reminded not to misuse and plunder the resources of nature.

11. Offering without selfishness (Ajyahuti)
Several offerings to the fire are made with the

words 'It is not for me' (Id na mum). Here Hindus pray for protection from anger, and ask for more light and less darkness. This also means more knowledge and less ignorance, more happiness and less misery for everyone.

12. Final offering (Poornahuti)
The final mantra says, 'God is perfect. God is infinite.' The Vedas say that God is infinite and perfect because he will never run out of energy. The prayer is for everything to be perfect and complete.

Hindus believe that there is a scientific basis for Havan Yajna. The aromatic oils and herbs offered to the sacred fire burn to create chemical substances such as ketones and aldehydes which produce disinfectants like Formaldehyde. It is a kind of fumigation process which cleanses the air of harmful germs. Many Hindus perform Havan Yajna at their homes for purification.

Making offerings with chants like 'It is not for me' is believed to be a kind of psychological training in performing a selfless act. It serves as a reminder of obligations towards God, nature and fellow human beings. Havan Yajna is performed at all Hindu weddings and sacraments.

Yajna emphasizes feelings of mutual obligation and reminds those who have forgotten about them.

IN THE CLASSROOM

The material in this section can be useful when discussing how people of different faiths pray. Two important points about Havan Yajna should be made clear:
• It is not a prayer for an individual. It is a prayer performed jointly for the benefit of all.
• There is a strong message about the protection and care of the environment and nature.

Typical questions/discussion points
1. What is the significance of the fire and water in the Hindu prayer of Havan?
2. Why do Hindus believe that Havan Yajna purifies the environment?
3. What is the main message of Havan Yajna?

Pilgrimage

There are many shrines and holy places in India which attract millions of Hindus from around the world. That is why India is believed to be the holy land by all Hindus. Pilgrimage to the holy land, also known as 'Tirth yatra', is not mandatory, but is considered to be an important practice carried out during the lifetime of a Hindu.

The aims of pilgrimage
The aims of undertaking pilgrimage – such as achievement of spiritual merit in visiting the shrines and holy places of one's faith, and doing penance for self-purification – are common to all faiths. These are applicable to Hindus, but in addition, and perhaps uniquely, the Hindu is seeking 'Moksha' – ultimate liberation of the soul from the bondage of life and death. Moksha, as explained earlier, can be achieved only through self-realization. Pilgrimage provides the Hindu with an ample setting for soul-searching and self-analysis. As a Hindu gazes at the Murtis (statues) depicting God in his manifold forms, and as a devotee prostrates before the shrines or bathes in the holy rivers, he or she is struck with wonder and awe and realizes that material possessions are transient in nature and must be cast aside if one is to achieve self-realization.

Pilgrimage also helps the devotee to develop a sense of humility and to discover their heritage. For Hindus living outside India, it creates a cultural link. At some holy places, priests maintain written records of the history of many Hindu families. Pilgrimages are also sometimes undertaken as fulfilment of a vow, or when there is a birth or death in the family.

Acts usually performed on a pilgrimage
A pilgrimage is not a holiday; for a Hindu, it is a serious affair. Pilgrimage is specifically undertaken with a lot of planning and with certain objectives. Typical acts performed on a pilgrimage are:
• Abstinence from all meat and alcoholic beverage. Purity of thought, word and deed is essential when approaching the shrines and holy places. A first-time visitor to India may find some of the places unclean or

uncomfortable, but after a while the atmosphere of devotion engrosses and material comforts are forgotten.

- Staying at the place of pilgrimage to take part in the acts of worship (Puja) both in the morning and in the evening after ablutions.
- Making offerings and donations in memory of one's departed ancestors. At some places there are special priests who help the pilgrims offer Puja to their ancestors with Pindas (rice balls). This special puja is called Shraadh.
- Circumambulation of the shrine or the holy spot. Sometimes it involves trekking for miles over hilly areas. Some devotees 'measure their length' around the temple, and some have their heads shaven to symbolize the cutting away of worldliness.

Devotees at pilgrimage: 'Measuring their length' around the temple.

- To have Darshan. The word 'Darshan' means 'viewing'. To a Hindu devotee, seeing is important. Pilgrims must view the image kept in the inner sanctum of the temple. During special festivals, they may have to wait for days because of the number of people.
- To visit their family priest, called Purohit. At some places, a centuries-long relationship is maintained between a Hindu family and their Purohits who keep a written record of the family lineage. All births and deaths are recorded by them.

Places of pilgrimage

India has a vast number of holy places and shrines. Even certain mountains and rivers are regarded with deep reverence. Some of the most famous places of pilgrimage are described in this section. (See also map on p.9.)

Kashi (Varanasi or Benares)

The ancient city of Kashi has been described by many as the microcosm of Hinduism. There are at present nearly 375 temples left from the original 1400. It is famous for the Golden Mandir whose 0.75-tonne gold plating was provided by the Sikh Maharaja, Ranjit Singh. The Golden Mandir is situated opposite the site of the original mandir which was destroyed by the Moghul invader Aurangzeb. He built a mosque on the original site but traces of the old mandir are still visible behind the mosque. The four temples of Vishwanath are the holiest shrines here, including the latest Vishwanath temple constructed recently by the Benares Hindu University. Temples such as Sankat Mochan and Tulsi Manas hold relics of the famous saint Tulsi Das whose version of the Ramayana is very popular. About 20 kilometres north of Kashi is Sarnath where Buddha preached his sermon on Nirvana, so it is a holy place for Buddhists.

Kashi has two well-known cremation grounds, called Ghats, on the banks of the River Ganga (Ganges). It is a Hindu belief that one's soul attains freedom if one is cremated at these Ghats. Sometimes corpses are brought from thousands of miles for cremation and immersion of the ashes in the holy Ganges.

The Holy Ganga (Ganges)

The holy River Ganga flows from the Himalayas in the north, through the plains and into the bay of Bengal in the east (see map on p.9). It is of special reverence to Hindus who regard it as the mother Ganga. There is an interesting mythological story about the Ganga.

Story of the Holy Ganga

King Bhagirath was a pious and noble king. His ancestors had committed sinful acts in the presence of the great sage Kapil, for which they were burnt to cinders through the wrath of that sage. Though dead for many years, their souls remained unliberated. Liberation could be achieved only if the holy flow of the Ganges would wash their bones. But the Ganges was in the high heavens. So King Bhagirath performed acts of penance and pleaded for Ganga to descend to earth to liberate his ancestors. The problem was that upon her descent the strength of her flow would have smashed the earth. So Lord Shiva accepted her into his flowing hair and gradually released her on to the earth for the benefit of mankind. This also liberated the souls of King Bhagirath's ancestors.

This story has lead to the belief that if a dying person sips the holy water of the Ganges, the soul will be liberated. The source of the river is known as Gaumukh, at the Gangotri glacier. There are many shrines there and some ascetics live in nearby caves. The temple of Garhwal is the nearest shrine to the river's source. It was built by the Nepalese general Amar Singh Thapa. There are many pilgrimage sites along the course of the river. The two most special places are Haridwar and Rishikesh, both in the foothills of the Himalayas. Here the flow is crystal clear and pure. Many Hindus take back home containers filled with the holy water.

Kumbha Mela

This is the largest gathering in the world. It is held at twelve-year intervals at Haridwar, Prayag, Nasik and Ujjain. Holy men emerge from caves and forests, religious leaders come to preach and Hindu devotees go there seeking purity and knowledge. Kumbha Mela is a symbol of unity. Mark Tully has given an enchanting insight into this unique and gigantic gathering in his book *No Full Stops in India*. Nearly 30 million people attend the Kumbha Mela: imagine more than half of Britain's population gathering at one event!

Rameshwar

Rameshwar is a small island situated at the

Hindus bathing in the River Ganga

The Kumbha Mela gathering at Prayag Raj

southern tip of India, from which a crossing to Sri Lanka could be made by sea. It is famous because it is believed that here Rama, Sita and Hanuman established two Linghams (shrines) dedicated to Shiva (see the story of the Ramayana on pp.134–138). Pilgrims often bring water from the River Ganges to pour on the Linghams. They also bathe at the temple's twenty-two wells, each one for a particular kind of sin. The construction of the temple began in the twelfth century. Its main corridor is 1219 metres long.

It is a pilgrimage site for Sikhs since it was visited by Guru Gobind Singh. It is also one of the four pilgrimages designated by the great philosopher Adi Shakracharya. The others are Badrinath in the north, Dwarka in the west and Puri in the east. The soil here is believed to be so sacred that the inhabitants do not plough the land.

Chidambaram

It is believed that Lord Shiva danced the Tandava dance of creation at this place. It is located in Tamil Nadu state in southern India. Here, the great philosopher Sage Patanjali wrote the Yoga Sutras; also, Rishi Tirumular,

the author of the scripture 'Tirumantiram', lived here. The main sanctum of the temple has a solid gold roof with 17,500 tiles.

Kedarnath

This temple of Lord Shiva, at a height of over 3500 metres, is believed to have been made by the five Pandava brothers (see the story of the Mahabharata on pp.138–143) after they won the war.

Mount Kailash

This is the most austere pilgrimage. High in the Himalayan range is Mount Kailash (also known as Mount Meru). At the foot of this sacred peak is Lake Manasarovara. It is an area of stunning natural beauty; within 80 kilometres of this place are the sources of four of India's most sacred rivers.

Ayodhya

This is the birthplace of Shri Rama (see the story of the Ramayana on pp.134–138). Originally the town was full of temples but many were destroyed by Moghul emperors. In the book *The Mosques of India*, published by the famous centre of Islamic learning, the

Nadwatal-Ulama of Lucknow, it is mentioned, 'There is a famous story about his [Rama's] wife Sita.It is said that Sita had a temple here in which she lived and cooked for her husband. On that very site a mosque-like structure was constructed by Babar [a Moghul invader].' New archaeological discoveries have identified the exact location of the birthplace of Rama (see Ramjanmabhumi published by Professor K.L. Lal, President of the Historian Forum) . Hindus are now trying to build a temple at the site. Further information about this controversial issue can be obtained from the book *Ramjanmabhoomi vs Babri Masjid* written by Koenraad Elst who has presented a case study of this conflict as an outside observer.

Mathura

This is the birthplace of Shri Krishna. The nearby towns of Vrindavan and Gokula are popular visiting places as Shri Krishna grew up there.

Dwarka

This is located at the extreme western tip of the state of Gujarat. Shri Krishna set up his capital here after leaving Mathura. Earlier cities (now submerged) have been revealed at the site by archaeological excavations. It is renowned for Janmashtami (birth of Krishna) celebrations.

Somnath

The temple was originally built of gold. It was raided, looted and razed by the Muslim invader M. Ghazni. In 1950 it was rebuilt in the traditional style on the original site by the sea.

Puri

This is famous for the 900-year-old Jagannatha temple. Here is held one of the most impressive festivals, in which devotees pull a 12-metre-long wooden chariot by ropes some 500 metres long. This mammoth and spectacular event is called the Jagannath Yatra (the march of Jagannath). This is the origin of the English word 'juggernaut', meaning a heavy lorry. Nearly a million people participate in this event and about 6000 men are employed for mandir functions and rituals.

Badrinath

This is a Vishnu temple situated at a height of 3000 metres in the Himalayas. It is famous for its statue of Lord Vishnu with many priceless gems and a large diamond over his third eye.

Tirupati

This is perhaps the richest temple in India. On average 30,000 pilgrims come every day to have Darshan (sight) of the sacred 2-metre tall, jet black idol of Shri Venkateshwara, also known as Bala ji. Usually the pilgrims have to wait nearly twelve hours in queues to enter the temple. Many pilgrims have their heads shaved at this holy place.

Pilgrimages for the goddesses

Right across India there are many temples devoted to goddesses. At Kanyakumari, the southernmost tip of India, is the temple of goddess Parvati, consort of Shiva. Also there is the Vivekananda Rock Memorial which commemorates the famous Hindu monk Swami Vivekananda. It is believed that he found divine enlightenment here to spread the message of humanity.

Madurai is famous for the 985-pillared temple of Meenakshi, a manifestation of Parvati.

North of Jammu, hidden deep inside a cave is the temple of Vaishno Devi, a devotee of Lord Vishnu. She defeated a demon called Bhaironath. Vaishno Devi is regarded as the divine power and strength which protects from evil. In spite of the hilly area and long climb, nearly 20,000 pilgrims a day visit this temple throughout the year.

Many Westerners visit Hindu holy places seeking spiritual experiences. A devotee has her forehead smeared with sandalwood paste at Kumbha Mela.

IN THE CLASSROOM

This topic can be introduced from KS2 onwards. It can be started by a general discussion about the need to travel. Do we need to travel to seek truth and happiness or to discover something new? Introduce the idea that Hindus have to travel to far-off places when they go on pilgrimages. A map of India can be shown to help pupils appreciate the vastness of the country. Point out the Himalayan range, the River Ganges and the distinctive southern tip of India. Pictures of temples and a large gathering of people at a riverside can be shown. Ask them to look at the *Guinness Book of Records* to find the largest gathering of people – the Kumbha Mela.

At KS3 and KS4, pupils should be able to grasp the idea that the Hindu way of life is a series of stages of a journey. Pilgrimages play an important part in the understanding of life as a progression towards God.

Typical questions/discussion points
1. Why is the River Ganges regarded as a holy river by Hindus?
2. What is the significance of the Hindu ritual of bathing in a holy river or a temple well?
3. Why does the Kumbha Mela attract so many people?
4. Which Hindu place of pilgrimage has given us the English word 'juggernaut'?
5. Why do religious people go on pilgrimage?

Hindu Temples and Rituals

India is a land of temples. The Hindu temple is a house of worship with unique features. This is because it is symbolically designed in such a way that the place where it is built, the manner of its construction and the rituals that are traditionally enacted within it all have spiritual significance and enormous scientific merit. All these aspects are so formulated as to indicate the spiritual path man has to follow to achieve self-realization, which is the ultimate goal of human existence.

Many of the main temples in ancient India were situated on the tops of mountains or hills. The paths to these temples were narrow and rugged and the pilgrims had to walk up the hill in single file; they had to face many difficulties before reaching the temple shrine. They carried with them fruit and flowers to offer to the Lord in the temple. What is the symbolic significance of these features?

The hilltop site
The high altitude signifies that spiritual development is above everything in this world and that to gain self-realization one needs to put in a great deal of effort. The high location also made the temple visible from all around. Nowadays the altitude aspect is overcome by having a high-domed construction.

The narrow, rugged path
There is a need for great effort, determination and single-mindedness if the pilgrim is to overcome the temptations and challenges that he comes across on his spiritual journey. Today roads and transportation have been improved to reach the temples and this age-old spiritual practice has been lost.

Carrying fruit and flowers to offer to the deities
The offering of fruit and flowers represents an expression of love and devotion which helps to unfold the inner self. An individual without any desires is fully liberated and has realized the self. The visit to the temple therefore signifies exhaustion of one's desires and realization of God.

The purpose of temples
- They create a religious atmosphere and turn the mind towards pious and pure thoughts.
- They generate a feeling of peace and mental calmness.
- They encourage congregational worship, which creates a religious purity in the community and solidarity in society, decreases confrontation and quarrels, and promotes an atmosphere of coexistence.
- The deity is treated as a king of kings living in his palace (temple). That is why temples are built in an ornate manner which look so magnificent in their decor. The priest is there to serve the deity.

These functions of a temple fall into three main categories: religious, social and educational. By organizing the celebration of festivals, often involving the display of deities in public marches (Ratha Yatra), they help to maintain cultural identity. Temples also run charitable programmes to give aid to orphans and the poor and needy. In addition, they are places of learning where the study of ancient scriptures takes place. In former times, usually the king provided the necessary funds for temple activities. Nowadays, temples are built and run by members of the public without any assistance from the government.

> *Mandirs preserve the cleanliness of the soul and keep it from becoming diseased. Some diseases cannot be seen, only experienced. Our scriptures have shown the medicine to be mandirs.*
>
> (HIS DIVINE HOLINESS PRAMUKH SWAMI MAHARAJ OF THE SWAMINARAYAN MOVEMENT)

The symbols of a temple

- A saffron flag on top of the dome signifies the Kingdom of God (just as the Union Jack denotes the United Kingdom). The saffron colour has always depicted purity, devotion and godliness because it is the colour of the sun and fire. The sun is the source of all existence and as such represents the Almighty. The saffron-coloured robes that Rishis and Swamis wear is to denote their attachment to this spiritual path.

- Images or statues of deities (see p.22) and various signs and symbols (AUM, see p.28) depict the various powers and attributes of the Almighty God. An image or a symbol (in the form of a god or a goddess) is not God but represents that divine all-pervading power and through it one contemplates God. Multiple heads and arms are often used to portray superhuman qualities. Even the gestures of their hands (Mudras) have meaning. The uplifted outward-facing palm bestows grace, while the downward palm signifies submission.

- The building has a tall dome (representing the sky) and traditionally there are three passages around the deity. The outer passage denotes the outer gross body, the middle

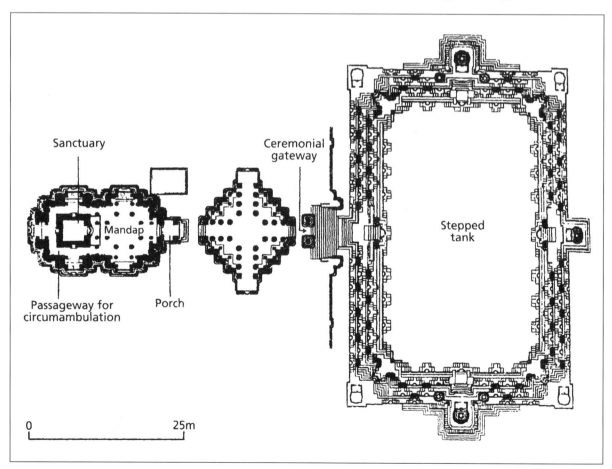

Plan of a Hindu temple

(a) Many big temples in India keep elephants, others have sculptures of elephants at the main gate.
(b) Pillars and arches inside the Jain temple in Leicester
(c) Details of a hand carved lime stone pillar
(d) Sikh gurudwara in Hounslow. Saffron flag (Nishan Sahib) is flown outside gurudwaras.

the subtle body, and the inner passage the causal body (the seat of ignorance and Vasanas). Within these lies the deity along with the burning lamp of ghee representing the Atman and the everlasting light of wisdom, which can be achieved only when one has gained mastery over these physical states – body, mind and intellect. Shikhara (pinnacles) represent a mountain symbolizing upward aspiration.

Temple architecture

The essential parts of a temple are: the 'Garbhagriha' (sanctum sanctorum); the Shukanasi (nose); the Antarala, which are the adjoining passages; the Navaranga or Mandap that serves as a multi-purpose hall for religio-cultural activities; the Dhwaja sthambha (flag-post); and the Balipith or the pedestal for offerings. Bigger temples also have smaller shrines for the minor deities associated with the chief deity, wells, water tanks and gardens. In Britain, some old church buildings have been converted into Hindu temples and gurdwaras and some new temples have been built (see p.57).

The architecture, the installation of deities, the worship and the other details of many temples are guided by religious scriptures known as Agama Shastras (see p.126) and Shilpa Shastra.

The structure of a temple is highly symbolic. Primarily it represents God as the cosmic person. The Garbhagriha or sanctum sanctorum is his head, the Gopura (tower at the main entrance) is his feet, the Shukanasi (lion) his nose, the Antarala his neck, the Prakaras (the surrounding high walls) his hands. Gavaksha (ornamental windows) represent the ears and Ghanta (bells) the tongue. Alternatively, it can represent the body of man, with God residing in his heart. The temple may also represent the whole creation. Images that are consecrated according to scriptural rites are considered to be 'alive'; hence formal worship is necessary. This worship ranges from one to nine times per day depending on the extent and resources of the temple. On special festival days, celebrations are conducted with much pomp and ceremony and thousands of people throng to the festivals to participate. Such celebrations are termed

Brahmotsava ('Brahma' means 'big'). The 'Rathotsav' or temple car festival is also held as a symbol of a moving temple.

Many temples in southern India arrange a floating festival. In this the deity is placed on a boat, which is lit by candles or lamps, and floated around the temple tank. This conveys the idea that the world is an uncharted ocean in which humanity has to sail. If God is the helmsman there is no fear, for he is the real saviour.

Generally, every temple has three prakaras or surrounding walls representing the three bodies – gross, subtle and causal. Some temples have five walls representing five sheaths of Atman – Anna, Prana, Mana, Vijnana and Anandamay. The seven walls in the seven-walled city of Srirangam, the abode of Lord Ranganath, represent the seven Dhatus (elements) of which the body is made (see p.155).

Every temple has a Bali-pith in front. It represents the fact that the devotee should sacrifice all his ego and desires before he enters the temple. The circumambulation done in some of the temples of Shiva is not in a clockwise direction; instead, the worshipper goes up to one half and then turns back and completes the circuit. Thus the figure of AUM is traced.

The temple as a social institution
In the past Indian temples were not only places of worship but were the very focus of society. They served as a centre of culture and education, a charitable institution, a feeding house, a hospital and an art gallery all in one. The temple, especially in southern India, is thus a unique institution, the like of which cannot be seen anywhere else in the world.

A temple took several years to build, providing work for many artisans and engineers. There were elaborate rites and rituals to be performed in the temples. Music formed a regular part of the service to the deity and about eighteen instruments were used. Even today the instrument called Nadaswaram is commonly used in all temples in southern India. At Suchindram there are musical pillars that produce different musical notes.

Several literary works originated and have been preserved in the temples of southern India. Periyapuran, Kandapuran, and Kamba Ramayana were released in the temples at Chidambaram, Kumarkottam and Srirangam respectively. Educational institutes were also run by the temples. A university with over a thousand students was founded by the temple in Trivendram. There was also a college of Vedic studies in Kanyakumari district.

The temple has also served as an orphanage and a feeding centre. This is a common sight when you visit Indian temples where food and clothes are distributed to the needy and poor.

Hospitals also functioned in some temples. Today there are temples which run dispensaries for poor patients where medicine is provided free of charge. In addition, temples played the role of village co-operative societies by helping needy villagers with loans that would be repaid in the form of various commodities required by the temples. Another function is as a sports arena. During the Onam festivals boat races are held on the river in front of the temple of Krishna at Aranmula in Kerala. Temples also acted as record offices. Two inscriptions dating from the tenth century and relating to King Paranthaka I of the Chola dynasty have been found in Utharamerur temple and give a detailed account of village self-government.

Temple administrators in the UK are aware of the temple's role as a social institution and have taken steps to fulfil this function. They have started day centres, drama and music classes, provide food for the elderly and many other activities. These are the needs of today.

Rituals in the temple
The mechanical performance of rituals without understanding is of no spiritual value. The purpose of ritual is to enable one to achieve deeper concentration and be engrossed in divine thoughts, thereby securing spiritual advancement. As mentioned earlier, a mandir represents the body of God – a living body. It is a supernatural superstructure; its every part is sacred and holy. This explains why footwear is removed on entering a mandir.

1. Ringing the bell
This is usually done upon entering the temple after first removing one's shoes. This signifies

to the pilgrim that he is entering the place of God and should therefore become alert and be conscious of him. It also represents sound which is carried through the air. Air is one of the five basic elements comprising the universe and all existence (the others are earth, fire, water and space, see p.40).

2. Prostrate before the deity

The devotee prostrates before the chosen deity in the temple. He lies flat on his stomach with arms stretched over his head and his palms together. His head (intellect) and his heart (mind and feelings) are at God's feet. The ritual of prostrating signifies humility and the desire to serve God.

3. Worship and Puja

This takes various forms, including prayers, singing of religious hymns (called Bhajans), recitation of scriptures and Mantras, meditation (see p.114), lectures and religious dissertations by the priest. For details about the rituals of Puja, see p.101.

4. Offering of flowers

The ritual of offering flowers (representing desires or Vasanas) is done in a particular way. First, the five fingers of the right hand are used to pick up the flower gently. The fingers are then turned upwards with the flower which is gently offered at the statue's feet. The five fingers represent not only the personality sheaths or koshas but also the five senses. When picking up the flower the fingers are turned downwards which represents the senses picking up desires or vasanas. If, however, the senses are directed to the higher self, indicated by the fingers turning upwards, then the desires may be eliminated.

5. Offering of fruit

This also signifies the ridding of desires. The usual fruit that is offered is the coconut. The outer skin of a coconut represents the gross physical body, the core below the skin represents the desires and various entanglements (subtle body), and the hard shell denotes the seat of vasanas (causal body). The kernel denotes the supreme self. Usually the coconut is given to the priest with a tuft of its outer shell remaining. The priest breaks the shell and tears the tuft to expose the white kernel. The removal of this tuft signifies the exhaustion of all desires.

6. Aarti

This is the singing of a special prayer to God and is a call from the devotee's heart to reach him and to seek blessings from him. The prayer recites God's praises. A lamp or a tray of lamps is moved in a circular, clockwise motion whilst the prayer is sung. The circular motion represents the cyclical nature of the entire creation. It represents perfection and endless power. The Aarti (see p.123) is said and performed to instil the virtues of God in oneself. It is often accompanied by the ringing of bells.

7. Burning of camphor

The camphor is solid but when left in the open it vaporizes and gives out a fragrance. The camphor represents the human personality. Man is nothing but desires which determine his personality (which gives off his fragrance or smell). When desires are burnt or evaporated what remains is the pure self or Atman.

8. Prashad

This is the offerings made to the deity in the form of fruit or sweets. It is distributed after the Aarti or visit to the deity (Darshan). Prashad in Sanskrit means calmness, peace of mind, equanimity. Taking of Prashad, therefore, represents the achieving of the supreme bliss of self-realization.

9. Jyoti or Deep

This is a lamp lit in the temple or the prayer room in the house to create an atmosphere of purity, serenity and calm by its soft glow. It portrays the sun and fire (another basic physical element without which life is impossible).

10. Kalash

This is a spherical-based container (usually of copper) on which is placed a coconut and some leaves. The spherical shape represents the entire creation (macrocosm) which therefore encloses space (another physical element). The leaves and the coconut symbolize fruit and vegetation which are a product of the sun's light (photosynthesis) and mother earth (one of the five elements). The Kalash contains water which is sprinkled on the devotees as a sign of purity and the faith of the devotee. It is also a recognition of the importance of the fifth physical element, space (see pp.40–41).

IN THE CLASSROOM

The concept of the Hindu temple can be introduced by linking it to the Christian church. A church is a place for prayer by the Christians who congregate there on Sundays or other religious or festive days. They do this for worship and for various ceremonies like weddings, christenings and funerals. It is regarded as the house of the Lord and a place for communal activities. In the same way, the temple is a house of God for Hindus, where similar activities are conducted. However, it has much more symbolic representation in the form of images of gods and goddesses and the various rituals that are conducted there. Explain that a temple is not only a place for worship but is also a place for learning, like a school.

Another approach is to talk about being in the dark, when we are not aware of our surroundings because we cannot see anything. The darkness can also be frightening. It is like being totally blind. How can we remove this darkness? We can switch on a light or a torch which then allows us to see things around us. No longer are we frightened. For Hindus, a temple is a place of prayer which is a means of removing this darkness, represented in the temple by symbolically lighting a Deep (lamp). Light a candle and let all the pupils in the classroom sit silently and watch it for a few minutes. Then ask them about their experience.

Typical questions/discussion points
1. What kinds of ritual can you observe in a Hindu temple?
2. Hindus believe that God is everywhere, so why do they have a temple?
3. How can we be affected by buildings?

Personal Worship

In Hinduism, there are many different forms of worship. It can be personal or it can be offered in public. Forms of public worship are described later on pp.118–120. In this section, we look at three important aspects of personal worship: prayer, Yoga and Japa.

Prayer (Prarthana)

There is an eternal struggle raging in man's breast between the powers of darkness and the powers of light. He who has not the sheet-anchor of prayer to rely upon will be a victim to the powers of darkness.

(MAHATMA GANDHI)

This is the basic tenet of Hinduism. Prayer is a path by which God can be reached. Man thinks of God with devotion and prayers are a call from the heart of the devotee during which he asks for God's help and guidance and at the same time sings his praises. Prayers, therefore, stand for asking, requesting, appealing. The purpose of prayer is first to cultivate godly attributes in oneself, secondly to rid oneself of evil thoughts and desires (Vasanas) by meditating on God, and thirdly to express gratitude to God. Prayers therefore strengthen one's resolve, decrease fear, lead to peace of mind and set one on the path of righteousness; all this will eventually lead to self-realization. To help in this process, one utilizes images of deities (see p.21), symbols (see p.28), Mantras, Japa, meditation and eventually contemplation of the absolute.

Yoga as personal worship

Yoga comes from the Sanskrit word 'Yuj' which means to join, meet, come together. Yoga, therefore, represents the union of man with God and embraces the threefold nature of man (physical, mental, intellectual). Hindus believe that when prayer or meditation is engaged in the soul becomes engrossed in thoughts about God. At that moment the soul unites with the almighty. This is Yoga. The aim of Yoga, therefore, is the realization of God. It is a form of personal worship. There are many branches of Yoga which can be followed according to one's interest and ability. These were scientifically developed by the Rishis and sages in ancient times, based upon their spiritual experiences. The following four main Yoga systems have already been described on pp.44–45:

- Raj or Dhyan Yoga – Yoga of meditation.
- Karma Yoga – Yoga of action. This entails doing good to others based on selfless action.
- Jnana Yoga – Yoga of knowledge. This path leads to the truth by means of intelligence and logic.
- Bhakti Yoga – Yoga of devotion. Here man is endowed with the feeling of love and devotion and thus takes total refuge in divinity.

Ashtanga Yoga – the eightfold path of self-realization

Yoga is the control of the thoughts and desires of the mind. The mind thinks and creates wishes, desires and cravings and thus remains entrapped in the pleasures of the senses. On this account man becomes unable to differentiate between good and bad and displays anger, jealousy, hatred, greed and pride. If such thoughts and desires are removed the mind becomes tranquil, controlled and ready to fix itself to one object. The mind must be drawn away from these pleasures of the senses to achieve peace and concentration.

Patanjali Rishi, a very revered sage, devised eight techniques or courses. These are referred to as the eight (Ashta) limbs (Anga) or steps of Yoga (Ashtanga Yoga). They set out clearly the path of self-realization (see p.52). The eight steps are:

1. Yama

This comprises moral and disciplinary matters: truthfulness, non-violence, non-stealing, celibacy, non-covetousness.

2. Niyama

This entails physical discipline. It includes purification, contentment, austerity, study and devotion to God.

3. Asanas (Yoga postures or physical exercises)

The aspiring individual must undergo a period of preparation by keeping the body fit. This is achieved through a system of exercises to make all parts of the body strong and healthy. These exercises also help to keep the mind calm. There are over sixty Asanas. An example is Padmasana which is a posture for meditation. It entails sitting cross-legged on the floor, keeping the body erect, arms straight and resting on the knees and keeping the eyes closed for meditation.

4. Pranayama

This is a special method of breath control with which the Prana (life-force, breath) is brought under control and made regular. There is a close link between the mental state and breathing: if breathing is irregular the mind is agitated, whilst regularity leads to mental calm and composure. Pranayama tunes up breathing and provides the right mental state for meditation. Breath is a gross manifestation of a subtle life-force. All bodily functions contain five vital airs (life-forces): Prana (breathing – the main life force); Apana (force for waste excretion via the kidneys and intestines); Samana (force involved in digestion); Vyana (blood circulation); Udana (brain and nerves). Normally our breathing is shallow and irregular. Breathing should be deep and systematic. Pranayama has three stages:

(a) Inhalation (Puraka): breathe in slowly through one nostril while the thumb closes the other. Never breathe quickly.
(b) Retention (Kumbaka): hold the breath for as long as you can comfortably do so. Both the nostrils are closed by pressure of thumb and fingers.
(c) Exhalation (Rechaka): breathe out slowly through the opposite nostril to the inhalation. Never breathe out quickly.

5. Pratyahara (sense control)

This means the ability to withdraw the senses or internal organs from objects to which they are attached. Just as a tortoise withdraws all its limbs in the face of danger, an aspirant must completely withdraw his senses from all objects.

These three (Asanas, Pranayama, Pratyahara) represent the external yogic steps in controlling the mind. The three internal ones are Dharana, Dhyana and Samadhi, described below.

6. Dharana

This is when the mind is withdrawn from external objects and is totally fixed on an idea or a centre and is said to be concentrated.

7. Dhyana (meditation)

Meditation involves engaging the mind in a particular thought or idea without interruption. In this state (called Dhyana) one forgets the surroundings and physical pleasures or pains. During meditation the mind is fixed on the form, attributes and work of God. Thoughts are fixed by reciting a Mantra together with its meaning or by meditating on the symbol AUM. During this time one could also meditate through Japa (see below) which must be done with feeling, understanding and single-mindedness. The meditative techniques are varied but by and large entail choosing a quiet, clean spot, adopting a comfortable, cross-legged sitting posture, with eyes closed, mentally releasing body tension and then meditating on the deity or symbol or contemplating the ocean or sunrise.

As a prelude to meditation, Asanas and Pranayama are performed. Before meditating one can also undertake baby Pranayama or Ham-Sa, which literally means 'swan' (the swan symbolizes purity and tranquillity). In this technique one actually 'watches' the incoming and outgoing breaths without interfering with the rhythm of breathing. During this process the Mantra Sah-Aham is chanted. Sah (whilst exhaling) and Aham (whilst inhaling). Sah-Aham means 'He is I'. Pranayama is the basic yogic technique which calms the mind and helps concentration.

8. Samadhi

This is the final state of meditation when complete fixation of the mind is achieved without interruption. Samadhi is the final step when the person experiences oneness with the Supreme God. It confers absolute bliss and happiness and an end to all sorrows. This is Yoga.

Japa

There are three forms of worship: Kayik (physical), Vachik (verbal) and Manasik (mental); i.e. external worship, invocation by praises and prayers, and meditation. The first mode of worship is almost non-existent in the modern life-style, owing mainly to the stress of activity and lack of time. Hindu scriptures have laid great emphasis on verbal and mental worship, particularly the former since it is easier to practise. Manu, the famous law-giver, says: 'The seeker after truth reaches the highest goal by Japa (chanting of God's name repeatedly).' The Mahabharata, the great epic of India, has also stressed that Japa is said to be the best of all spiritual practices. Vishnu Purana (see p.150) supports this view when it observes: 'That one obtained through meditation in Satya Yuga (the Golden Age), through sacrifice in the Treta Yuga (the Silver Age) and through worship in the Dwapar Yuga (the Bronze Age), may be achieved in the Kali Yuga (the Iron Age) by Nam Japa, reciting the names of God.'

This practice still exists in modern times. If you go to any temple, you will see the devotees continuously chanting the name of the God they believe in. Hare Krishna devotees can be seen in many city centres chanting the mantra:

Hare Krishna Hare Krishna,
Krishna Krishna Hare Hare,
Hare Rama Hare Rama,
Rama Rama Hare Hare.

Sound and thought are inseparable: sound is the expression of thought. The spiritual aspirant uses the sound symbol to help awaken the holy thought in his mind.

During meditation the mind wanders and loses concentration. To avoid this, a Japa Mala (or rosary) of 108 beads has been evolved by the sages and Rishis. The 108 beads are on a single cord with a space between the beads. The number 108 represents the product of twelve (twelve months of the year = cyclic time) and nine (nine planets, representing space or the universe) and denotes the omnipresent and omniscient qualities of God in relation to his entire creation from time immemorial. So long as one chants a Mantra, rotation of the beads continues, as the mind wanders, the rotation stops. The intellect becomes aware of a change, the mind resumes the chant as well as the rotation and the concentration returns.

Mantras are recited during Japa just as they are during religious ceremonies and prayers. The word 'Mantra' comes from 'Manan' (to meditate, contemplate) and 'Tran' (protection, preservation). Mantra therefore represents that which protects the meditative stance to enable one to reach the self.

Mantra is a word symbol or symbols representing and expressing a particular view of God and the universe. It is an aid to meditation advocated by seers and Rishis who realized its deep significance and importance. A Mantra is a combination of letters which are sounds. These sounds, with spiritual potential, awaken the power centres in the body (the Yogini Chakras, anatomically represented by the various nerve plexuses). Mantra science is based on sound waves and frequencies and each combination is in harmony with a power centre in the human body. Mantras affect the thinking and intellect (by reflection on the meaning), awaken the power centres (through the sound waves) and through recitation energize the body.

AUM is the symbol of the supreme Brahman and represents the most powerful word symbol for meditation. AUM is the highest mantra, representing the divine ideal. It stands for pure consciousness and appears at the start of all mantras; it is like a railway engine without which the train (the rest of the mantra) cannot function (see p.29).

The Gayatri Mantra is composed of fourteen words. It is the most important Vedic mantra. Its meaning is given on p.123, along with some other selected mantras.

Idol worship

Hindus do not worship an idol, they worship God through an idol. An idol worshipper is one who considers an idol to be God, as though God is nowhere else but in the idol. Hindus believe that God is everywhere, therefore they are not idol worshippers. In temple worship, God's presence is invoked in the statue during the time of the worship (Puja). This is meant to help the human mind that needs to focus on a name and a form for support.

Different ways of worship

Hindus worship God or meditate upon God in many different ways:

- God as Nirguna-Nirakara (God has no physical qualities and no form). This is an advanced state of worship where the devotee is able to transcend his or her mind.
- God as Saguna-Nirakara (God has qualities such as compassion, knowledge, etc. but is formless). This concept is also found in other religions.
- God as Saguna-Sakara (God has qualities as well as personal form). This form of worship is very popular.
- God can be worshipped through forms, symbols, names (Mantras) and idols (Murtis).

Vrat or Upvaas (Fasting)

Vrat literally means vow. There are many ways that Hindus undertake Vrats: for example, a vow of fasting, a vow of silence, a vow to chant a particular Mantra or name of God, a vow of celibacy, and so on. There is spiritual, physical and mental significance in observing Vrat. It trains and conditions the body to be worthy of divine realization, and in fact Hindus believe that the soul acquires a human body for this very purpose. Physically, the vow of fasting promotes good health by giving rest to the internal organs. Mentally, it controls passion, improves will-power and self-discipline.

There is no uniform practice in fasting; each individual undertakes it according to his or her ability and commitment to a particular purpose or as selfless dedication to God. In the Bhagavad Gita is the advice: 'Vow or penance undertaken to impress others, or causing self-torture or with an aim to destroy others is foolish.' (Gita, 17-19)

Some Hindus fast on all Ekadashi days (11th day of the lunar fortnight). Many fast during the Navaratri festival. Some devotees take a vow of refraining from eating a favourite food as part of 'Vairaag' (vow of dispassion). Devotees also fast on some special days like the Shivaratri and some fast regularly on a particular day of the week. Some traditional Vrats are associated with myths and legends. One of the most popular is the 'Karwa Chauth' Vrat which falls on the 4th night of the dark fortnight in October. Married women fast for their husbands' welfare to reinforce relationships, and virgins undertake this Vrat for the peace and prosperity of their prospective husbands.

IN THE CLASSROOM

The following ideas can be used to introduce the concept of personal worship:

1. Our mind is constantly full of thoughts and wanders from place to place in an instant. How do you try to concentrate? The mind is very agile and runs after objects to fulfil its desires. Evil thoughts arise in the mind. By saying prayers we try to reduce these thoughts. Personal worship can help the mind to concentrate.

2. When we receive something from someone we thank them. God gives us everything: how do we thank him? We can praise him in our prayers and express our thanks and gratitude towards him.

3. When a child is in trouble or frightened he immediately shouts for his mum or dad. Similarly, a child experiences happiness, peace and comfort in her mother's lap. Compare this with people who consider themselves to be God's children. They go to him to seek comfort and happiness. Should you go to your parents or to God only when you are in trouble, or do you keep them in your mind always?

The following exercises can be tried in the classroom to introduce the concept of Yoga:

1. Do deep-breathing exercises (see Pranayama on p.115).

2. Try the postures of the Suryanamaskar (Salutation to the sun), shown on p.45. It can be done as part of a PE lesson.

Typical questions/discussion points
1. Do you think a prayer can help to calm your mind?
2. Whom do you turn to when you need help? What do you give back in return?
3. Why do people pray to God?
4. Is there only one way of praying to God or can different people use different ways of praying?

Public Worship

Divine Grace helps man to surmount the crisis, Divine Grace makes the mute eloquent and the disabled cross mountains.

(TULSI RAMAYANA)

In all ages and in all religions, spiritual aspirants and devotees have given natural vent to their innate desires and noblest sentiments in hymns, psalms, praises and prayers. Sometimes they sing and pray out of the fullness of their hearts, dwelling in celestial moods untouched by cares and wants. However, in most cases it is a consciousness of misery and helplessness that makes the weary and struggling souls turn to God for solace and succour. The Gita says:

Four kinds of persons worship God: the distressed, the seeker of knowledge, the seeker of enjoyment, and the wise.

(GITA 7-16)

In this section we look at three main forms of public worship: Kirtan, Pravachan and Yajna.

Kirtan

Supreme love for God expressed through a devotional form of worship is known as Bhakti. Bhakti is an expression of the most intense form of devotion to God. The highest Bhakti or what is called 'Para Bhakti' is classified into five types:

1. Shanta Bhakti (silent worship);

2. Dasya Bhakti (worshipping as his servant);

3. Sakhya Bhakti (worshipping God as a friend);

4. Vatsalya Bhakti (worship of God as pure as motherly love for the child);

5. Madhur Bhakti (sweet devotion).

When this form of devotional worship is performed as a congregational singing of 'Bhajans' (religious songs or hymns), it is called 'Kirtan'. This means singing the glory of the Almighty in hymns or psalms. Devotees gather in groups and sing Bhajans written by famous saints and poets (see p.61), such as Meera Bai, Surdas, Tulsi, Guru Nanak, Narasi Mehta, Namdev, Kabir and Tukaram. These Bhajans narrate the glory and might of the Almighty. Many singers from India travel round the world and sing to large audiences. They congregate to perform Kirtans regularly at temples and on special occasions in people's own homes.

Pravachan

This is a form of worship in which devotees go to listen to discourses on Hindu scriptures. These are often given by learned scholars who come specially from India. A very popular form of religious discourse is 'Katha' (story-telling). This involves narrating stories from the Ramayana and the Puranas, such as Srimad Bhagwatam. The Kathakars (story-tellers), Swamis (holy men) and Acharyas (scholars) travel round the world giving discourses and thousands of people gather to hear these Kathas. The duration of the Katha may sometimes be for a day, while at other times it could last for a week or a month depending on the circumstances and convenience of the organizer. These holy books provide people with a sense of religion and an understanding of moral values and how to live a moral and simple life, by devoting time to the good of society, protecting the oppressed and so on. Discourses by holy men and scholars also help Hindus to maintain their religious traditions. In 1994, Shri Morari Bapu recited Ramayana Katha in London for a week and his discourse was televised by satellite.

Yajna

Work performed in the right frame of mind is called Yajna. When a large number of people gather to act in unison at the same altar of grace, for the total glory of all, that form of public worship is Yajna. The act of Yajna is the united act of a whole community, not of an individual.

The spirit of Yajna is doing things without expecting any reward. The sun converts sea-water into an invisible vapour and in its turn the vapour becomes rain. Rubbish consigned to the fire changes itself into invisible carbon dioxide; it then forms food for plants which they assimilate through their leaves. All these things serve the world to make it what it is, and none of them seems to demand even a passing recognition from the people who benefit by it. They all do their duty without expecting any reward. The importance of working together, and worshipping together in the form of Yajna, is described in the Gita: 'The creator (Prajapati) after having created mankind together with Yajna said, "By this shall you create: this shall be the fulfiller of all your desires."' (Gita 3-10). Thus Yajna is handed over to mankind by the creator himself. It means that people should work together for the achievement of their goal; function in this co-operative spirit, be selfless and dedicated and all will prosper.

The message of Yajna is to act as a team. To work co-operatively, each will have to sacrifice his ego and personal desires. If anyone in a team asserts his ego or grows anxious for his own desire, the rhythm in the work is lost and the co-operative schemes break down.

The essential Hindu thought behind Yajna is that the efforts we put into our work will be successful if the environment and the circumstances are beneficial. A farmer may work hard but if the weather does not favour him then the harvest will be ruined. Hence it is imperative that nature also works well so that humanity's efforts become a success. We have our doubts about whether cosmic forces obey us or whether we have any command over them.

Cherish the Devas [Deva means the one who gives] *with the Yajna Spirit and those Devas shall in turn cherish you; thus cherishing each other, you shall gain the highest good.*

(GITA 3-11)

Hindus regard the Yajna as divine law, a universal truth and a scientific fact that the greatest prosperity is achieved by helping each other.

In the UK massive Yajnas have been performed in London, Leicester, Birmingham, Manchester, Coventry and other places under the guidance of renowned saints like Swami Shri Satyamitranandji, Swami Chinmayanandji and other religious scholars. Part of the Yajna is 'Havan' which involves lighting a sacred fire (see p.102). When such Yajnas are performed the substance that is put in the sacred fire of the Yajna Kunda purifies the air and thus makes the environment free of all pollution. Such Yajnas serve as destroyers of pollution.

IN THE CLASSROOM

The best way to introduce public forms of worship like the Kirtan and the Yajna is for pupils to see them being performed. If possible, take them to a local temple or show them a video. The pupils may not be able to understand the language and the meaning of the prayers but the material presented in this book can be used to explain the significance of the rituals they will observe.

At KS1 and KS2, pupils can look at and even try to play the musical instruments which are used during a Kirtan. At KS3 and KS4, they can carefully observe a Yajna being performed, then, with the help of the material given on pp.102–104, they can try to offer an explanation for the rituals performed during a Havan Yajna.

Typical questions/discussion points
1. Why is it important to perform Havan Yajna collectively?
2. How do Hindus in Britain learn about their religious traditions?

The Hindu Calendar

It is necessary to understand the Hindu calendar in broad outline in order to understand the dates of Hindu festivals. Hindus have very ancient solar and lunar calendars. S.S. Apte, in *Vedic Astronomy and Mythology*, states that long before contact with the Arabs in the eighth century and with the Greeks about 1000 years before that, Hindu astronomers had discovered the truth that all heavenly bodies, including our earth, were spherical and glowed in reflected light. They had also calculated the diameter of the earth and were aware of its movements on its own axis, and they could calculate the dates and times of occurrences of eclipses. A Hindu priest has to fix the exact time and place of a Puja, which he does by reciting the

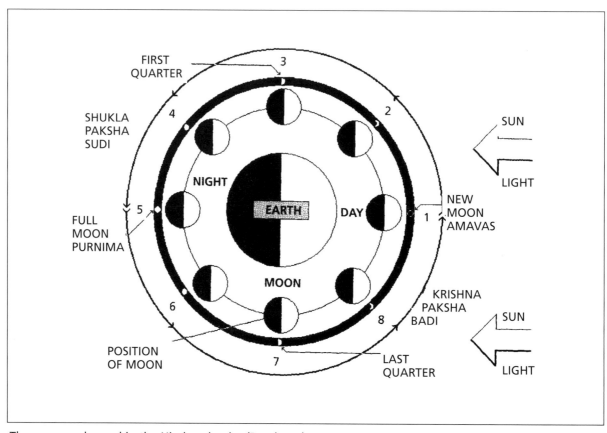

The moon cycle used in the Hindu calendar (Panchang)

geographical position of the place, the sun's position in the zodiac, the time of day, the day of the month, the name of the month and the year in the Vikram Samvat. The Vikram Samvat started in 57 BCE and is the most popular calendar in India (see p.100).

With the exception of the Makar Sankranti (see p.101), the dates of all major Hindu festivals are based on the lunar calendar, called the Panchang. The calculation of months and years is based on the movement of the moon around the earth. The twelve months of the Hindu year are based on the lunar month, that is, from the time of one new moon to the next, which is about twenty-nine days long. The months are named after the star which ascends during the full moon time of that month. They are as follows:

1. Chaitra (March/April)
2. Vaisakh (April/May)
3. Jyeshth (May/June)
4. Ashad (June/July)
5. Shravan (July/August)
6. Bhadrapada (August/September)
7. Aswayuja (September/October)
8. Kartik (October/November)
9. Margaseersha (November/December)
10. Poushya (December/January)
11. Magh (January/February)
12. Phalgun (February/March)
13. Adhik (once every two-and-a-half years)

The thirteenth month is necessary because the twelve lunar months do not add up to 365 days as in the Gregorian calendar. The lunar calendar falls short by one day every month. So, after thirty months (two-and-a-half years) there are thirty days short. This is the extra thirteenth month called Adhik. Adhik is a very favourable period for Hindus to undertake fasts and other spiritual practices.

The bright and dark fortnights
Each month in the Hindu calendar is divided into two parts: the bright and the dark fortnights (Paksha). These are called Shukla Paksha and Krishna Paksha. The bright half is

DAYS OF THE WEEK	
Sunday	Ravivar
Monday	Somvar
Tuesday	Mangalvar
Wednesday	Budhvar
Thursday	Guruvar
Friday	Shukravar
Saturday	Shanivar

SIX SEASONS (Ritus)	
Shishir	Pre-spring
Vasanta	Spring
Grishma	Summer
Varsha	Rainy
Sharad	Autumn
Hemant	Winter

HINDU ZODIAC	
Maysh (ram)	Aries
Vrashubh (bull)	Taurus
Mithoon (couple)	Gemini
Karka (crab)	Cancer
Simha (lion)	Leo
Kanya (virgin)	Virgo
Toola (scales)	Libra
Vrashchick (scorpion)	Scorpio
Dhanu (bow)	Sagittarius
Makar (crocodile)	Capricorn
Kumbha (water carrier)	Aquarius
Meen (fish)	Pisces

when the moon is 'increasing' in size, or becoming brighter. This period extends from the day after the new moon up to the full moon day. This is the first half of the month (Shukla Paksha). The dark half is when the moon is 'getting smaller' or becoming less bright. This takes place from the day after the full moon up to the new moon day. This is the second half of the month (Krishna Paksha).

The full moon day which occurs at the middle of each month is very auspicious for Hindus. On every such day one of the Hindu festivals is celebrated. The day of the full moon is called Poornima.

Universal time

Just as normal time is calculated in terms of days and nights, Hindu scriptures present the ideal of universal time being calculated in terms of divine days and nights. The period of creation (Srishti) is termed a divine day and that of dissolution (Pralaya) a divine night. Thirty such divine days (day and night combined) make one divine month and twelve divine months make one divine year. The difference is at the level of the duration of the day and night. One human day is of twenty-four hours, while a divine day is of 8640 million years. Out of this time, 4320 million years (1 Kalpa = 1000 Mahayugas = 4320 millions years) is the period of creation (Srishti), which is called a divine day, and 4320 million years the period of dissolution (Pralaya), called a divine night.

Time is divided into four Yugas or cycles:

Satyayuga	1,728,000 years
Tretayuga	1,296,000 years
Dwaparyuga	864,000 years
Kaliyuga	432,000 years
	4,320,000 years

One divine day is made up of 1000 Chaturyugis (i.e. 4320 million years) and similarly 1000 Chaturyugis, 4320 million years, make one divine night; that is to say, once God creates the universe it remains there for 4320 million years. There may be small changes here and there during this period – some destruction, some new

---

> ## SPIRITUALITY IN NUMBERS
>
> In Hindu scriptures, the following names are often associated with numbers and dates:
>
> 1 Brahman (One ultimate reality, see p.34)
>
> 2 Eyes (Seer/creator/light)
>
> 3 Vishnu (all-pervading, three Gunas, see p.41)
>
> 4 Four Vedas (see pp.130–132)
>
> 5 Five physical elements (see p.40)
>
> 6 Six Darshan Shastras (see p.158)
>
> 7 Seven Rishis (see p.162)
>
> 8 Vasus (eight abodes)
>
> 9 Anka (the largest single digit)
>
> 10 Ten attributes of Dharma
>
> 11 Rudra (eleven names of air)
>
> 12 Aditya (twelve names of the sun)

---

appearances – but that is all the result of the natural law. The total annihilation created by God comes only after the period of creation is over.

As far as the present universe is concerned, it has already completed six out of fourteen Manvantara, twenty-seven out of seventy-two Chaturyugis in the seventh Manvantara, three Yugas in the twenty-eighth Chaturyugis, and by 1995 had completed 5097 years in the fourth Yuga, known as Kaliyuga. Based on the calculations given in Hindu scriptures, about 2000 million years have passed since the creation of the present universe.

IN THE CLASSROOM

Talk about the zodiac signs. Tell the pupils that these are very similar to the signs developed by ancient Hindu astrologers. How many pupils believe that the movement of planets and stars can influence their lives? Is it possible for planets and stars to influence us? Look at the way the movement of the sun and the earth regulates our lives by creating days and nights.

At KS3 and KS4, investigate how mankind has come to understand the heavenly bodies. How have people expressed feelings of awe and wonder at the sight of objects in space? The difference between astrology and astronomy can be discussed. When comparing the study of planets and stars with religious faith, point out that astronomy has played an important part as a scientific investigation in ancient Hindu scriptures, whilst astrology has been left to an individual's faith. Many Hindus consult astrologers before starting an important project, going on a journey or opening a new building. How are such beliefs formed?

Typical questions/discussion points
1. Do you believe in astrology?
2. Compare the ancient Hindu zodiac with the one you know. Can you explain why there is so much similarity?
3. Do you believe in destiny? Do you think that the motion and position of planets can determine your future? If not, what determines your future?
4. Why do people study the planets and the stars? Why are such objects related to religious beliefs and stories?

Some Common Hindu Prayers

There is a difference between 'Mantra' and 'prayer'. The pure Mantra has an inherent effectiveness called 'Mantra shakti' that is the power contained in inarticulate or intonational sound. It may or may not have any meaning. It becomes a prayer when it has a philosophical meaning and the advantage of articulate sound. In this section, we introduce some of the common prayers which pupils and teachers are likely to hear when visiting a Hindu temple or a Hindu home.

Gayatri Mantra
The Gayatri Mantra is said to be one of the oldest of the divine hymns. It is referred to as the mother of the Vedas. Parathasarthy, in his book *The Symbolism of Hindu Gods and*

Rituals, explains that the Gayatri has both the power of Mantra and the power of prayer. It has a compelling charm of its own to millions of Hindus. The repetition of this Mantra with the right understanding of its sacred meaning is believed to have the power to dispel all the negative tendencies in the human mind and thereby unfold the supreme self within. It is also known by two other names: Guru Mantra and Savitri Mantra.

AUM bhur bhuvah swah. Tatsavitur varenyam bhargo devasya dhimahi. Dhiyo yo nah prachodayat.

O God (AUM), the giver of life (bhur), remover of pains and sorrows (bhuvah), bestower of happiness (swah), and creator of the universe (tatsavitur), thou art most luminous (devasya), pure (bhargo) and adorable (varenyam). We meditate on thee (dhimahi). May thou (yo) inspire and guide (prachodayat) our (nah) intellect (dhiyo) in the right direction.

Shanti Paath (Prayer for peace)

AUM dyauh shantir antarikshagwam, shan-ti Prithivi shanti rapah, shanti roshadhaya shantih vanaspatayah shantir, vishwe devah shantih, brahma shantih sarvagwang shantih shantireva shantih sama shanti redhi. AUM shantih shantih shantih.

May there be peace in heaven
Peace in the atmosphere
Peace across the waters
May there be peace on earth
May peace flow from herbs, plants and trees
May all the celestial beings radiate peace
May peace pervade all quarters
May that peace come to me too
May there be peace, peace, peace.

Aarti
Aarti is the singing of a special prayer to God. The devotee sings the hymn of God's attributes and seeks refuge in him. Devotees seek protection from evil deeds and thoughts and freedom from sin. Below are the words of the Aarti with the English translation.

Om Jai Jagadish hare, swami jai Jagdish hare
Glory to the Creator of the world.
Bhakta jano ke sankat, kshana mein duur kare
Who quickly removes the difficulties of the devotees;
Jo dhaavae phal pave, dukh vinashe man ka
He who prays eats the fruit; troubles of the mind are set at peace;
Sukh sampati ghar ave, kashta mite tan ka
Peace and prosperity come home, bodily pains disappear;
Mata pita tum mere, sharan gahun mein kiski
You are my parents, where else shall I seek the shelter;
Tum bina aur na duja, aas karu mein jisaki
Without you there is no one else I can rely upon;
Tum pooran Paramatma, tum antaryami
You are Supreme Soul omnipresent, and omnipotent;
Paar Braham Parmeshwar, tum sab ke swami
You are the Supreme Lord; you are everyone's Master;
Tum karuna ke sagar, tum palan karta
You are extremely merciful; You are the protector;
Mein sevak tum swami, kripa karo bharta
I am your servant, you are my Lord; Have mercy on me;
Tum ho ek agochar, sab ke pran pati
You are the one invisible; you are the master of all souls;
Kis vidh miloon dayamay tumko mein kumati
How could I meet you, O compassionate one, I being so ignorant;
Deen bandhu dukh harta tum rakshak mere
O friend of the poor, remover of all sorrows, O my protector;
Karuna hath uthao, dwar pare tere
Raise your merciful hands; I am at your doorstep;
Vishaya vikar mitao, paap haro deva
Remove all my worldly passions and desires; free me from sin;
Shraddha bhakti barhao, Santan ki seva
Enhance faith and devotion in me and in the spirit of service for the saintly beings.

Tan man dhan sab, Kuchha hai tera
Tera tujhko arapan, Kya lage mera
O God, the body, the mind, the wealth – all belong to you and I offer you all that back, because nothing belongs to me.
Parabrahma ki aarti, Jo koi nar gaave
Kahata Shivanand swami, mana vanchhit phal paave
The blissful indicates that one who worships the Supreme Lord regularly has his wishes fulfilled.

Other selected prayers

Prayer for guru (teacher)

Gurur Brahmaa gurur Vishnu
Gurur devo Maheshvarah
Gurursackshaat para Brahman
Tasmai sri gurave namah

The guru is Brahmaa, the guru is Vishnu,
The guru is Shiva,
The guru is verily the Supreme Brahman.
I bow down to that guru.

Prayer for self

Tvameva mata cha pita tvameva
Tvameva bandhuscha sakha tvameva
Tvameva vidya dravinam tvameva
Tvameva sarvam mama deva deva

You are my father and mother
You are my brother and friend
You are the knowledge and the wealth
You are everything, O my God of gods.

Prayer for the well-being of all

Sarve bhavantu sukhena
Sarve santu niraamyaa
Sarve bhadraani pashyantu
Ma kashchit dukhbagh bhavet

O God, grant happiness to all
May all be free from misery
May all possess good things in life
Let no one suffer from any sorrow.

Prayer for community

Asato maa sad gamayaa
Tamaso ma ajyotir gamayaa
Mrityorma amritam gamayaa

O God, lead us from untruth to truth
Lead us from darkness to light
Lead us from death to immortality.

Prayer for family

Maa bhraataa bhraataram dwikshan
Maa swasaara mutas swasaa
Samyanchah savrataa bhootvaa
Vaacham vadata bhadrayaa

Brother should not fight with brother,
sisters should be kind. All should speak
gently with each other and generate an
attitude of truth, service and
co-operation.

School assembly prayer

AUM sahnaavavatu sahanau bhunaktu
Saha veeryam karva vaahai
Tejasvinaa vadheetamastu
Maa vidwishaa vahai

Let us protect each other. Let us eat
together. Let us work together. Let us
study together to be bright and successful.
Let us not hate each other.

Mealtime prayer

AUM annapate annasya no dehyanami-
vasya shushminah. Prapradataram tarisha
urjam no dhehi dvipade chatushpade.

O Lord, the giver of food, may you provide
us with healthy and nutritious food. Grant
happiness to those who give food in charity.
May all living beings be blessed with
nutritious food.

Rangoli patterns

CHAPTER FIVE
SCRIPTURES

Family Tree of Hindu Scriptures

*H*indu scriptural literature gives an insight into the progress of Indian thought through the ages. The Hindu scriptures are the product of relentless investigations into the facts and truth of life carried out by the ancient sages of India. They contain systematic treatises on varied subjects in the fields of science, religion, metaphysics, philosophy and spiritual knowledge. They are not limited to a few books because Hinduism does not confine ideas; therefore the scriptures have become a home of many different schools of thought. There is not room to mention here all the sacred books of Hindus, but for the sake of brevity, a family structure of some of the important books is shown in the figure on p.129.

In Hinduism, there are two categories of books: 'Shrutis' which deal with never-changing, eternal principles, and 'Smrutis' which often deal with the practical application of those eternal principles. Shruti means 'what is heard' or 'what is revealed by God' and Smruti means 'what is remembered'.

It has been said that the Vedic literature is the most ancient record of any people of the world and forms the source of the earliest history of the Hindus. The oldest and best known are the four Vedas, which are described in detail on pp.130–132. The language of the Vedas is old Sanskrit which is different from modern literary Sanskrit. The Vedic language is marked by an extreme economy of expression and because of its compactness it becomes almost cryptic, therefore the interpretation of the Vedas has assumed great significance. A lot of literature has been produced in which attempts have been made to clarify the meanings of the Vedas.

The contents of each of the Vedas can be categorised into two: Karma Kanda and Jnana Kanda. The Karma Kanda has two sections: the Samhitas (Mantras) consisting of hymns and prayers, and the Brahmanas describing the rituals. There are nine principal Brahmana Granths (books): Aitareya, Ashvalayana and Kaushitaki, Sankhyayana, Shatapatha, Panchvinsha, Shadvinsha, Tandya, Jaiminya and Gopatha.

The Jnana Kanda contains the contemplative literature of the Upanishads and Aranyakas. The Upanishads are described briefly on pp.146–150. The Aranyakas are those Upanishads which were propounded in the forests; 'Aranyaka' means belonging to the forest. There are over 100 Upanishads with 11 main Upanishads which provide a philosophical interpretation of the Vedas rather than a ritualistic description. The Upanishads or the Aranyakas form the basis of most of the philosophies and religions of India.

Despite the multitude of scriptures trying to explain the original Vedic material, there always remained some confusion because every commentator interpreted the passages to suit the interests of his own community. The Buddhism and Jainism sects deny the authority of the Vedas because the explanation of the Vedas offered by their contemporaries could not satisfy their curiosity. In Sanskrit, those who accept the authority of the Vedas are called 'Astika' and those who reject the Vedas are called 'Nastikas', hence Buddhist, Jain and Charvaka (materialism) scriptures are often termed 'Nastika' literature, though they remain firmly within the fold of Hinduism (see additional discussion on pp.47–49). Dharmpad and Tripitakas in Buddhism and Kalpa Sutra in Jainism are the main scriptures.

The basic teachings of Buddha are contained in the 'Tripitakas', literally meaning 'three boxes'. These are:

1. Sutta-Pitaka: consists of five collections of talks and condensed gospel called 'Dhammapada'.

2. Vinaya-Pitaka: contains the books of discipline.

3. Abhidhamma-Pitaka: teachings related to the righteous path of man, mental processes and sense consciousness.

The Noble Eightfold Path of Buddhism is similar to the Eightfold Yoga of sage Patanjali mentioned on p.45. The moral principles of Jainism are similar to the five 'Yamas' described on p.52.

The Smrutis, the scriptures dealing with the practical application of eternal principles, are even more numerous. In this class, first came the six Vedangas. 'Anga' means limb. The following Vedangas were designed to aid in the correct pronunciation and interpretation of the Mantras:

1. Shiksha (the science of proper articulation and pronunciation).

2. Chhanda (the science of prosody).

3. Vyakarana (grammar).

4. Nirukta (etymological explanation of difficult Vedic words).

5. Jyotisha (astronomy).

6. Kalpa (ritual, insititutional or ceremonial).

The most important of the six is the Kalpa, which is subdivided into three famous Kalpa Sutras, namely Shrauta, Grihya and Dharma. The Grihya Sutra contains details of the sixteen 'Sanskaras' (sacraments) which Hindus perform from conception to death (see p.65).

There are also writings which are subordinates of the Vedas and are called Upavedas:

1. Ayurveda (medicine) This is perhaps the best-known Upaveda. The form of medicine it describes is based mostly on natural herbs and is now recognised by many medical authorities around the world. Sushrut Samhita, Charaka Samhita and Ashtanga Hridya are other scriptures which describe medical treatment for various ailments.

2. Dhanurveda (military science).

3. Gandharvaveda (classical music).

4. Shilpa or Sthapatyaveda (mechanics or architecture).

Most of these were written in the post-Buddhist period. A Shilpa shastra found recently describes the essentials of architecture of the type used to build the Taj Mahal. In *Riches of the East,* John Keay points out that in building architecture, the dome and the voussoir arch first appeared in India and are of Hindu origin.

In philosophy, the grandeur of the scriptures is even more awe-inspiring. There are six Astika (Vedic) philosophical schools, details of which are given on pp.158–160. In addition to these, an atheistic school known as Charvaka or Lokayata also existed and had its own theories regarding the origin of the universe. Other Hindu philosophical schools initiated by Gautama Buddha and Mahavira Jain are also recognized but they do not follow the Vedas. The most popular school in modern times is the Vedanta, mainly owing to the efforts of Swami Vivekananda.

The ancient sacred law codes of the Hindus are called Dharma Shastras or Smrutis. Law-givers such as Manu, Yajnavalkya and Parasara laid down rules to maintain certain manners and customs. Manu Smruti is the best known; it elaborates the four stages of life (Ashramas) and the division of labour through a class system (Varna Vyavastha). Further details are given on pp.152–153. With the passage of time, the laws were amended and up to now eighteen Smrutis are known to have existed. In addition to the law codes, there are Niti Shastras by Chanakya, Vidhur and Shukra which give advice on codes of conduct and policy. In this class of scriptures, Kautilya's Arthashastra is a work of exceptional interest and value. It was written by Chanakya under the pseudonym 'Kautilya' during the period 321–296 BCE. It provides guidance to a king, a code of conduct and a penal code all rolled into one treatise.

Tamil is the oldest of the Dravidian group of languages. It has both Shaivism and Vaishnavism in its classical literature. On the Shaivite side are the four great teacher-saints: Appar, Sundarar, Thirujnanasambandhar and Manikkavacagar. Their compositions are known as 'Thevaram' and 'Thiruvacakam'. Another literary masterpiece describing idealistic forms of behaviour, conduct and ethics is the Tirukkural. 'Tiru' means holy and 'kural' means 'short' or 'brief'. This anthology of three-line verses, numbering 1330 in all, was written by Tiruvalluvar in the Tamil language and is very popular among the Shaivite sect, who worship Lord Shiva. It is also read by followers of Jainism because it exemplifies the ideals of Ahimsa (non-violence). The most popular Vaishnava literature in Tamil is 'Nalayira Divya Prabandham' which is a collection of 4000 verses and comprises the devotional songs written by the great poet-saints known as 'Alvars'. In the Telegu language, musical compositions of the famous saint Tyagaraja are very popular.

The Puranas are another class of Hindu scriptures which describe the teaching of the Vedas through myths, legends and examples of great men. They were created to popularize and simplify religious teachings. There are eighteen main Puranas and many other lesser Puranas, which are discussed on pp.150–152. There is also the Devi Mahatmya which describes the worship of God as the Divine Mother. It is read by the followers of Durga Mata.

Similar to the Puranas are the Itihasas (epics). 'Itihasa' means historical text. The best-known epics are the Ramayana and the Mahabharata, which are written in the form of beautiful songs and poems. The Ramayana was first written by Rishi Valmiki and in it he told the story of Shri Rama. The Mahabharata, written by Rishi Veda Vyas, is sometimes called the fifth Veda. It is the longest poem in the world, with 100,000 verses. Shri Krishna is the central figure of this epic. The Gita, which is probably the most famous Hindu scripture, is a part of the Mahabharata. The stories of both these epics are given on pp.134–143.

Agama Shastras are also part of Hindu scriptures. They are unique amongst religious scriptures in that they deal with temple architecture, the installation of deities and describe how to worship and perform ceremonies for those sects among Hindus who worship images of God. There are many Agamas but the three main ones are for the Vaishnava, Shaiva and Shakta sects. The religious aspect of the temple is guided by these Agamas and the nature of the temple is decided by the specific Agama traditionally followed by the authorities running the temple.

As mentioned earlier, Hinduism is not a closed book; from time to time sages in India have given new impetus to the faith by removing bad or misleading practices and re-establishing the teachings of the Vedas according to the demands of the time. One example is Sikhism, which was founded by Guru Nanak Dev about 500 years ago. The Guru Granth Sahib is the main scripture of Sikhism. It is written in Punjabi, but in spite of its different language, its philosophy is based on the Vedas (see p.48). The concept of 'Ek Omkar' taught by Guru Nanak Dev is the concept of the Vedas.

Another example is the Arya Samaj movement started by Swami Dayananda more than 100 years ago. His mission was to open up new vistas in rediscovering the meanings of the Vedas. He also wanted to instigate social reforms such as education for women, abolition of the caste system based on birth, removal of superstitions and unsound customs like dowry. He wrote in Sanskrit and Hindi. His best-known books are the Satyarth Prakash (Light of Truth) and commentaries on the Vedas, particularly the Bhashya Bhumika on the Rig Veda.

There are many other popular movements like 'Swadhayaya', 'Sai Baba', 'Krishna Consciousness' and 'Swaminarayana', each with their own holy books. For example, the 'Vachanamritam' and 'Shikshapatri' are the two main scriptures of the Swaminarayana sect. Devotees of Krishna Consciousness follow the Teachings of Chaitanya based on Bhakti Yoga.

There are many more books, some lost in the past, some still being written, and there will no doubt be many in the future. This is how Hinduism remains dynamic. Unity in diversity is the strength of Hinduism, enabling it to survive as the world's oldest religion and yet remain modern. In a way, even this book can be treated as a Smruti because it has interpreted and explained the teachings of Hinduism for modern society.

IN THE CLASSROOM

Teachers can start a discussion by asking pupils to recall the first book they read. Usually it will be the book from which they learnt the alphabet. Ask them to describe the books they study in primary school and in secondary school. Can they guess what kind of books they will study when they go to university or college? The idea is to demonstrate that older students have more books to study. Similarly, Hinduism, being the oldest religious faith, has many scriptures and holy books which have been written at different periods over thousands of years.

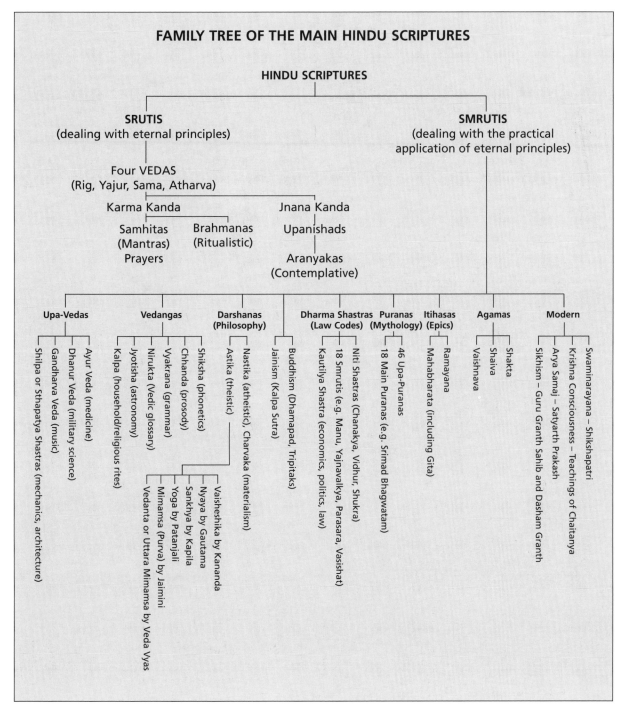

FAMILY TREE OF THE MAIN HINDU SCRIPTURES

Typical questions/discussion points
1. Is Hinduism based on one book or on many books?
2. Should there be freedom of thought for religious believers? If so, can a single book be prescribed?
3. What do you expect to find in religious scripture? Do you expect to find lists of things you can and cannot do, or do you expect to find knowledge to help you cope with everyday life?

The Vedas – the Oldest Books

The Veda has a twofold interest: it belongs to the history of the world and to the history of India ... As long as Man continues to take interest in the history of his race, and as long as we collect in libraries and museums the relics of former ages, the first place in that long row of books which contain the records of the Aryan branch of mankind, will belong for ever to the Rig Veda.

(F. MAX MULLER)

The Vedas are accepted as the direct or indirect source of all sacred books pertaining to Hinduism. Since Hinduism is recognized as the oldest formal religion in the world, it comes as no surprise that Max Muller, the great Indologist, declared the Vedas to be the oldest books in the library of mankind. Hindus believe that their knowledge was first revealed by God at the beginning of human creation for the benefit of mankind. There are four Vedas:

- Rig Veda deals with general knowledge;
- Yajur Veda deals with knowledge of action (Karma);
- Sama Veda deals with knowledge of worship (Upasana);
- Atharva Veda deals with knowledge of science: machines (Yantra), formulae (Mantra) and techniques (Tantra).

The word 'Veda' comes from the root 'vid' meaning 'to know'. Together the four Vedas contain over 20,000 Mantras (hymns) revealing words of divine knowledge. The above classification was done by Rishi Veda Vyas who compiled the original hymns into three categories, namely prose, poetry and song. Veda Vyas was only the compiler, not the originator of the Vedas. The learned men to whom the knowledge was first revealed are called 'Rishis'. (See p.162 for more details about 'Rishis'.)

The contents of each of the Vedas can be categorized into two: Karma Kanda and Jnana Kanda. The Karma Kanda has two sections: the Samhitas (Mantras) consisting of hymns and prayers and the Brahmanas describing the rituals.

The first Veda is the Rig Veda which has 1028 hymns (Sukta) containing 10,589 verses (Mantras) which are arranged in ten separate books (Mandals).

The Yajur Veda, also known as the Veda of Liturgy, explains how to perform rituals and even describes rules and regulations about how to make an altar. It has in total 1975 verses spread over forty chapters. Yajur Veda was very popular among the priests so it has many versions. Two well-known versions are Shukla (white) Yajur Veda and Krishna (black) Yajur Veda.

The word 'Sama' means music. The Sama Veda is the Veda of Holy Songs. Classical Indian music originated from this Veda. The verses have been classified in a variety of different ways so the numbers vary from 1803 to 1875 verses, out of which nearly 1800 are variations of verses from the Rig Veda.

The Atharva Veda is a collection of 5977 verses spread over twenty books, and contains knowledge imparted by the sage Atharvana. This is the last of the four Vedas and contains hymns on miscellaneous subjects.

Hindus believe that these holy books were revealed by the Supreme Being so they are complete in all respects, perfect by all means; they are timeless because they contain no history, names of persons or places. They contain only Mantras by which divine knowledge is made known. The whole Vedic collection of truths has influenced all the religions, sects and sub-sects of Hinduism, which is why often Hindu Dharma is also known as Vedic Dharma. It is important to know that parents often chose words from the Vedas as names for their children. Hindus still follow this practice, but the Vedas themselves do not contain the history of any individual.

The Vedas are not just a collection of worship hymns; in fact, they are much more than that and contain text on various branches of science and arts. See pp.153–156 for further details.

The Vedas have been written in Vedic Sanskrit (believed by Hindus to be God's own language) and are considered as the ultimate scriptural authority. Owing to the compactness and poetic nature of the Vedic verses, they have been interpreted differently by various scholars. In the introduction to the English translation of the Rig Veda Samhita, published by the Veda Pratishthana, all the available commentaries are classified as follows:

1. Pre-Sayana commentaries
These commentaries have been written by scholars belonging to the ritualistic school of Hinduism. Most of them were written before 1300 CE.

2. Sayana's commentaries
Sayana was born in 1315 CE. His commentaries are often quoted by Western scholars. He mostly provided verbal interpretations without going deeper into the root-meanings. His writings were influenced by the Puranic myths and mythological events and he also mixed legends and history with the Vedas.

3. Commentaries by Western scholars
Max Muller, Wilson, Bloomfield and Griffith are some of the well-known Western scholars who have translated Vedic texts. Most of these translations relied heavily on Sayana's ritualistic and mythological interpretations, and in the process failed to notice the scientific and natural aspects of the Vedic literature. Some Western authors lacked sympathy and deeper understanding; writing during colonial times, it suited them to present the Vedas as ritualistic books of a primitive, barbaric society.

4. Commentaries by Dayananda
The first credit goes to the great social reformer and scholar of Vedic Sanskrit, Dayananda for raising a voice against the misinterpretation of the Vedas. He re-established the Vedas as living religious scriptures and showed that they contain religious, ethical and scientific truths. He undertook the enormous task of translation and proved that Vedic teaching is monotheistic and the so-called Vedic gods or demi-gods are nothing but different descriptive names of one God. He believed that an understanding of the Vedas could lead to scientific truths discovered by modern research.

5. Post-Dayanand commentaries
Aurobindo Ghosh is one of the notable contributors to the Vedic commentaries. As new translations are written it is being shown that none of our modern scientific discoveries has contradicted the teachings of Vedic literature.

The Vedas have had a major influence on many Western thinkers and writers such as Ralph Waldo Emerson, Henry David Thoreau and Professor Friedrick Max Muller.

Quotations on the Vedas

MANUSMRUTI (2-13): *'For they who want to acquire true knowledge, the Vedas are the highest authority.'*

UPANISHAD (MUNDAKOPANISHAD): *'Fire is the head of Him (God) and his eyes are the Sun and the Moon, the quarters His organs of hearing and the revealed Vedas are his voice.'*

MAHABHARATA (12-232-24): *'In the beginning of the world Self-existent God revealed the Vedas which are eternal and divine. They are the sources or guides of all human activity.'*

LAVI, AN ARABIAN POET (SON OF AKHTAAB AND GRANDSON OF TURFA, LIVED ABOUT 170 BCE): *'What a pure light do these four Revealed Books afford to our mind's eyes like the charming and cool lustre of the dawn. These four, God revealed to his prophets (Rishis) in Hind (India).'*

BUDDHA (535 BCE, IN SUTTANIPATA 292): *'He who attains true knowledge of Dharma (righteousness) through the Vedas, attains a steady position. He does not waver.'*

GURU NANAK (MAHLA 1 DAKHANI OMKAR, P.930): *'Omkar is He who created the Vedas.'*

JAIN ACHARYA KUMUDENDU (BHOOVALAYA 2-6):
'The Rig Veda is eternal and the Word of the Omniscient in the beginning. Various languages have been derived from it. The message of the Omniscient Supreme Being is one and the same for the speakers of all languages.'

PROFESSOR M. BLOOMFIELD: *'Vedas are the most ancient ... One must remember that even after the changes which had taken place in our ideas, language and religion over the past so many centuries, there is abundance of knowledge present in the Vedas even today.'*

WRITING OF COUNT LEO TOLSTOY, MR ALEXANDER SHIFMAN OF TOLSTOY MUSEUM IN MOSCOW SAID: *'Tolstoy not only read the Vedas, but also spread their teachings in Russia. He included many of the sayings of the Vedas and the Upanishads in his collections* Range of Reading *and* Thoughts of Wisemen *and others.'*

NOBEL PRIZE-WINNER, RAVINDRANATH TAGORE: *'Perhaps the most significant thing that strikes the reader as he goes through some of the Vedic hymns is that they do not read like so many commandments enjoined by priests or prophets, which in the European mind are identical with this Oriental religion, but as a Poetic-Testament of a people's collective reaction to the wonder and awe of existence. A people of a vigorous and unsophisticated imagination, awakened at the very dawn of civilisation to a sense of the inexhaustible mystery that is implicit in life.'*

IN THE CLASSROOM

The material presented in this section can be used when covering the topic of holy books. It is important that pupils understand that Hinduism is not based on any one book. At KS1, ask pupils what makes a book special. Do they have a special/favourite book and why is it special? Discuss how a special book is treated. KS2 pupils could be asked to find the meaning of the word 'Vedas' in an English dictionary. They can be encouraged to find out about the age of these books.

Draw pupils' attention to their future.

What do we need to know now in order to be prepared for the future? From where is that knowledge going to come? Hindus, over thousands of years, have written books to preserve their knowledge and experiences.

Some hymns in the Vedas are very beautiful; they describe the beauty of dawn, the wondrous creation of the world, the journey of life like a flight of swans, for example. At KS3 and KS4, pupils can be introduced to the hymns which state scientific theories (see p.155).

Typical questions/discussion points
1. Name the main holy books of the Hindus. Can you guess how old they are?
2. How did Hindus come to know about the Vedas?
3. Why do Hindus believe that the Vedas are religious as well as scientific texts?
4. Why do religious people see sacred writings as special?

The Bhagavad Gita

The Bhagavad Gita is the essence of Vedic knowledge and has been crystallized into 700 concise Shlokas (verses) in Sanskrit, which provide a definitive guide to the science of self-realization. In one short verse, Shri Krishna states all that one needs to know and to do:

To action alone you have the right,
never to the fruit thereof.
Let not the fruit of action be your motive;
Nor should you desire to avoid action.
(CHAPTER II, VERSE 47)

The Gita is universally renowned as the jewel of ancient India's spiritual wisdom, representing the history of India and the Battle of Mahabharata 5200 years ago. The knowledge of the Gita was imparted by Shri Krishna to Arjuna on the battlefield of Mahabharata, as contained in the Vedas and the Upanishads.

The Bhagavad Gita is today taught and read all over the world with veneration and ranks among the foremost scriptures of mankind. It represents one of the finest collections of spiritual thought and has caught the imagination of many scholars. To all those who are unhappy and unsure as to what is true and right, the Gita provides both light and refuge.

The word 'Gita' means the celestial song. The knowledge is presented in the form of questions and answers. This style of writing, in the form of a dialogue between a teacher and a student, is a typical style of the Upanishads (see pp.126 and 146). The Gita itself is considered to be an Upanishad.

For a Hindu (of any sect) the Gita is as important as the Bible is to Christians. The Gita is used in law courts in Britain and India for oath-taking and every Hindu home and temple, both in India and abroad, is guided by this holy book.

The Gita's main task is to remove the illusion of material entanglement and the sense of personal attachment. It reveals the supreme truth and provides rational solutions to the problems and mysteries of life and death, the duties and obligations of human beings. It reiterates the indestructible nature of the soul which is described in detail in the Upanishads. The secret of the teachings of the Gita is selfless activity: the performance of actions and deeds without attachment to the reward. The Gita has attracted the attention of scholars outside India and it has been translated into all the major languages of the world. In Europe the first translation of the Bhagavad Gita from Sanskrit into English was by Sir Charles Wilkins (1750–1836) of the East India Company in the year 1785. This translation influenced the Western mind and accelerated the study of Vedic literature and the Sanskrit language.

Summary of the Bhagavad Gita

1. Don't be afraid. Stop worrying uselessly. No one can kill you. The soul within you is immortal. The soul is never born nor does it ever die.

2. The past has passed away, the future will depend on the actions performed now and today. Don't repent the past, don't worry about the future, make the present full of worthiness.

3. Empty-handed you came into this world and empty-handed you will go. God has created you to be trustee of his gifts. Remember you are only a trustee not an owner. The material things will not remain with you. What is yours today will belong to some one else tomorrow. The happiness you get from owning these is only temporary and this greed will eventually become the cause of your sorrows.

4. Change is the law of nature. Death is just another name for life. One can be rich for a moment and become poor the next moment. Remove selfishness and vanity from your mind and then all will be yours.

5. Neither you belong to the body nor does the body belong to you. It is made up of five elements: fire, water, earth, air and space. It will finally merge back into them. Only the soul is indestructible.

6. Your refuge lies in offering yourself to God. This is the best choice. Those who trust in God have no fear, no worry and no grief.

Selected Quotations from Gita

Just as a man gives up old garments to put on new ones similarly the soul casting off worn out bodies enters into new ones.   (2:22)

Senses are said to be superior, mind is greater than the senses, the reason is greater than the mind. What is beyond reason is He (the Self).   (3:42)

Whensoever there is decay of Dharma (righteousness), I bring forth myself to restore Dharma.   (4:7)

I serve people in the way in which they approach me. (4:11)

One should uplift oneself by self help and should not degrade oneself, because one is one's own friend and enemy.   (6:5)

Translation by Dr Mira Parikh, Universal Gita Foundation

7. Your salvation lies in offering all your actions to God. While doing so you will realize a sense of supreme bliss.

(Translated by the late Pt. Angira D. Prinja from the original published by Mauji Ram Memorial Trust, New Delhi)

Stories from the Ramayana and the Mahabharata

The Ramayana

The Ramayana has been, from time immemorial, a source of guidance, instruction and solace to the many millions of Hindus in India as well as in other countries. It is not only a work of art of the finest magnitude, but is a cultural analysis of the highest of ideals of the Hindu life narrated through the characters of Rama and Sita. The epic Ramayana, originally written by the sage Valmiki in Sanskrit and later, in the seventeenth century, translated by Goswami Tulsidas into Hindi, is very popular among Hindus, who often arrange for uninterrupted readings of the whole epic.

The version written by Tulsidas is also known as Ramcharit Manas. During the time of Tulsidas, the Moghuls had established their rule in India and the Indian population was full of despair at their political defeat. There was a fear that, along with political rule, they would lose their religion and culture. Tulsidas dispelled that fear and the social and religious antipathy of his time. He placed before the public in the Hindi language the cream extracted from the whole range of scriptural and philosophical literature of Hinduism and paved the way for lay society to bring into practice the basic tenets of the religious scriptures. The Tulsi Ramayana is sung with love, devotion and reverence by millions of people all over India and by Indians living abroad even to this day. It is appreciated alike by every class of the Hindu community, whether high or low, rich or poor, young or old. In fact, the importance of Tulsidas in the history of India cannot be overrated. Putting the literary merits of his work aside, the fact of its universal acceptance by all classes is a clear acknowledgement of its value.

In the Valmiki Ramayana is found the true Aryan life-style that existed in the age of the Vedas and the Upanishads. This is the epic dealing with the factual story of Rama centred on the ancient city of Ayodhya thousands of years ago. The Ramayana features a world of ideal characters like Rama, Sita, Lakshmana, Bharata, Hanuman, etc. It is the religious literature of the Hindus. For countless centuries this epic has influenced Hindu religion and society and has inspired family and social life. For thousands of years too, literary authors have written plays based on the lives of characters in this epic. Hindus have used the Ramayana to inculcate the importance of good character and morality in youngsters by narrating the story and enacting it on stage as 'Ramalila' (see p.63). It has enchanted generations of Hindus because poetry and morality are charmingly united in this holy poem.

The Ramayana presents Rama as an ideal son, an ideal student, an ideal brother, an ideal husband and, above all, as an ideal king. Sita, the heroine of the Ramayana, the very embodiment of chastity, presents the highest ideals of Indian womanhood; she showed strength and resolve when she underwent the unmerited tortures of prison life in the land ruled by Ravana and she advised even Rama on the principles of the code of human conduct. Sita has become an unforgettable name for all Hindus and is respected as mother.

The story of the Ramayana (suitable for KS1 and KS2)

The birth of Shri Rama
Thousands of years ago there lived in India a great king called Dasharatha. He was the ruler of the kingdom of Kaushal. The capital of his kingdom was Ayodhya. King Dasharatha had three queens. The eldest queen was Kaushalya, the second was Kaikeyi and the youngest was Sumitra. King Dasharatha was getting old. He had no heirs. Therefore he was always very worried.

One day a great saint came to the court of the king. He performed an important religious ceremony. The queens were asked to eat the Prasad (offering made to God) after the ceremony was over. In time all the queens were blessed with sons. Kaushalya gave birth to Rama, Kaikeyi to Bharat and Sumitra was blessed with twins; Lakshman and Shatrughna. The citizens of Ayodhya were overjoyed to hear of the birth of the princes.

The four brothers lived very amicably and enjoyed one another's company. Rama and Lakshman were always in the company of each other. Bharat and Shatrughna were always seen together. When they were of school age, they were sent to the Gurukul (school) where they were placed in the care of their teacher Vashishtha. At the Gurukul the princes were trained in the art of warfare and received a thorough grounding to become just and righteous kings in the future.

Protection of the Yajna

When Rama was born there were some barbaric tribes living in the forests of India. They were called Rakshasas. They often attacked the civilized people. They used to raid the villages and take away valuables from the homes of the villagers. Very often they killed the people.

In those days holy men lived in the forests, in dwellings called 'Ashrams'. In their Ashrams the saints meditated and wrote holy books. Young children also received their education at the Ashrams. These schools were called 'Gurukuls'. The children not only gained knowledge at the Ashram but also lived with their guru until their schooling was over.

At that time there lived a great Rishi (saint) by the name of Vishwamitra. Once, when he was engaged in the performance of a great Yajna (involving studies and prayers), the Rakshasas began to interfere with his work. They began to throw meat and blood to defile the prayer place. Rishi Vishwamitra visited King Dashratha for help and, at his request, the king agreed to send Rama and Lakshman with Rishi Vishwamitra to protect his Yajna.

As they travelled through the forest they met a female demon called Taraka. She was a woman but she was very cruel. She used to torture people and then kill them. Therefore, on the instruction of Rishi Vishwamitra, Rama killed her.

Rama and Lakshman arrived at the Ashram of Vishwamitra and there they began protecting the Rishi against the foul acts of the demons. They chased any Rakshas coming near the Rishi's abode. Marich and Subahoo

were the leaders of the demons. Subahoo was killed by Lakshman. Marich was so afraid of the deadly arrows of Rama that he was never seen there again. After this the attacks of the demons came to an end and Vishwamitra was able to complete his prayers in peace.

The marriage of Sita

During the time of King Dasharatha there also lived another king in the kingdom of Mithila. He was King Janaka. He had a daughter, Sita, who was very beautiful, intelligent and gentle.

When Sita grew up to be a very beautiful young woman, King Janaka decided that she should choose a suitable partner for herself. He invited many young princes to this occasion. Princes and kings from far-off places arrived. Rishi Vishwamitra also came, along with Rama and Lakshman. The mighty King of Lanka (Ceylon), Ravana, was also present.

King Janaka made it a condition that the prince who could lift the bow of Shiva and string it would receive the hand of Sita in marriage. Many of the princes made an attempt but failed to lift the bow. Ravana also failed to do so. In the end Vishwamitra ordered Rama to accept the challenge. Rama lifted the bow effortlessly, and as he began to string it, he bent it so much that it broke. All expressed surprise at the amazing strength of Rama. King Janaka was very happy indeed. Sita garlanded Rama, which meant that she had chosen him as her bridegroom.

The news reached Ayodhya. King Dasharatha went to Mithila to attend the wedding of Rama and Sita. Sita had three cousins and they were married to Bharat, Lakshman and Shatrughna respectively. Parshuram, a great devotee of Lord Shiva, became very angry when he heard about the breaking of the bow, but when he saw Rama, his anger went away.

The exile of Rama

When King Dasharatha became very old, he decided to hand over his kingdom to his eldest son, Rama. The approval of Guru Vashishtha was obtained and preparations for the coronation of Rama began. The citizens of Ayodhya were bubbling with joy at the news.

Manthara was the maidservant of Queen Kaikeyi. She also learnt of the coming coronation. She was a very evil woman and she began to poison the mind of Kaikeyi. She told the queen that once Rama was crowned King of Ayodhya, her son Bharat would become the slave of Rama. Something should be done so that Bharat could become the king.

Queen Kaikeyi fell into the trap laid by Manthara. This is the result of keeping evil company. Kaikeyi began thinking that her son Bharat should become the king instead of Rama. She did not even consult Bharat. At that time both Bharat and Shatrughna were at their maternal great-uncle's home.

When King Dasharatha visited Kaikeyi he found her in an angry mood. Kaikeyi then reminded the king that he had once promised two requests to her. The king said, 'Ask and you shall have them.' Kaikeyi then asked that her son Bharat should be made king and that Rama should be sent to spend fourteen years in the forests.

The king was deeply shocked to hear such a request, but he did not want to break his promises. Rama came to know about this unhappy incident. He believed that following the path of truth is true religion. He felt that it was his duty to fulfil his father's promise and therefore he accepted the demands of Kaikeyi. He immediately gave up the desire to reign and began to prepare himself for his journey to the forest. When Rama was about to set off, Sita insisted on joining him. Sita said that it was the duty of the wife to be with her husband, both in happiness and in sorrow. Lakshman decided to accompany them, to be of service to his brother and sister-in-law. Thus three of them left for the forest. The people of Ayodhya were in tears. King Dasharatha died in agony, thinking of his sons and daughter-in-law.

Meeting with Bharat

When Bharat and Shatrughna returned to Ayodhya, they learnt of what had happened in their absence. Bharat was very grieved. He told his mother bluntly that he would not accept the throne. In his opinion, Rama was the elder and more suitable to be the king in every respect.

Bharat immediately set off to look for Rama. Guru Vashishtha and the queens also decided to accompany him. At this time,

Rama, Lakshman and Sita were living in the forest of Chitrakoot. When Bharat arrived there he and Rama met each other very cordially. Tears of happiness rolled down their cheeks. Bharat pleaded with Rama to return to Ayodhya and rule. But Rama was not prepared to go against his father's commands. When Bharat could not get Rama to agree, he asked Rama to give him his (Rama's) sandals. Bharat returned with the sandals. He placed them on the throne and began ruling on behalf of King Rama. Bharat himself lived in a hut like a hermit just as Rama was living in the forest.

The abduction of Sita

Rama, Sita and Lakshman continued on their journey southwards. After travelling for a few days they came to the banks of the River Godavari. At Panchvati they built a hut and settled there. This place was frequented by lions and tigers and there were many demons to be found in these forests. Therefore Lakshman used to remain awake at night to guard and protect Rama and Sita. Sita always did her household chores herself. She taught the tribal women all the good things in life. She lived very happily among them.

In the forest lived Shrupanakha, sister of Ravana. One day she came beautifully dressed and asked Lakshman to marry her. When Lakshman refused, she went to Rama. Rama also refused. Being very angry she went to devour Sita. Lakshman punished Shrupanakha by cutting off her nose and ears. She went weeping to her brother, Ravana.

Ravana came to Panchvati accompanied by Marich who was the most cunning of all demons. He disguised himself as a golden deer and began to graze near Sita. Sita thought that the deer was really golden and she sent Rama to capture it. Rama followed the deer for a long distance, but when he could not get the deer alive, he shot at it. Marich, to deceive Sita, cried out, 'Oh Lakshman, Oh Sita.'

When Sita heard this, she became very worried. She thought that Rama was in grave danger. She sent Lakshman to help her husband. As soon as Lakshman had gone, Ravana came disguised as a hermit begging for food. When Sita came forward to give alms, Ravana grabbed her. He abducted her, forced her into his chariot and rode away. On the way they came across Jatayu, the king of vultures. Sita screamed, 'Oh, good bird, help me.' As Jatayu came forward, Ravana brutally cut off its wings. The noble bird fell down to the earth.

In the meantime, having killed Marich, Rama and Lakshman returned to their hut. When they did not find Sita, they grew anxious and set out to search for her.

In the forest, near a lake, lived a very poor old woman named Shabri. When she came to know that Rama and Lakshman were in that part of the forest, she started to make preparations to receive them. The only thing the poor woman could find were wild berries. She plucked some and, to ensure that they were ripe and sweet, she took a small bite. When Rama and Lakshman walked past, she invited them in and offered the berries as a sign of respect. Lakshman warned Rama to be careful in accepting half-eaten berries from an old woman. But Rama was touched by the love and devotion shown by Shabri and he happily accepted her gift.

The search for Sita

Looking for Sita from place to place, Rama and Lakshman arrived at Kishkindha. Here a race called the Vanara lived. Their leaders were Bali and Sugriva. Bali had taken the kingdom of Sugriva and expelled him. The Minister in Sugriva's court was Hanuman, who was very learned and noble. Hanuman met Rama and Lakshman and brought to Rama the hand of friendship of Sugriva. Then Rama killed Bali and restored to Sugriva the kingdom of Kishkindha. Sugriva, in return, promised to help in finding Sita. In their search they found the brave bird Jatayu who was fatally wounded. At his direction, Hanuman and many other Vanaras went southwards looking for Sita. They came to the southern sea, beyond which there was an island called Lanka (known as Ceylon). The King of Lanka was Ravana. Hanuman crossed the sea and reached Lanka. There he found Sita imprisoned in a park called Ashoka Vatika. He conveyed to her the news of Rama.

Ravana wanted to make Sita his queen. To achieve his desire, he used to visit her often to win her over. When he saw that Sita was not prepared to agree to his wishes, he

threatened her with death. But Sita always held Rama dear to her heart. She could never think of anyone else but her husband. She gave a sigh of relief when she heard about Rama through Hanuman.

Some of the Rakshasas (demons) saw Hanuman and began to attack him, but Hanuman killed many of them. Ravana's son, Meghnad, came to fight him. He caught Hanuman and took him to Ravana. Ravana set Hanuman's tail alight, but Hanuman escaped and set Lanka alight. The beautiful city and its buildings were in ruins. Hanuman returned to Rama to give him the news of Sita. Rama was very pleased to hear of her safety.

The Battle of Lanka

Having learnt of the whereabouts of Sita, Rama made preparations to fight Ravana. Thousands of Vanaras joined the army. With this big army Rama arrived at the seashore. They built a bridge to link India with Lanka and then the army marched to Lanka.

Vibhishan, the brother of Ravana, also lived in Lanka. He was a holy and righteous person. He advised Ravana to return Sita to Rama. But Ravana was so furious that he turned Vibhishan out of his house. Vibhishan joined Rama and helped him against Ravana.

On both sides preparations for a battle began. The Rakshasas and the Vanaras began fighting with their weapons. Hanuman showed great valour and killed many demons. Then Ravana sent his brother Kumbhakarna to lead the battle. He was very powerful. He used to eat a lot and was a heavy sleeper. He succeeded in making the Vanaras run, but Rama saw this and beheaded Kumbhakarna. As soon as Kumbhakarna fell, the demons fled.

The following day Ravana's son, Meghnad, assumed the leadership in the battle. He was very mighty indeed. Lakshman had a duel with him, but Meghnad possessed a secret weapon and he used it on Lakshman. This made Lakshman unconscious and his life was in danger. Everyone was sad and Rama wept for Lakshman. Then Hanuman came forward to help Rama. On the advice of the doctor Sushena, Hanuman fetched Sanjivani, a medicinal herb, from a mountain. Lakshman recovered after taking this medicine and the next day he was on the battlefield to challenge

Meghnad. A fierce battle took place; this time Lakshman killed his foe.

After the death of his son, Ravana led the battle himself. Rama and Ravana fought very fiercely until finally Rama killed Ravana and rescued Sita. Rama was not interested in taking possession of Lanka so he handed over the reign of the island to Vibhishan. By now, the fourteen years of Rama's exile had come to an end so Rama, Sita and Lakshman returned to Ayodhya. Bharat, the mothers and the citizens of Ayodhya rejoiced at their arrival. They lit clay lamps in the evening to celebrate the occasion. This day is celebrated as Diwali. Rama began ruling as the King of Ayodhya and everyone was very happy in his kingdom. His perfect kingdom came to be known as Rama Rajya.

IN THE CLASSROOM

There are many smaller stories within the Ramayana, and each one carries a moral message. For example, the meeting of Rama and Shabri in the forest demonstrates that every one is equal in front of God; he is there for the poorest of the poor. Use the example of Lakshman's and Bharat's love for Rama to demonstrate an ideal relationship between brothers. Use the story to point out that strength should be used to protect the weak and, if required, to punish the wicked. Select one story and explain it to the pupils and ask them to enact the story.

Typical questions/discussion points
1. What are the duties of a son? Husband? Brother? Wife?
2. Is it good to have a picture/notion of the ideal man/woman on which to base ourselves? Who is your ideal or hero?
3. Discuss the importance of the Ramayana in providing a model of how Hindus should live their lives.

The story of the Mahabharata

> *Bowing in devotion to the Most High,*
> *To Common and Ideal Beings as well;*
> *To Goddess of Learning, so great and high,*
> *The epic named Jaya, would I tell.*
>
> SAGE VYASA

The origin of the name Bharat
The story of the Mahabharata starts with the most famous and powerful Kaurava ruler named Dushyant who married Shakuntala, the foster daughter of Saint Kanva. Shakuntala was the daughter of Menaka and Saint Vishwamitra.

As the result of a curse put on her by Saint Durwasa, Shakuntala was deserted by her husband after a brief honeymoon and had to remain in the forest, where a son was born to her. Growing up among the fierce animals of the forest, Shakuntala's son became unbelievably brave and courageous. As the blood of a great king like Dushyant flowed in his veins, he possessed enviable dignity, charm and captivating manners as well. This son of Shakuntala was named Bharata.

Even as a small child of five or six, Bharata used to play with lions, tigers, leopards and elephants. He was brave and Shakuntala was convinced that her son was bound to be a very great ruler one day.

Eventually, Durwasa's curse was over and Dushyant brought Shakuntala and their son to his palace. In the course of time, Bharata succeeded to the throne of his father. He emerged as a very powerful ruler who made large conquests and, as a result, his fame spread far and wide. He assumed the title of Chakravarti Samrat (a universal emperor) and so India came to be called Bharatvarsha after his name.

Emperor Bharata is credited with initiating the institution of democracy in those distant times. He was a very far-sighted ruler. He desired that his dynasty should have the ablest possible rulers by electing or selecting every new king on the basis of his merits.

The story goes that none of Bharata's sons was worthy of succeeding to his powerful throne. They all lacked the qualities that were essential to make a successful and popular ruler. So Bharata decided to break with the old practice regarding the succession to the throne. In other words, he chose to go against the dynastic tradition in the interests of his empire. After consultations with his nobles and under the guidance of the royal priest, Bharata started searching for a suitable candidate who could produce a successful heir to his throne, in place of one of his own sons. His search ended when he found that the eldest son of Saint Bhardwaj was quite fit to be his successor. He made an unusual and surprising announcement in his court: 'I Bharata, the universal emperor, set aside the claim of my sons to my throne because of their incapability and appoint the eldest son of Saint Bhardwaj as my heir so that he may succeed me as the next ruler of my empire.'

Unfortunately, after the death of Bharata, things did not go well for long. His successors failed to preserve the integrity of his large empire and in due course, it came to be reduced to a mere principality – a kingdom of medium size. This kingdom had its capital at Hastinapur.

The writing of the Mahabharata

The divine epic of the Mahabharata was composed thousands of years ago by Vyasa Muni, the son of the great sage Parashara Muni and the grandfather of the Pandavas. He is known as Veda Vyasa. The original epic as related by Vyasa Muni had 8800 verses or stanzas and is probably the longest poem in the world.

The Mahabharata is a whole literature in itself, containing a code of life, a philosophy of social and ethical relations, and speculative thought on human problems. Above all, it has for its core the Gita. There is so much knowledge in the Book that it is called the 'Fifth Veda'.

In response to the prayers of Vyasa Muni, Lord Ganesh appeared and agreed to act as a scribe for writing the Mahabharata on the condition that his pen should never stop until the sublime task was over. Vyasa agreed, guarding himself, however, with a counter stipulation: 'Be it so, but you must first grasp the meaning of what I dictate, before you write it down.' Ganesh smiled and agreed to this condition. Then Vyasa narrated the story of the Mahabharata.

The great battle of Mahabharata flared up in Kurukshetra (northern India) between the two armies of the Pandavas and the Kauravas. It lasted eighteen days and there were eighteen army divisions involved. There were also eighteen warriors of high fame on the side of the Pandavas. On the cessation of the battle, the number of Pandavas and Kauravas left was

eighteen. The Book has eighteen volumes and the Gita has eighteen chapters. In this way the number eighteen is of special significance.

The battle was so devastating that it eliminated the cream of Hindu society: the most learned scholars, the bravest of warriors, the most capable administrators, the most highly skilled technicians and craftsmen were all killed. Only the lowest strata of society were left behind. This situation led to a decline in noble thinking and practice in that part of the world. The result was the arrival of cheap religiosity, low moral values and a general degradation of Hindu society.

In the following sections, the story of the Mahabharata is summarized.

The solemn vow of Bhishma

About five thousand years ago, a great king named Shantanu ruled over a kingdom in northern India with Hastinapur as its capital. He was born in the Kuru dynasty. King Shantanu had a son named Devavrata who was a very promising lad.

One day King Shantanu saw the beautiful daughter of a fisherman. Her name was Satyavati. The king wanted to marry her. Her father asked the king to make a promise that the son born of Satyavati would be the only heir to his throne. Only under this condition would he allow his daughter to marry the king.

Devavrata was the legitimate heir to the throne. For this reason, the king could not give his word to the fisherman. The king was sad because he could not marry the woman he liked. Devavrata learnt of the reason why his father was so sad. Because he was a devoted son he could not bear to see his father suffering.

Devavrata called on the fisherman and on behalf of his father he gave the fisherman the assurance that Satyavati's son would be his father's heir. In order to avoid any trouble in the future for the throne, he even vowed that he would not marry at all. This was a very great promise. His vow came to be regarded as Bhishma Pratigya, which means Great Promise. From then onwards, Devavrata became famous as Bhishma.

The birth of Krishna

During the period of Bhishma, another great person was born in India. He is remembered even today by millions of Hindus throughout the world and many believe that he was a reincarnation of God. This great person was Shri Krishna. His birthday is celebrated as Krishna Janmashtami.

Krishna was born in the family of the Yadav dynasty. Vasudev was his father and Devaki his mother. Devaki's brother Kansa was very wicked and cruel. Kansa imprisoned his own father and became the king of Mathura. His sister Devaki and his brother-in-law protested at such an unjust action; as a result he imprisoned them as well. In the prison, seven children were born to them. Kansa killed them all. The eighth son, Krishna, was also born in the jail, but Vasudev secretly sent him away to a place called Gokul (see p.145).

Krishna was cared for by Nanda and Yashoda at Gokul. As a child, Krishna worked as a cowherd. He was also a very skilful flute player. When he grew up, he visited Mathura and in a dramatic duel he killed Kansa. Vasudev and Devaki were then set free from the prison. Ugrasen was also set free and restored to his throne. Krishna left Mathura and took his people away to Dwarka. There, on the shore of the sea, he established his kingdom and began his reign.

The childhood of the Kauravas and the Pandavas

King Shantanu had two grandsons, Dhritarashtra and Pandu. Dhritarashtra was blind from birth, therefore Pandu became the king. Pandu had two queens. The first queen, Kunti, had three sons: Yudhishthira, Bhimsena and Arjuna. The other queen, Madri, had two sons: Nakula and Sahadeva. Because the five brothers were the sons of King Pandu, they became known as Pandavas.

Gandhari was the queen of Dhritarashtra. They had a hundred sons. These sons were born in the dynasty of Kuru, therefore they were called Kauravas. Among the Kauravas, Duryodhana and Dushasana were the eldest.

In the course of time King Pandu died. Therefore the blind Dhritarashtra ascended the throne, but the step-grandfather of the Pandavas and the Kauravas, Devavrata Bhishma, managed the affairs of state.

The guru of the Kauravas and the Pandavas was Dronacharya. He taught them all the skills and art of war. Among the brothers and the cousins, Arjuna was the best archer. In the art of mace warfare (Gada-yudha), Bhimsena and Duryodhana were matchless. Yudhishthira was known to be the most intelligent and truthful. Since Kunti was the daughter of Shri Krishna's aunt, the Kauravas and Pandavas were Krishna's cousins.

Seeds of enmity were sown between the Kauravas and the Pandavas since childhood. Duryodhana and his brothers always envied the Pandavas. Bhimsena, who was also known as Bhima, was very strong and mighty. The Kauravas were always jealous so the feud between the cousins started in their childhood.

The marriage of Draupadi

To rid himself of the Pandava brothers, Duryodhana devised a cunning trick. He constructed a house of wax which was highly inflammable, then he asked the Pandavas to live there. They soon learnt of his guile, however, and with their mother, Kunti, they disguised themselves and under the cover of darkness, they escaped from the wax dwelling. Duryodhana set fire to the house at night. He and the others thought that the Pandavas had perished in the burning house.

Walking through dense jungles, the Pandavas came to the kingdom of Panchal, whose king was Drupada. The king had a daughter, called Draupadi, who was very beautiful. Drupada decided that she should marry, and in order to choose a suitable young prince who would wed his daughter, he arranged a contest. In this contest the suitor had to pierce the eye of a fish while it was revolving, fastened to a pole. The eye was to be pierced with an arrow, and the archer was to set his aim by looking at the reflection of the fish in a pool of water.

At this contest, princes from all over the country had gathered. Duryodhana and his brothers were there. The Pandava brothers, disguised as Brahmins, also attended this contest. Many of them attempted to pierce the eye of the fish but they failed. Karna, who was also there, came forward. Draupadi refused to wed him if he succeeded because he was not a prince, so Karna had to withdraw from the contest. No one knew that Karna really belonged to the Pandava family.

When the Kshatriyas failed to win the contest, Arjuna came forward as a Brahmin. He very ably fulfilled the conditions of the contest and Draupadi garlanded him. All those who were present realized that the Brahmins were none other than the Pandavas. The Kauravas then realized that the Pandavas had not died in the fire. As a result of this contest, Draupadi married into the Pandavas.

Jealousy between brothers

After the wedding of Draupadi, the Pandavas returned to Hastinapur. The Kauravas had to divide the kingdom into two and give one half to the Pandavas. The Pandavas established the city of Indraprastha which today is known as Delhi, the capital of India.

Yudhishthira, the eldest of the Pandavas, arranged a religious function (Yajna), to which he invited the kings and learned scholars from all the leading kingdoms. For this event, an artisan by the name of Maya built a very beautiful palace. He had so skilfully set and joined stone and glass that on the floor where there was water it appeared like solid ground, and where there was stone it appeared as if it was water. In place of the door, one would see the wall, and in place of the wall one would see the door. When Duryodhana was walking around in this palace, being misled by the work of the artisan, he fell into the water and dashed his forehead against the wall. At this, Draupadi laughed and teased Duryodhana and this increased the bitterness between the Pandavas and the Kauravas.

Defeat at a game of dice

When Duryodhana returned home, he began to think of ways and means of ruining the Pandavas. He sought the help of his uncle, Shakuni, and Karna to achieve his aim. Karna was very brave. Duryodhana made him his ally by granting him the kingdom of Anga. Shakuni was an expert dice thrower. At his instance, Duryodhana invited Yudhishthira to a game of dice.

Yudhishthira was a lover of the game of dice and he agreed without hesitation. The condition of the contest was that the party that lost would have to spend twelve years in the forest and then another year was to be spent in hiding. If they were discovered during that year, then the forest dwellers would have to spend another twelve years in the forest.

Shakuni was gambling on behalf of Duryodhana. Gradually Yudhishthira was beginning to lose. As the game progressed he lost diamonds, rubies, pearls, gold and silver and all the wealth that he possessed. He lost his palace and his kingdom. Gambling is a very bad habit. The gambler loses his sense of reasoning: the loser always believes that he will win the next round. Yudhishthira was thinking along these lines. He even gambled away his brothers. Having lost them, he wagered Draupadi as a bet. He then lost that game. Now the five brothers and Draupadi became the servants of the Kauravas.

Duryodhana ordered his brother Dushasana to drag Draupadi by her hair. She was insulted in the presence of the courtiers. He attempted to remove her clothing and jewels from her body, but the honour of Draupadi was saved by Shri Krishna. According to the rules of the gambling contest, the Pandavas had lost, and they had to leave their kingdom and go away to the forest. Draupadi also accompanied them.

Exile in the forest

In the forest the Pandavas lived like hermits and ate the roots and fruits that grew there. They moved from one place to another and during the twelve years they travelled throughout India. But while they were living in the forest they endured a lot of hardships. Duryodhana had made their lives almost intolerable. They lived in the company of saints and Arjuna meditated for a long time in the forest. He spent his exile in the Himalayas learning how to use various kinds of weapons in times of war.

When the twelve years had expired, the Pandavas began making preparations to live secretly for another year. They changed their appearance, so that they would not be discovered, and came to the district of Virat. They began living in the house of King Virat as his servants. Yudhishthira used to advise the king on state matters. Bhima was in charge of the kitchen and he was the chief cook. Arjuna began to teach Uttra, the king's daughter, the art of dancing. Nakula and Sahdeva worked in the stables of the king. Draupadi became the queen's maid.

Duryodhana did his best to seek out the Pandavas. When the year was about to end, Duryodhana suspected that the Pandavas might be living with the King of Virat so he attacked the kingdom. Arjuna joined the battle on the side of the king and they defeated the army of the Kauravas. Then the Kauravas came to know of the whereabouts of the five brothers, but by now the year had already passed.

The peace efforts of Shri Krishna and preparations for war

The Pandavas revealed themselves once again. Throughout the country everyone rejoiced. King Virat married his daughter Uttra to Abhimanyu, the son of Arjuna.

Now it became the desire of everyone that the Pandavas should regain their lost kingdom. After great thought, it was decided that Shri Krishna should be asked to bring about peace between the two. Shri Krishna visited Hastinapur. He explained to Dhritarashtra and Duryodhana that they should return the kingdom of the Pandavas. But Duryodhana was very stubborn: he was confident that the Pandavas would not be able to defeat him in war. He refused to accept the pleas of Shri Krishna, so Krishna returned disappointed and empty-handed.

Now preparations for war were being made on both sides. Bhishma and Guru Dronacharya knew that the cause of the Pandavas was just. They desired the victory of the Pandavas. But they had grown up in the kingdom of Duryodhana; they had eaten the food of Duryodhana. Therefore, they remained on the side of Duryodhana.

The Kauravas and the Pandavas both sought the help of Shri Krishna. Krishna said that he would remain unarmed on one side, and his army would join the other side. The Pandavas accepted Shri Krishna on their side, while his army went over to the side of the Kauravas. Duryodhana was very glad. The Kauravas thus had eleven army divisions and the Pandavas had seven divisions.

The Battle of Mahabharata

The armies of the Kauravas and the Pandavas assembled at the battlefield of Kurukshetra.

The commander of the Kaurava army was Bhishma. The commander of the Pandava army was Dhrishtadumna, but Arjuna was their chief warrior. Shri Krishna served as the charioteer of Arjuna. Shri Krishna brought the chariot between the armies as they faced each other.

Arjuna was very shocked when he saw that his grandfather, Bhishma, his teacher, Dronacharya, and other close relatives were in the army opposing him. Then he reflected that in this war he would have to slay his grandfather, teacher, uncles and cousins. He said, 'I shall not fight against my teachers and my elders. I will never be able to strike my own relatives.' Saying this, he lowered his bow (called Gandeev) and refused to fight.

Shri Krishna then reminded him of his duty and gave him wonderful advice. His teachings to Arjuna have been called the Bhagavad Gita or 'The Song Divine'. The Gita is a sacred book of Hinduism (see p.132) and is read with great respect throughout the world.

The teachings of Krishna inspired Arjuna and he thus realized his duty in life. He lifted his bow and decided to fight. A fierce battle then ensued. Great destruction took place and many soldiers were killed. The battle went on for ten days. Bhishma was badly wounded by the arrows of Arjuna.

After Bhishma, Dronacharya took command of the Kauravas' side. He arranged his army in the form of a circle which had seven enclosures. At this time Arjuna was busy fighting at another front. Arjuna's son Abhimanyu faced Dronacharya and his men. He was as brave as his father. He broke through the defences of the enemy and fought very bravely. The rules of war allowed only one-to-one fighting, but seven warriors from the Kaurava army jointly attacked Abhimanyu and killed him. This was another unjust act.

The death of Abhimanyu enraged Arjuna. He began killing the Kauravas mercilessly. Dronacharya had been the guru of both sides so it was difficult to defeat him. He also began killing the Pandava soldiers mercilessly. Bhima had killed an elephant by the name of Ashvatthama and he shouted that Ashvatthama had been killed. Dronacharya's son was also named Ashvatthama. To find out the truth,

Dronacharya enquired whether his son had been killed. Yudhishthira replied that the elephant Ashvatthama had been killed and not his son. But owing to the noise around him, Dronacharya could not hear correctly. In a moment of sadness, he lowered his weapons and was killed.

The battle had been in progress for fifteen days. Karna now commanded the Kaurava army. Duryodhana had placed all his hopes in Karna. But without much difficulty Bhima wounded Dushasana and inflicted a shattering blow on his chest with his mace. Bhima thus kept his vow to avenge Draupadi's insult. After this, Karna and Arjuna fought a duel. Both were very brave. During the fighting Karna's chariot became stuck in the battlefield. Taking advantage of this, Arjuna killed him.

On the seventeenth day, King Shalya became the fourth commander of the Kaurava army. Shalya and Yudhishthira fought fiercely until Shalya was killed. Sahadeva killed his uncle Shakuni, the dice thrower. Bhima killed the remainder of the Kaurava brothers. In this way most of the brave warriors were killed; only Duryodhana remained.

On the eighteenth day Duryodhana hid himself in a lake, but Bhima challenged him to come out. Both fought with maces. Bhima crushed the thighs of Duryodhana and fulfilled his vow. In the battle of the Mahabharata the Pandavas were victorious. Almost every soldier on both sides was killed. The best warriors had died in this war. Only the Pandava brothers and Shri Krishna remained.

Death of the Pandavas
After the battle was over, Yudhishthira was the ruler of India. He ruled the country with the help of his brothers, but he was very depressed.

After many years Yudhishthira performed Ashvamedha Yajna. This involved setting a horse free and to protect the horse, an army was sent. All the kings of different states allowed the horse to pass through their kingdom. Thus they accepted Yudhishthira as their ruler and he was proclaimed the Emperor of India.

Yudhishthira ruled for thirty-six years, at the end of which he handed over the reign to Parikshita, the son of Abhimanyu. The Pandavas then settled in the Himalayas with Draupadi. They meditated there for many years. And in the Himalayas they died one after the other.

Thus ends the Mahabharata – the story of the great Pandava brothers who fought against injustice.

<u>IN THE CLASSROOM</u>

The various stories from the Mahabharata can be used to develop ideas of right and wrong. The concepts of fairness, forgiveness and punishment can be discussed by considering how the Kauravas cheated the Pandavas, and how Krishna tried to resolve the conflict. The Mahabharata, particularly its part called the Gita, can be quoted as an example of the scriptures which have helped to develop Hindu values of righteousness and duty.

Typical questions/discussion points
1. Why do we enjoy stories about 'goodies and baddies'?
2. Who usually wins in such stories? Is it true to life?
3. Why do we need such stories?

Stories of Krishna

The stories of Krishna are very interesting, and tell us how attractive and powerful he was. Even though he was a man, because of his extraordinary nature, he was regarded as an incarnation of God (see p.26). He was born in a prison where his innocent parents were locked up by his cruel uncle Kansa (described on p.139). Krishna's father smuggled the baby out of prison and left him with cowherds in a beautiful village near Brindavan in the north of India. Krishna was very genial and liked by all. There Yashoda brought him up and often adorned him with a peacock feather in his long hair.

Krishna always carried a flute and his music attracted everyone. With his elder brother, Balram, and all their friends, he took the cows to graze. In the forest they had a wonderful time. As a young boy, Krishna played many mischievous tricks. He often took butter from the stores and distributed it among his friends. He teased the Gopis and had light-hearted fun. All this is considered as the mischievous expression of divine play (Lila). While he was a hero to all his friends and all the people in his village, he was a threat to all evil-doers. One by one, he killed all the demons who were sent by Kansa to kill him. Even though they came in disguise, Krishna found them out and punished them for their bad intentions. He readily excused those who surrendered to him and repented for their sins.

Krishna's life was dedicated to protecting innocent people. He was very wise and a brave fighter. He was an expert in using several weapons. Sudarshan was his magic disc and Kaumodaki his mace (club). The sound of his conch, Paanchjanya, made his enemies tremble. He killed thousands of demons. Many of Krishna's stories are about fighting for justice. He supported the Pandavas, who were good and innocent. They suffered a lot from their cousins, the Kauravas, who were wicked. When there was a great war between them at Kurukshetra (in what is now northern India), Krishna helped the Pandavas in many ways and secured their victory. His preaching to Arjuna on the battlefield is popularly known as the 'Gita' – a poem of philosophy. The Gita is a sacred book for Hindus and is discussed on pp.132–134.

The devotees of Krishna have described his glorious character through their compositions of stories, songs and plays. The River Yamuna, the city of Mathura, the beautiful Brindavan, the harbour of Dwaraka and Kurukshetra are some of the places in India which are associated with the events in Krishna's life. Meera Bai and Surdas (see p.61) are among the prominent poets who were devotees of Krishna.

Several Hindu festivals celebrate different but significant incidents in the life of Krishna. During Diwali, people commemorate his slaying of the demon Narakasur and the freeing of many women slaves kept by the demon. During Holi celebrations, people remember and sing about the divine love between Radha and Krishna. Statues of Radha and Krishna are often found in Hindu temples,

but it should be pointed out that Radha was not Krishna's wife but a devotee. In Govardhana Annakuta, which comes in the Diwali period, people remember how Krishna saved the village of Gokul from torrential rains and floods, helping them to take shelter under a hill called Govardhana. In Navaratri, people dance Raas to commemorate the eternal love between Krishna and the Gopika maidens at Brindavan. In Gita Jayanti, the holy Gita is read with devotion. The birth of Krishna – Krishna Janmashtami – is celebrated every year on the eighth day of the month of Shravan in the Hindu calendar.

RADHA AND KRISHNA
And when the Infinite whispers Its secrets to the finite – as happens sometimes to all of us in loving – the moment is expressed, in Indian poetry, as the speech of Krishna the Cowherd with Radha, leader of the gopis.
(SISTER NIVEDITA IN *CRADLE TALES OF HINDUISM*)

Krishna's fight against Kansa for justice
Thousands of years ago, King Ugrasena ruled the city of Mathura in northern India. He was very gentle by nature. His son Kansa, who was very strong, became aggressive. Being greedy for the throne, he put his own father in prison and declared himself to be the king. People did not like this but were afraid of his brutality. Kansa made friends with several wicked kings and they were ruthless with the people who opposed them. People's rights and freedom were curbed and those who opposed the cruel kings were killed. All the innocent people, sages and holy men began praying to God to rescue them and they yearned to establish natural justice. They remembered the eternal assurance given by God that he would be reincarnated whenever there was a crisis as a result of injustice or lack of Dharma.

Kansa celebrated his sister Devaki's marriage to Vasudeva, who was a good man and a great devotee of God. When the wedding procession was on the march, Kansa laughed loudly at his success, but a voice from the sky warned him that his good days would soon be over and that the eighth baby born to Devaki would kill him. He became furious and drew his sword to kill his sister, but Vasudeva begged him not to do so. Kansa agreed to spare her life but threw the couple into jail, locked in chains, and kept a very secure watch over them. After a year, a baby was born to Devaki. As soon as Kansa heard the news he went to see the baby and killed it. The same happened to the next six babies born to Devaki.

When Devaki was pregnant for the eighth time, Kansa, remembering that this baby would kill him, tightened the security around the prison even more. It was the month of Sharvan, the month of the terrible rainy season in India. On the eighth night after the full moon of that month, Devaki gave birth to a son. Like Vasudeva, she was anxious and sad about the fate of the baby. But God's will is always very powerful. All the prison guards fell into a deep sleep. The baby was dazzling, with a shining complexion: he was named Krishna. A divine voice ordered Vasudeva to take Krishna away and leave him in the house of Nanda at a village called Gokul and to bring Nanda's child back. Vasudeva wondered how this could happen when he was chained up in a secure prison, but suddenly his chains fell away and the doors opened. When all the watchmen were asleep, Vasudeva took Krishna in a basket upon his head and walked out. When he reached Yamuna, the river, which was in full flood, miraculously gave way to him.

Nanda's wife, Yashoda, was fast asleep when Vasudeva arrived at their house. Beside Yashoda a female baby was lying and smiling at Vasudeva and Krishna. Quietly Vasudeva put Krishna in the place of the baby girl and took her. Unnoticed by anybody he returned to Mathura and entered the jail, where all the doors and chains returned to their previous locked state.

When Kansa took the child and was about to smash it against the wall, she slipped from his hand, flew in the sky and told him that his enemy was growing in the village of Gokul. Kansa was very frightened, yet he thought it would be easy to kill his nephew, who was just an infant. Being afraid to go there himself, he sent assassins to kill Krishna.

The first of the assassins was Putana, a horrible woman who was notorious for killing babies by poisoning them, under the pretext of breast-feeding them. Poor Yashoda was too innocent to recognize the plot and happily handed over Krishna to her. When Yashoda was out of sight, Putana prepared herself to kill Krishna. But Krishna gave her no chance to add poison to the milk; he bit her. Putana screamed and fell down, bleeding to death.

Then Kansa sent Shakata, a demon who came into the village in the form of a cart. Unknowingly, Yashoda laid Krishna down under the cart. Before the demon could crush him, Krishna gave a powerful kick which thrust Shakata whistling up into the sky and when he fell to the ground he was shattered into pieces.

Shakata was followed by Maya and Dhenuka, but they were crushed by Krishna. Each of these monsters, although equipped with some magical or mystical power, was unable to fool God in the form of Krishna.

When all his assassins had failed miserably, Kansa wanted Krishna to be brought to his city. He thought this would be safer than going to Gokul to kill Krishna. This time, he sent a virtuous man, Akrooha, who did not know of Kansa's vicious intentions.

When Akrooha arrived at Brindavan, he saw the handsome Krishna, now fourteen years old, surrounded by many young maidens. Krishna was playing the flute, while all the villagers danced Raas (folk dance) to his tunes. The whole scene was charged with the spark of divine ecstasy. Krishna decided to go and meet Kansa.

As Krishna and his brother entered the city of Mathura, a demon appointed by Kansa attacked them in the form of an elephant. But the demon, named Gajasura, was successfully grounded by Krishna and Balaram. When they entered the royal court, Kansa ordered a powerful wrestler, Chanoora, to fight with Krishna, but the mighty blows of Krishna defeated Chanoora. Finally, Kansa attacked Krishna himself, but he was no match at all and Krishna killed him. Krishna did not forget to tell his uncle that Kansa was only paying the penalty for all the wrong deeds he had committed throughout his life. After killing Kansa, Krishna released King Ugrasena from prison and restored him to the throne at Dwaraka, which is now a place of pilgrimage in Gujarat.

IN THE CLASSROOM

At KS1 and KS2, pupils will find the stories of young Krishna fascinating and full of adventure. One of his best childhood friends was a disabled boy with whom he played many games, and he never forgot his friendship with a very poor boy, Sudama, who was his schoolmate. Videos about the life of Krishna are available with English subtitles (the programme about the Mahabharata televised on BBC2 is a very good source).

Typical questions/discussion points
1. Why do we regard Kansa as a bad person?
2. By what name do Hindus celebrate Krishna's day of birth?
3. What do they do on Krishna's birthday?
4. Did Krishna fight to save himself? What was his aim when he fought with so many demons?
5. In your opinion, do Hindus believe that Krishna was: (a) a son of God; (b) a messenger or a prophet sent by God; (c) God himself, who came into the world in the form of man; (d) a great national hero with many qualities he used for the benefit of others?

Stories from the Upanishads

The word 'Upanishad' comes from 'upa' (near) 'ni' (down) and 'sad' (to sit). The meaning of this word is therefore to find knowledge by sitting near the feet of the teacher. Hinduism allows questioning, and these scriptures record the conversations between students and their gurus.

There are eleven major Upanishads, enumerated in Vedic tradition as follows: Isha, Kena, Katha, Prashna, Aitareya, Taittiriya, Mundaka, Mandukya, Brihadaranyaka, Chhandogya and Shevtashvatara.

There are a host of minor Upanishads, less important, sectarian in character and of post-Buddhist and post-Sankaracharya period. The eleven major Upanishads preceded the six systems of Hindu philosophy and are authoritative. The philosophy of the Upanishads is the philosophy of Brahman. The reality of Brahman and its identity with the individual soul, the falsity of the world and its

objects, and the attainment of immortality through the realization of Brahman or Atman are the fundamental doctrines of the Upanishads. These scriptures contain a vast collection of spiritual insights into Brahman, the self of man, the nature and origin of the universe, and philosophical knowledge, as well as questions and answers discussed in great depth between different Rishis (teachers) and disciples (students) on various aspects of Vedanta.

The Upanishads are known as Vedanta, the conclusion of the Vedas. They give open expression to all that was held in the symbolic Vedic speech as mysterious and secret. They contain the highest and ultimate goal of the Vedas as they deal with Moksha or emancipation. The Vedic philosophy has been developed in the Upanishads, and as such, without the Upanishads one cannot think of the Vedic philosophy. They are the basis of the enlightened faith of India.

The Upanishads were composed by sages and Rishis prior to the advent of Buddha in the seventh century BCE. The Isha Upanishad is fundamental and concise and constitutes the last chapter of the Yajurveda with slight variations. The Brihadaranyaka is the longest and contains philosophical thought and spiritual inspiration. These Upanishads are rich in elevating expressions, and Hindus believe that these will live for all time and provide solace to soul and mind in the wilderness of advancing cultures and civilizations.

In the whole world, there is no study, except that of the original Vedas, so beneficial and so elevating as that of the Upanishads. It has been the solace of my life, it will be the solace of my death. They present the fruit of the highest knowledge and wisdom and contain almost superhuman conceptions whose originators can hardly be regarded as mere men.
(SCHOPENHAUER)

Yajnavalkya–Maitreyi dialogue
Yajnavalkya, the greatest seer and sage, said: 'Maitreyi, I am going away from this house into the forest to enter another order of life (Sanyasa); therefore let me divide my property between you and Katyani.'

Maitreyi said: 'My venerable Lord, if this whole world with all its wealth belongs to me, tell me truly, could I attain immortality?'

'No,' replied Yajnavalkya, 'Like the life of rich people will be your life, but there is no hope of attaining immortality by wealth.'

Maitreyi said: 'Of what use would wealth be to me, if I do not thereby become immortal? Tell me, O Venerable Lord, any means of attaining immortality of which you know.'

Yajnavalkya replied: 'Come, sit down, my beloved Maitreyi, I will explain it to you; try to understand what I say.'

Yajnavalkya said: 'Verily, not indeed for the husband's sake the husband is dear, but for the sake of the self the husband is dear. Verily, not indeed for the wife's sake the wife is dear, but for the sake of self the wife is dear. Verily, not indeed for the sake of the son the son is dear, but for the sake of the self the son is dear. Verily, this all-pervading Atma or Brahma is to be seen, heard, reflected and meditated upon, O Maitreyi.

'O Maitreyi, when there is duality, one sees the other, one smells the other, one tastes the other, one salutes the other, one speaks to the other, one touches the other, one knows the other; but when the self or Atma is all this, how could one see the other, how could one smell the other, touch the other, know the other? How could he know him by whom he knows all this? That self cannot be described.'

Nachiketa–Yama dialogue (Katha Upanishad): Young boy meets the Lord of Death

Nachiketa's father was a king. He was always giving away gifts. Once Nachiketa asked if he would also be given away. 'Yes' replied the king in anger, 'I give you to Yama, the Lord of Death.' Nachiketa dutifully went to Yama, but Yama was not there to receive him. Nachiketa waited for three days and nights. When Yama returned, he felt sorry.

Yama: I have failed my duties as a host. I must undo the wrong. Since you are my guest and have not been treated as such, I shall grant you three boons to make up for my lapse of duty.

Nachiketa: Thank you, O Lord. For my first boon, I request that you grant my father peace of mind. Let him not be angry.

Yama (*with his right hand raised, palm facing out*): Tathastu, so be it. You shall be welcomed with open arms and your father shall live in peace. What else?

Nachiketa: O Lord, it is said that in heaven there is no hunger, thirst, old age or death. Teach me the ritual that takes one to heaven.

Yama (*with his right hand raised, palm facing out*): So be it. I shall teach you precisely how to perform this sacrifice. What is your third boon, my son?

Nachiketa (*with hands folded*): O Lord, when a man dies, some believe he exists and others believe he does not exist. Tell me, O Lord, who is right?

Yama (*smiling*): You are too young to be asking this question. Even the gods have this doubt. The answer is not easy. Ask me for another boon.

Nachiketa (*firmly*): Who else but the Lord of Death can make it understandable? Please teach me.

Yama (*with a wave of his hand*): Don't inquire about death, dear boy. Look, Nachiketa, I will give you all the wealth in the world, every pleasure that you desire and a long life to enjoy it all. As a bonus I will give you something which no other mortal has. Take these celestial nymphs to serve you. How can you refuse such an offer?

Nachiketa (*unperturbed*): O Lord, man is never satisfied with wealth. All pleasures bring only momentary happiness. Human desires can never be quenched. I seek only that which brings everlasting happiness. I do not want anything else.

Yama: There are two ends in life. The wise choose the path which brings everlasting happiness. The others foolishly choose the path which brings only temporary happiness. Finding no fulfilment, such people are trapped in the never-ending circle of birth and death.

Nachiketa (*earnestly*): Tell me, O Lord, about this self which is beyond good or bad, beyond cause and effect.

Yama (*showing a picture of a chariot*): Look at this chariot, Nachiketa. The body is the chariot, the intellect is the driver, the mind is the reins, and the sense organs are the horses. And the self is to be the master.

Nachiketa: But is the self not the body or the mind or the intellect or the sense organs? Who is the self? I am confused, O Lord. Please teach me the nature of the self.

Yama: My child, the self does not live in the body, but the body is an object of the self. Now, are you the subject or the object?

Nachiketa: O Lord, I am the subject.

Yama: Can a subject ever become an object?

Nachiketa: No, my Lord.

Yama: Do you see your own physical body?

Nachiketa: Yes. I see my physical body.

Yama: That means the body is an object of your perception. How can the self be the object, the physical body?

Nachiketa: No. I, being the subject, should always be the subject. I cannot be the physical body. Similarly, I see, I objectify my sense organs. Therefore I cannot be the sense organs. I see, I objectify my mind, my thoughts, my emotions. Therefore I cannot be the mind. I see, I objectify my intellect, my knowledge, my ignorance. Therefore I cannot be the intellect. Who am I? What is my nature?

Yama: Your nature, Nachiketa, is pure awareness. You are Sat-Chit-Ananda (true, conscious and blissful), not bound by time, place or attribute. The subject, I, is awareness, which objectifies the physical body, the mind and the intellect. It is in awareness that the intellect is, the mind is, the sense organs are, the body is, the tree is, the river is, the stars are, in fact the whole creation is in awareness.

Nachiketa: I am the basis of the whole creation. I am not separate from the Lord. Moksha, or liberation, is the knowledge of this profound truth. I am Sat-Chit-Anand.

Deva-Yaksha dialogue (Kena Upanishad)

In the fight with the Asuras, the Devas were victorious. The Devas thought that they won through their own power and prowess and forgot that it was divine help which brought victory to them. Lord Brahma wanted to teach them a lesson. He knew they were puffed up with vanity and appeared before them in the form of a Yaksha (great spirit), the beginning and end of which were not visible. They did not know him and Agni was given the job of finding out.

Agni ran up to Brahma, and Brahma said, 'Who are you?' He replied, 'I am Agni, Jatveda.' Brahma asked Agni, 'What power do you have?' Agni replied, 'I can burn whatsoever there is on earth.' Brahma placed a blade of grass before Agni and said, 'Burn this.' Agni approached it with all his power, but he could not burn it. Next came Vayu (God of wind). Brahma asked Vayu, 'What powers do you have?' Vayu replied, 'I can blow away all the universe and all that is on the earth.' Brahma placed a blade of grass before Vayu and said, 'Blow this away. Vayu approached it with all his power and was not able to make it move an inch from its place. Last of all the chief of the Devas, Indra himself, came. But when he reached the spot he found that the Yaksha had vanished. Indra was in a state of great dilemma; he was confused and perplexed. When he was standing there, bewildered and ashamed at their defeat, Uma (Haimavati), the daughter of Hemavan (Himalaya) and the consort of Lord Shiva appeared before him and revealed to him the real identity of the Yaksha. Only then did Indra know the 'spirit' to be Brahma.

On account of egoism, you think that you do everything and that is why you are bound. Feel that you are an instrument in the hands of God. God works through your hands, sees through your eyes, hears through your ears, smells through your nose. You will be freed from egoism and the bondage of Karma. You will attain peace and become one with God. This is the secret of Karma Yoga and Shakti Yoga.

Yajnavalkya–Gargi dialogue (Brihadaranyaka Upanishad)

Gargi, daughter of Vachuknu, was very intelligent and no one could beat her debating power. Once, when she met sage Yajnavalkya, she said, 'I shall ask you two questions. Will you answer me, O venerable sage?'

Yajnavalkya said, 'Ask, O Gargi.'

Gargi said, 'O Yajnavalkya, tell me what is above the heavens, beneath the earth, embracing heaven and earth, past, present and future, tell me, in what is it woven, like warp and weft.'

Yajnavalkya replied, 'In ether or Akasha.' Gargi said, 'I bow to you. In what is the ether woven and re-woven like warp and weft?'

Yajnavalkya replied, 'O Gargi, in Brahma is the ether woven and re-woven like warp and weft. Sages call this the Akshara (the Imperishable).

'It is neither coarse, nor subtle, neither short nor long, neither red nor white. It is neither shadow nor darkness. It is without ears, eyes, mind or breath, without speech, smell or mouth. It has no within and no without.

By the command of this Indestructible Being, O Gargi, sun and moon, heaven and earth, stand upheld in their places. By the command of this Akshara, O Gargi, minutes, hours, days, nights, weeks, months, seasons and years stand apart.

Whatsoever, O Gargi, without knowing the Akshara, departs from this world, becomes a miser. But he who departs from this world knowing this Indestructible Being is a true Brahma or liberated sage.

'That Brahma, although unseen, but he sees; although unheard, but he hears; although unthought, but he thinks; unknown but he knows. There is none that sees but he, there is none that thinks but he, there is none that knows but he.

'In the Akshara, then O Gargi, the ether is woven and re-woven like warp and weft.' On hearing these words of wisdom from Yajnavalkya, Gargi became silent.

Uddalaka-Shwetaketu dialogues (Chhandogya Upanishad)

Uddalka was father and guru of Shwetaketu. There are some very interesting dialogues between them. Two of the stories, which explain the concept of all-pervading Brahma, are given on pp.35 and 36.

Rama–Vasishtha dialogue (Yoga–Vasishtha)

Shri Rama asked, 'Venerable guru, what is attraction? What is non-attraction? What is attraction which leads one to bondage? What is that non-attraction which tends to freedom? How can I destroy this bondage? Please enlighten me on these points.'

Vasishtha replied, 'If anyone believes that this body is permanent, if he fails to discriminate between the body and its presider or in-dweller or inner ruler who is eternal and if he thinks always of body only, he is a slave to attraction and he is bound by attraction. This is attraction. This will undoubtedly lead to bondage. The belief that everything is Brahma or Atma only, and that there is nothing for one to love or hate in this universe is non-attraction. This non-attraction will lead to Moksha or final emancipation.

'Jivanmuktas are endowed with non-attraction. When there is non-attraction, the mind abandons the pleasures of the world, egoism vanishes and attachment for anything perishes. The state of non-attraction leads to Moksha. Those who have attained the state of non-attraction relinquish the fruits of actions, they seek neither action nor inaction. Attraction entails one in rebirth.

'The attraction is of two kinds – Bandhya (binding) and Abhandhya (non-binding). The former belongs to the ignorant, while the latter is the ornament of those who have attained self-realization. The former produces objects while the latter generates discrimination and knowledge of the self. Lord Vishnu and the hosts of Siddhas protect this earth by performing various actions through the Abhandhya attraction.

'A Jivanmukta is not attached to actions, although he performs manifold actions for the well-being of the world. He is quite indifferent, although he associates himself with the objects. He has no attraction to the objects. His mind is ever fixed in the Supreme Self only. He regards this world as an unreality. He never lives in future expectation, nor does he rely on his present possession. He does not live on the pleasure of his past memory. Sleeping, he is awake in his vision of Supreme Light; and waking he is plunged in the deep sleepless sleep of Nirvikalpa Samadhi. He does actions and remains as if he has done nothing. He does all actions without the error of believing himself as the actor. He neither rejoices nor grieves at anything. He behaves himself as a boy with boys and as a veteran with old people. He is youthful in the society of young men and is sincere in the company of the wise. He rejoices at the happiness of others. He is sympathetic with the people who are in distress.'

The material selected from the Upanishads will be suitable for pupils at KS4 and KS4+. The dialogues convey philosophical ideas and will require further explanation. The dialogue between Shwetaketu and Uddalaka in which the example of salt and water is given to explain the idea that God is everywhere (p.35) can be enacted in the classroom at KS2 and KS3 level.

The story of Nachiketa meeting the Lord of Death can be used to convey the Hindu philosophical idea about the self (spirit or soul). The dialogue could be spoken aloud in the classroom.

A discussion can be held on the forces of nature experienced through the wind and the sun. What is driving these forces? Why does the wind blow? From what does the sun get its energy? Scientific laws can explain it all, but who made the laws of nature? Use the Deva-Yaksha dialogue (p.148) to convey the Hindu belief that God is the power behind all the forces of nature.

Can God be seen? Ask pupils to discuss their ideas about God's nature and qualities. Can God be described? Use the Gargi–Yajnavalkya dialogue (p.148) to explain the Hindu view that God is indescribable. Finally, teachers should note that the Upanishads provide very useful material in the form of questions and answers, and these can be used to help develop an enquiring attitude in pupils.

Typical questions/discussion points
1. The Upanishads are full of questions and answers. Why is it important to ask questions?
2. Should you believe in something without asking questions? Do religions encourage questioning? Does Hinduism give freedom to question?
3. Study the story of 'Nachiketa meeting the Lord of Death' and explain what you understand about the self (spirit or soul).
4. What authority does anyone have to say, 'This is true'? What are the powers and limits of human reason?

The Puranas (Hindu Mythology) and Dharma Shastras (Law Codes)

The origin and purpose of the Puranas

Right up to the Battle of Mahabharata 5200 years ago, worship of an impersonal and formless God was prevalent. After the Mahabharata, when the cream of society was lost, the teachings and practice of the Vedas came to a halt. Ignorance and illiteracy prevailed amongst the general masses and the worship of a formless God declined. After a great many changes had taken place in the observance of Vedic Dharma, there emerged the Jains, from Rishabdev to Mahavira (the founder of Jainism), who propounded the theory that there was no God as a creator of the universe because the concept of God had already been effaced from human thinking at that time.

Then came the collection called the Puranas which endeavoured to reform, inasmuch as they are an attempt to take stock of the religious myths, legends, doctrines and rites current at that time and to give them the sanction of a purified and spiritual form. Their main idea is to popularize abstract truths or higher ideas in imagery and tales to make them more accessible to ordinary people.

There are eighteen main Puranas and many minor Puranas. Amongst these the most famous are the Vishnu Purana, the Shiva Purana, the Garud Purana, the Skanda Purana and the Bhagavata Purana.

The stories and the teachings of the Puranas have come to us through the tradition of guru and disciple. They have undergone changes according to time and place, and similarly there have been many interpolations in these stories. Several stories found in the Puranas are very ancient and interesting. Some of them were current even during the period of the Upanishads.

The subject matter covered in Hindu mythology (i.e. the Puranas) pertains to the creation and dissolution of the universe, stories about various deities and the portrayal of the kings of the solar and the lunar dynasties as well as their histories.

The Puranas are denoted by the word 'Smruti' and their authority is accepted as far as they are in agreement with the Vedas, although a supersensuous vision of truths is to be met with in some measure in them. The doctrine that God incarnates again and again in human form for the protection of the Dharma and the doctrine of Bhakti is well established in the Puranas. The ideal of Bhakti in the lives of saints and kings is illustrated here. To the ordinary person, the Puranas convey the message of Bhakti, and wonderful stories of Dhruva and Prahlada and of a thousand other saints.

Some Hindus believe in the scientific accuracy of the Puranas while others generally regard them as attempts to explain the mysteries of the universe through interesting mythological stories. Either way, the Hindu way of life has been influenced by stories of the Puranas. The teaching of Bhakti in the Puranas was to make religion practical, to bring it from its high philosophical imagery into the everyday lives of common people.

The Puranas were written in the language of the people of that time, what we would call modern Sanskrit. They were meant not for scholars but for the ordinary people who could not understand philosophy. The sages made use of the lives of saints and kings and historical events, and with symbolic illustration, tried to explain the eternal principles of religion.

The eighteen main Puranas

The eighteen main Puranas comprise six Puranas for each of the Hindu trinity of Brahmaa, Vishnu and Shiva (Mahesh).

BRAHMAA
(Creator)
Brahma, Brahmanda,
Brahma-Vaivasvata (Vaivarta)
Markandeya, Bhavishya,
and Vamana

VISHNU
(Preserver)
Vishnu, Narada,
Shrimad Bhagvata,
Garuda, Padma and Varaha

SHIVA (MAHESH)
(Destroyer)
Matsya, Kurma, Linga,
Shiv (Vayu), Skanda and Agni

A brief description can be given of each of the eighteen main Puranas:

1. **Brahma Purana** Describes the qualities of the sun and answers questions on the Sankhya school of philosophy. Many parts are similar to the Mahabharata.

2. **Brahmanda Purana** 'Brahmanda' means universe. It talks about the wonder of the entire universe and shows that Shiva and Vishnu are different facets of the same God.

3. **Brahma-Vaivarta Purana** Describes how the power of nature is manifested through goddesses like Durga, Lakshmi, Saraswati and Radha. Includes a very entertaining description of the birth of baby Krishna.

4. **Markandeya Purana** Narrates the story of sage Markandeya who realized that the universe was functioning by the power of God. Emphasis is put on a combination of knowledge with action (Karma).

5. **Bhavishya Purana** 'Bhavishya' means future. This Purana includes stories about the future. Also details about worship of the sun and some medicines are given.

6. **Vamana Purana** Gives the story related to the incarnation of Vishnu as the short man 'Vamana'. Also describes the wedding of Uma and Shiva. An interesting story about the birth of Lord Ganesh is found in this scripture.

7. **Vishnu Purana** This Purana follows the Vaishnav tradition. It includes a description of the Ashram system.

8. **Narada Purana** Views on Varna (class), the Ashram system and penance are given in this scripture.

9. **Shrimad Bhagvata Purana** This is a very important scripture to Hindus and is considered as an authority on Vaishnavism. In 18,000 stanzas, contained in ten chapters, it narrates the stories of all the avatars of Lord Vishnu. In total twenty-two avatars are described, including the one named 'Kalki'

which some Hindus believe is the avatar for the space age and expect it to come in the future. There is also a vivid picture of Pralaya (doomsday) in the last chapter.

10. **Garuda Purana** Includes the story of creation as narrated by Vishnu to Garuda. Includes a summary of 'Gita' and gives a view about what happens after death.

11. **Padma Purana** Contains stories about different levels of the world similar to the idea of heaven, earth and hell.

12. **Varaha Purana** This is related to the 'Varaha' incarnation of Vishnu in the form of a boar. It is believed to represent that stage in the evolution of life when the first mammals arrived.

13. **Matsya Purana** Includes the stories about the fight between Shankar (Shiva) and a demon, Tripurasur. The first incarnation of Vishnu as a fish, believed to represent the start of life in water, is presented. The importance of pious places like Kashi, Prayag and River Narmada is mentioned.

14. **Kurma Purana** This is related to the second avatar of Vishnu in the form of a tortoise, believed to represent the start of life on dry land as the first amphibians arrived. It includes a description of the Hindu trinity: Brahmaa, Vishnu and Mahesh. Emphasis is on the worship of power (Shakti) in female form. It identifies the goddess Lakshmi as Shiva's consort, Parvati.

15. **Linga Purana** Specifies the worship of Lord Shiva (also known as Shankar) in the form of Shiva Linga. Twenty-eight avatars of Shiva are mentioned. The creation of the world is narrated by Lord Shiva and this creative power is represented and worshipped in the form of Shivalinga. Some writers have misunderstood the significance of this symbol and have wrongly described Shivalinga as a phallic symbol. (See p.31 for more details on Shivalinga.)

16. **Vayu Purana** In four parts, it describes the whole universe, the earth, space and the eras.

It includes the history of sage Kayshap. Details of knowledge relating to music and different branches of the Vedas are found in this Purana.

17. **Skanda Purana** This Purana, containing 21,000 verses, is mostly related to the worship of Shiva. It includes a discussion on Vedanta philosophy. Stories related to holy places like Kashi, Avanti, Maheshvari and the River Reva are found here, as is the story of Satyanarayana, which is popular among Hindus.

18. **Agni Purana** This Purana is considered by some Hindus as a storehouse of all stories. The epics Ramayana and Mahabharata are described. Astrology and rituals associated with keeping different types of fasts are specified. It is highly regarded by many Hindus because it includes details of the eightfold path of Yoga (see p.115).

The Dharma Shastra (Law Codes)

The knowledge revealed to the Vedic Rishis and compiled in the Vedas was orally transmitted by succeeding generations of worthy pupils (disciples), learnt by recitation and repetition, and memorized. Later it was recalled and recorded in the voluminous body of religious literature called the Smruti texts. The term 'Smruti' means knowledge acquired by memorization. Sages such as Manu, Yajnavalkya, Parasara and Gautama were the first law-givers of Hinduism. Their books, known as Dharma Shastras or Smrutis, have had an everlasting influence on the Hindu way of life. The most popular is the Manu Smruti, the Law Codes of Manu.

The Manu Smruti

The Manu Smruti is the oldest and the most authentic of Smruti texts and was compiled and written by the great Vedic Rishi Manu. It contains nearly 2700 verses (Shlokas), running into twelve chapters. Manu is known as the first law-giver of mankind and is also known as the patron saint of social thinkers. This Smruti (text) incorporates the basic Vedic doctrines and philosophy at a practical level, covering the life of a man from the time of birth until his death, ethical behaviour, character and morality, jurisprudence, social etiquette, habits of hygiene, social organization, statecraft, etc. In addition, the fourfold division of society (classification or Varna Vyavastha), the four stages of life (Ashramas), the four objectives (Dharma, Artha, Kama, Moksha), customary practices, religious duties, rights of a child, rules of adoption, inheritance and division of property, etc. are discussed and categorized. The organization of the army, ethics of war, the laws of statecraft, functions of kings and ministers, the organized espionage system and state spies, etc. are also surveyed in great detail and featured in this Smruti.

Manu was a great Rishi and lived in an era preceding that of the Ramayana and Mahabharata; references to Manu appear in these two epics. Some Hindus believe Manu's Laws to be eternal and say that Manu reappears at the beginning of every creation. According to one mythological story, Manu appears fourteen times in a Kalpa, which is equivalent to 8640 million human years.

The Manu Smruti is an authoritative and informative text dealing with the most fundamental of all issues which confront mankind. The influence of Manu and the Manu Smruti was fairly extensive in the then known world, predominantly in Western Asia, Europe and also in the territories of the East Indies. It has attracted the attention of many researchers, though unfortunately some of them have misinterpreted this ancient law book of Hinduism. Throughout this book extensive quotations from the Manu Smruti have been included.

IN THE CLASSROOM

Start a discussion about how human beings try to explain or understand the mysteries of God and creation. Can science offer an explanation for everything? When science fails, what do we depend on? Do some of the early explanations offered by our ancestors turn into myths? Discuss the role of mythology. Hindu mythology is full of fascinating stories and ideas, and each one offers an explanation of the mystery surrounding God and creation.

With younger pupils you could use an example from a fairy tale (such as 'The Three Little Pigs') to illustrate that, though fairy tales or myths may not be real, they often carry an important message.

Talk about the need to have some rules, codes of conduct and laws. Can society function without any rules and regulations? Introduce the ancient Law Book of Manu (the Manu Smruti) to make pupils aware that the need to organize society for the benefit of all was recognized a long time ago. Point out that some laws have to change with time and place whereas other laws do not change.

Typical questions/discussion points
1. What is mythology? Discuss the role it plays in developing religious faith.
2. Why does society need rules and codes of conduct?
3. Investigate in what areas modern scientific thought agrees with the messages given by stories from Hindu mythology.
4. The Manu Smruti put forward the idea of a division of labour depending on the qualities of each individual. Does this still happen in our society? Are we divided into social groupings according to our profession, skills, income, etc.?

Vedic Knowledge and Modern Science

In Hinduism, there is no conflict between science and religion. The Vedic scriptures are not just old religious books, they are books which contain many true scientific facts. This aspect of the Hindu scriptures has not been acknowledged by many Western scholars, mainly because these books were written in Sanskrit and even today not many people understand this language. Moreover, all the Hindu scriptures were written in Bharat (India); when non-Hindu rulers such as the Moghuls and the British ruled over India, they had some influence on the translations of the Hindu scriptures (see the discussion on various commentaries on pp.130–131). The real value of these scriptures is only now emerging.

The most ancient and the best-known scriptures in Hinduism are the four Vedas. Below are some selected examples which illustrate the presence of many branches of science in the Vedas. Further examples can be found in *Sciences in the Vedas* by Acharya V.N. Shastri.

Mathematics

Multiplication tables and the concepts of zero and decimal (derived from the Sanskrit word 'Dasham luv') appeared first in the Vedas. In Mantra 15-1-11 of Artharva Veda the 'ten times table' is set out and it is explained how the value can be increased by placing a zero in the right place. Yajur Veda explains multiplication, division, fractions and square numbers. In the Rig Veda many numerical problems and patterns are discussed; for example, if any number is multiplied by 9 and then all the digits in the answer added together, the sum will always be equal to 9. These are the types of pattern that mathematics teachers often ask pupils to find.

In *Vedic Mathematics*, Shankara Acharya of Puri, Swami Bharati Krishna Tirthaji Maharaja, has described sixteen Vedic Sutras (compact one-line verses) which can be used to perform complex mathematical computations. For example, the conversion of a vulgar fraction (1/19 or 1/29) to its equivalent recurring decimal number involves eighteen or twenty-eight computational steps, but requires only one simple step of mental working using the Vedic Sutra. These mathematical formulae are never wrong. Today the whole world uses systems based on this knowledge of zero and decimals expounded in the Vedas. This is one reason why Hindus believe that Vedic knowledge is true and will never become outdated or meaningless.

In Vedic mathematics there are sixteen Sutras or formulae and about thirteen Sub-Sutras. The word 'Sutra' (pronounced 'sootra') is from ancient India and means a thread of knowledge. The English word 'suture', meaning the thread doctors use to stitch wounds together, comes from 'Sutra'. The mathematical Sutras are short and simple statements setting out formulae for solving mathematical problems. Each Sutra has a large number of uses at all levels of mathematics.

One of the Vedic Sutras is 'Nikhilam Navatascaraman Dasatah', which means 'All from nine and the last from ten'. This simple formula, known as 'Nikhilam Rule', relates any

number back to unity, or one. It does this by showing what must be added to the number to make it up to the next base of ten.

This rule can easily be used to multiply large numbers. The following is an example of multiplying two numbers which are close to 100.

1. Suppose we need to multiply 97 by 94. We write the base (100) above and set the sum out as shown.

$$\begin{array}{r} (100) \\ 97 \\ \times\ \underline{94} \end{array}$$

2. To obtain the complement of 97, using all from nine and the last from ten: 9 from 9=0 and 7 from 10=3, which gives 03 to be put down on the right with the connecting minus sign.

$$\begin{array}{r} (100) \\ 97{-}03 \\ \times\ \underline{94{-}06} \\ / \end{array}$$

3. Cross-subtract for the left-hand part of the answer:

$$\begin{array}{r} (100) \\ 97{-}06 = 91 \qquad\qquad 97{-}03 \\ \text{or } 94{-}03 = 91 \qquad \times\ \underline{94{-}06} \\ 91/ \end{array}$$

4. Multiply 3 and 6 for the right-hand part of the answer: 3 x 6 = 18

$$\begin{array}{r} (100) \\ 97{-}03 \\ \times\ \underline{94{-}06} \\ \underline{91/18} \end{array}$$

5. The answer is 9118.

Further examples can be found in *Vedic Mathematics for Schools – Book 1* by J.T. Glover.

Psychology

Different states of mind and behaviour are explained in the Vedas. The Yajur Veda defines mind as: 'That which is endowed with power of cognition, recollection and cohesion and that which is the perpetual light amongst all the sensuous susceptibilities and that without whose agency no act can be performed' Yajur Veda (34-3).

The Mandukya Upanishad describes the following four states of mind:

1. Jagrata (wakeful);
2. Swapana (dreaming);
3. Sushupti (dreamless, deep sleep);
4. Tureeya (the essential phase).

There are many more statements in the Vedic texts which show a deep understanding of the human mind and behaviour.

Physics

The Vedas state that all matter is made up of particles and these particles have three types of quality – Satvik, Rajsik and Tamsik. Scientists have now proven the same thing through experiments, i.e. that all matter is made up of atoms and each atom contains three types of particle – positive protons, negative electrons and neutral neutrons.

The Rig Veda (10-73-5) clearly states that the earth came into being from the sun. The Vedic view of the creation of the world (see pp.157–158) and the composition of matter agree very well with the theories proposed by modern scientists.

Sage Kanada's definition of motion is almost identical to modern concepts of mechanics. He defined acceleration (Ksanika), momentum (Vega), vibration (Spandana) and various types of motion.

Verses 10-45-1 and 10-45-3 in the Rig Veda clearly state that 'Agni' has properties of light, heat, electricity and magnetism and is found in all three regions of earth, atmosphere and space. It was recognized that light, heat and sound require a medium to travel, and this medium has been defined as 'Akasha' or ether. In the first Mandal (book) of the Rig Veda several references are found which define the rain cycle. 'Maruts' of various shapes have the function of carrying water from the seas to make rain; these 'Maruts' are simply clouds that form in the air.

Chemistry

In Mantras 1-2-7 and 7-33-7 of the Rig

Veda, different qualities of air (gases) are mentioned. It is stated that two different types of air (hydrogen and oxygen) mix to make water. In fact, the famous Ayur Veda, which explains about medicines, is part of the Rig Veda.

Astronomy

Astronomy is one branch of Vedic science that has received international acclaim. The Vedas recognized the sun as the source of energy. In the Yajur Veda, Mantra 23-9, it is explained that the sun moves about its own axis and the earth rotates around the sun, whilst the moon rotates around the earth. The Rig Veda (8-12-30) states that the earth is held by the sun's attraction. The most amazing fact is the mention of 'Navagrahas' (nine celestial bodies) which are often worshipped in some Hindu rituals. Including the sun and the moon, this accounts for the seven planets in our solar system. The names of the weekdays are derived from the names of the planets (see pp.120–122). The position of the stars and various planets in the twelve constellations of the zodiac were noted in the Vedas. The scriptures include calculations about the movement of the planets and scientists today agree with these explanations.

Environmental Sciences

The Rig Veda says, 'Do not destroy the trees because they give life.' The importance of ecology and the balance of nature was recognized thousands of years before scientists started to express their concern about the 'greenhouse effect' and depletion of the ozone layer. Al Gore, currently Vice President of the USA and a known environmentalist, has quoted the Vedas in his book *Earth in Balance*. He has said that the Vedas of Hinduism consider the protection of the environment a duty of every human being.

Medicine

A description of vital parts of the body, including the heart (Hridaya) and the brain (Mastiska), are found in Atharva Veda (10-9-15 and 10-2-26). Both Yajur Veda (39-10) and Rig Veda (8-28-5) define seven formative constituents of the human body (chyle, blood, fat, flesh, bone, marrow and semen), with seven kinds of strength. The identification of many diseases and their cures can be found in the famous Upaveda called 'Ayurveda'. In the history of medicine, Ayurveda has a distinct place. It influenced the growth of medical knowledge in Greece and Arabia, which schools were the forerunners of modern medicine. Dr Royle, MD, FRCS, of King's College and Hospitals, London, in his book *Antiquity of Hindu Medicine*, states: 'Hippocrates, the father of western medicine, borrowed his materia medica from India'.

The 'Charak Samhita' and 'Sushruta Samhita' (medicine and surgery) are two important classical texts dealing with medical sciences. As early as the sixth century BCE, Hindu surgeons had attained a high degree of proficiency in surgical procedures such as excising, incising, scarifying and puncturing. A large number of surgical instruments are also described in the Vedic texts. Modern-day plastic surgeons still refer to rhinoplasty, the method developed by ancient Hindu surgeons which involved turning down a flap of skin from the forehead to cover a gross defect in a patient's nose.

In his book *The Story of Medicine*, Dr Kenneth Walker writes: 'In Ayurveda, we find a description of the vascular system which strongly suggests that Hindus of this period anticipated Harvey's discovery of the circulation of blood. Ayurveda also contains the highly intelligent observations that plague is likely to appear when many dead rats are found lying about, and malaria is caused by mosquitoes. It gives a description of pthisis, a disease characterised by persistent cough, fever, and the expectoration of blood. Over seven hundred medical plants are mentioned in the great Hindu Ayurveda and information given about the dispensing of a number of useful ointments, inhalations, and sneezing powders.'

IN THE CLASSROOM

It is important to inform pupils that all these ancient scriptures or books are not simply religious books. They also contain scientific knowledge and can be treated as scientific texts. A few examples of Vedic mathematics can be tried. At KS3 and KS4 they can be used to perform complex mental arithmetic. A good source for this material is Glover's book, referred to earlier.

A few examples from the Ayurveda scripture will be of interest to students who are studying biology and topics related to health and medicine and may lead to further discussion.

Typical questions/discussion points
1. What do holy books contain?
2. What evidence of scientific thinking do you find in the Vedas, known to be among the oldest books?
3. Is there any conflict between the teachings of Hindu scriptures and science?
4. Is freedom to investigate and ask questions important for discovering the truth? Is this freedom allowed in Hinduism?
5. Look at herbal medicines and find out how knowledge from the Hindu scripture Ayurveda has influenced medical treatment.

The Creation of the World

Hindus have many different ideas about the creation of the world. Some of them are based on the mythological stories found in the Puranas whilst others are based either on scientific facts quoted in the Vedas or on philosophical arguments presented in the Upanishads. The mythological and the Vedic concepts are discussed here.

Hindu myths about creation
Most of the Hindu myths about creation are found in the Puranas and are related to the Trimurti, Brahmaa, Vishnu and Mahesh. They mention the cyclic creation of the universe. At the end of each 'Kalpa' (aeon), the universe is destroyed and remains submerged in cosmic waters till Brahma wakes up from his sleep to begin another creation.

One legend suggests that Brahma created the cosmic waters and deposited in them a seed which became a golden egg. From the egg, Brahma himself was born as 'Purusha', the cosmic man.

Another myth tells the story of Vishnu sleeping on coils of an endless snake called Anant Naga, whose thousand heads make a canopy over him. Brahma emerges on a lotus flower from the navel of Vishnu in the presence of Lakshmi who is goddess of wealth and prosperity. Together they create the world. At the end of the creation, the snake destroys the world with its venom.

Some authors, like Arthur Cotterell in *A Dictionary of World Mythology* and W.D. O'Flaherty in *Hindu Myths*, have wrongly translated the Hindu scriptures and portrayed a highly inaccurate story in which Brahma is alleged to have committed an act of incest with his own daughter for the purposes of creation. Such stories are not only false but Hindus find them to be derogatory and sinful.

According to Vishnu Purana, Brahma creates all objects (animate and inanimate) from his body. He creates opposites like night and day. He abandons his own body and takes on another body to create a whole variety of objects with diverse functions.

There are many more myths about creation in Hinduism, but they are no more than symbolic explanations of the wondrous and mysterious act of creation.

The Vedic concept of creation

The concept of creation enunciated in the Vedas, the oldest Hindu scripture, is very similar to the theory accepted by many modern scientists that the state of the Universe at the start is indescribable, it was so hot and so dense that all known physical laws breakdown. The famous creation hymn in the Rig Veda says:

*In the beginning there was neither nought
    nor aught
Then there was neither sky nor atmosphere
    above
What then enshrouded all this universe?
In the receptacle of what was it
    contained?
Then was there neither death nor immor-
    tality,
Then was neither day ,nor night, nor light,
    nor darkness,
Only the Existent One breathed calmly, self-
    contained.*

(RIG VEDA,10-121-1)

Pandit S. Vidyalankar, writing in *The Holy Vedas – A Golden Treasury*, explains that in the beginning of the present order of things, in some far-off period, at some distant point of time, the whole universe existed in a state which was invisible, subtle and unmanifested. That which we now know as the earth, the sun, the moon and the stars was then, in the beginning of the Kalpa, formless matter in its most elemental state – ether. Hindu philosophers called it 'Asat', meaning non-being. From Asat, one only without a second, proceeded the state of being. That single point, which scientists call singularity, where all the mass and energy of the entire universe was stored, is called in Vedic language 'Hiranyagarbha' – the womb of energy or shining light. 'In the beginning was Hiranyagarbha, the seed of elemental existence' (Atharva Veda, 4-2-7).

At the beginning of time, all known physical laws of science break down. The Hindu view is that eternal laws (called Reeta in the Vedas) always exist and one God, without a second, uses these laws to create the world and all forms of life. This view is illustrated in the Yajur Veda:

*God is the 'Purusha' (the cosmic man) with a
    thousand
(i.e. innumerable) heads, eyes and feet
    because in Him,
the all-pervading Supreme Being, there exist
    innumerable heads,
eyes, and feet of all living beings.
The Supreme Lord fills the earth and the
    'prakriti' (universe) from all sides.*

(YAJUR VEDA, 31-1)

According to the Hindu Vedic scriptures the sequence of creation is as follows. The indescribable phenomenon which starts the creation is Brahman. First, three types of building blocks of matter called 'Ahamkar' (Satva, Raja and Tama) were created. These are akin to the three elementary particles called Neutrino (Electron, Muon and Tau) by the modern physicists. Then came the five physical elements (panchbhoot): earth, air, fire, water and space. On the earth, first came the vegetation (vanaspati), often represented by lotus flower in Hindu mythology, and then the food (anna), living organisms (veerya), physical body (sharir), variety of life forms (animals and insects) and finally the human body with its five senses (indriyan), five sense organs and the mind (mana).

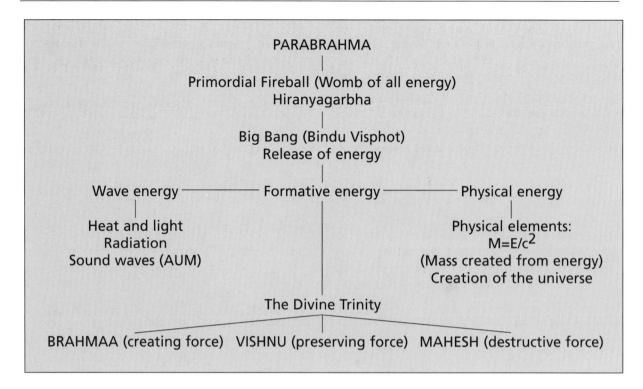

In *Hinduism, the Universal Truth*, Dr B.K. Modi explains that Hindus associate the scientific evolution of the universe with metaphysical and spiritual values. As the creator, the ultimate reality (Parabrahma) releases energy, the universe is created and also the three divine forces evolve. These forces have been given the form of Brahmaa (creator), Vishnu (preserver) and Mahesh or Shiva (destroyer). This idea of the evolution of the divine trinity with the creation is presented pictorially by Dr Modi:

IN THE CLASSROOM

At KS3 and KS4, ask pupils for their views about how the world was created. Let them decide if their view is based on myth or scientific evidence.

Invite a scientist and a believer to talk about their respective views of creation. Attempt to contrast the scientific view and the religious view. Do you see any difference? Should there be any difference? Can science always provide an explanation for the wonders and mysteries of the universe? It is important to realize that in Hinduism there is no conflict between science and religion. Science is treated as the study of nature. Hindus believe that the study of creation and nature can bring one closer to the truth and closer to God.

Typical questions/discussion points
1. Can human beings ever find out how the world was created?
2. Compare known religious views about creation with known scientific theories. Is there any conflict? Does the Hindu point of view conflict with science?
3. If scientific theories of the 'Big Bang' and evolution are right what are the implications for religious belief?
4. Am I more than a collection of chemicals?

The Six Schools of Hindu Philosophy: the Darshan Shastras

One can rightly speak of God only after one has seen Him. Only he who has seen God knows really and truly that God has form and that He is formless as well. He has many other aspects that cannot be described.

(SRI RAMAKRISHNA)

The Sanskrit word for philosophy is 'Darshan'. Darshan means seeing or direct perception; it means a view of life. In India philosophy is not considered as an intellectual exercise but a way of life leading to direct experience of God or reality.

Humans have a natural curiosity and want to understand about themselves and the world they live in. Who am I? What is the nature of this world? Is there a God? If so, what is his nature? Is there life after death? If so, how can we attain it? What is the meaning and purpose of life? Why is there so much suffering in this world? Is it possible for us to have permanent happiness?

These questions have been asked by all of us at some time or other. Their answers have also been sought by Hindu seers. After deep pondering some of the seers have found the answers and these answers are collectively called the Vedas (see pp.130–132). 'Veda' means knowledge – knowledge of God, of the other world, of the meaning of life and so on. We must remember that these answers are intuitive revelations and not intellectual cogitations. The essence of the Vedas is known as Vedanta. The Vedas have become the basis of Hinduism.

Later, some people tried to understand these revelations through intellect. Since reason has its limitations this has led to different interpretations. Thus came into existence several schools of Indian philosophy. Broadly all these different schools can be classified into six. Again, there is so much similarity between some of them that they are divided into three groups of two systems each.

These are:
1. Nyaya and Vaiseshika;
2. Sankhya and Yoga;
3. Mimamsa and Vedanta.

The six systems of Hindu thought are:

1. Vaiseshika Darshana by Kanada: dealing with atomic pluralism. His doctrine was that the world has originated from atoms (Paramanus).

2. Nyaya Darshana by Gautama: dealing with logical realism. He maintained that the world of matter consisted of five basic elements (Panch bhoot), namely earth, fire, water, air and sky or ether.

3. Sankhya Darshan by Kapila: dealing with the evolution of the universe. He propounded the dualistic theory of matter (Prakriti) and soul (Purusha). Purusha was to use Prakriti as a vehicle for its emancipation.

4. Yoga Darshan by Patanjali: dealing with the path towards perfection. The chief aim of Yoga philosophy is to teach the means by which the human soul may merge into divinity.

5. Mimamsa Darshan by Jaimini: dealing with the Karma Kanda of the Vedas. It also discusses various difficult points in the Vedic texts.

6. Vedanta or Uttara Mimamsa by Veda Vyas: dealing with one eternal principle, that of Brahma or the supreme spirit. It is called Vedanta because the word means 'end or summary of the Vedas'.

In addition to these, an atheistic school, known as Charvaka or Lokayata, also existed; this had its own theories regarding the origin of the universe. This materialistic philosophy was termed 'Lokayatam' and its basic tenet was: 'Since the existence of God cannot be proved through the senses, God does not exist.' For a number of centuries this philosophy continued to be held by a small number of rationalists, but Charvaka was the last in the line of materialist philosophers. This school lost ground in a free and fair fight with other philosophies. It was neither banned nor suppressed, however, and today there are still atheists in the Hindu community; they may not believe in God-the-Creator, but they remain Hindus.

Other Hindu philosophical schools initiated by Gautama Buddha and Mahavira Jain also exist but they do not follow the Vedas. The most popular school in modern times is the Vedanta, mainly as a result of the efforts of Swami Vivekananda. Vedanta has three branches:

1. Advaita Vedanta, believing in absolute non-dualism (monoism) and lead by Acharyas Shankara (788 CE) and Vidyaranya;

2. Visistadvaita Vedanta, believing in qualified non-dualism and lead by Acharyas Ramanuja (1027 CE) and Chaitanya.

3. Dvaita Vedanta, believing in dualism and lead by Archaryas Madhva (1199 CE) and Vallabha.

These six systems of thought are also called orthodox because they accepted the Vedas as authoritative and canonical. Strictly speaking, the seers like Kanada, Gautama and so on are not the founders because these thoughts were prevalent long before their time. They simply made those thoughts more systematic and disseminated them more widely.

Moreover, these six systems referred to above are not mutually contradictory, though in certain of their theories they would seem to be so. They really represent a progressive development from truth to higher truth to the highest truth. While Nyaya and Vaiseshika prepare the mind for philosophic thought, Sankhya explains the nature of the world and Yoga shows the way of concentration and self-control. Purva Mimamsa directs the mind of man to higher thoughts through rituals. Vedanta takes the best elements from all these systems and harmoniously combines them.

All the systems believe that the essence of humanity is the immortal self or Atman. All accept the fact that life in the world is full of misery. All accept that ignorance about reality is the cause of bondage and difficulties. All accept that liberation (Moksha) is the goal of life and that it can be attained either through mind-control or by the grace of God.

Although these systems seem to differ in many ways in fact they are talking about the same thing in different words, thus the confusion is only superficial. The point to remember is that God exists; life has a meaning and purpose; one can be happy only by realizing God and obtaining true knowledge about one's real nature. There are many paths leading to this realization and different religions of the world are different pathways leading to the same goal, i.e. God or reality.

Adherence to Truth

Mahatma Gandhi was a Hindu. He called himself a seeker after truth and he made practical use of Hindu philosophy. His practice of respecting all religions and his political strategy of 'Satyagraha' (adherence to truth) were based on Hindu scriptures such as the Bhagavad Gita. This earned him the admiration of millions throughout the world.

IN THE CLASSROOM

Ask pupils to observe different people – their classmates, perhaps. Some of them are

cheerful; some are gloomy. Some work hard; others do not. Some are born optimists; some are pessimists. All these varieties of behaviour, of course, stem from the particular view each person holds about life and its purpose. This 'view' about life is called philosophy. Our views remain confined, generally, to this world alone, but sometimes we wonder about higher things like God, life after death, etc. That is when serious philosophy begins.

Every nation has produced great philosophers and their views have often influenced the national way of life. However, no nation should think that it has answers to all questions; each one has grasped just a bit of the truth. Hence it would be wrong for any nation to think that what it alone has understood is the truth and that others are wrong. This type of thinking breeds fanaticism, hatred and wars. This is why people of different religions quarrel with each other. If we accept the fact that each one of us understands 'truth' in our own way, there would be more peace, harmony and co-operation on this earth.

Typical questions/discussion points
1. Do you think we need a philosophy about life?
2. What is the nature of true philosophy?
3. What is the meaning and the goal of life?
4. Are religions relevant these days?
5. Why is it that some people remain calm even under trying conditions while others cannot?
6. How can we know what is true? Can we ever be certain?
7. Are there different kinds of truth? Does truth remain the same for all time?

The Tantric Tradition

Tantrism is one form of the Shaktism branch of Hinduism. It is a system of practices used for spiritual uplifting. This topic is not included in any school RE syllabus but is briefly described here for the sake of completeness. Most of the Tantra literature is still kept secret and therefore often attracts the attention of researchers from the West.

Significance of geometrical patterns

Shri Yantra

Triangles, squares, pentagons and circles represent various forms and manifestations of energy. The three sides of a triangle represent the three Gunas (see p.41) and the three functions (creation, preservation and destruction) of divinity (see the Hindu Trinity referred to on p.22). The upward and downward triangles indicate the balance maintained by nature. The nine triangles of a Shri Yantra represent the various names of Shakti (strength). Shakti is one of the goddesses worshipped at Navaratri, the festival of nine nights (see p.99). The pentagon in the middle represents the five physical elements, the building blocks of this universe (see p.40). The circle depicts the cyclic nature of time and creation (see p.42).

Generally, most Hindus do not discuss Tantrism because parts of it deal with black magic and also with male and female sexuality. The Tantric tradition can be described as an experiment in exploring the human senses and using sexual energy for spiritual uplifting. Unfortunately, most Tantric literature, paintings and sculptures are viewed as erotic art. Erotic rituals are against the basic fundamentals of Hinduism.

Shakta Hindus worship the goddess called Shakti or Devi. In different parts of India different goddesses are popular. For example, the goddess Shri or Lakshmi, seen as the embodiment of good fortune and wealth, is popular in southern India, whereas in the north, particularly in Bengal, Kaali, the source of wisdom and liberation, is worshipped.

An important aspect of the Tantric or Shaktism tradition is the use of complex geometrical figures known as Yantras. These are based on mathematical forms. Yantras are pictorial representations of Mantras (thoughts). One of the most important Yantras is Sri Yantra or Yoni Chakra which is often seen in Shakti temples. The central focal point of a Yantra is a dot (Bindu) which represents the origin of all creation (see p.42).

The most positive aspect of Tantrism is its knowledge of the vast untapped Kundalini energy in the human body. This is a mysterious force which is believed to lie dormant in the human body until awakened through yogic practice. According to this system, there are seven psychic centres, called Chakras, in the body, starting from the base of the spine to the topmost point of the head. These Chakras, also known as gates of subtle energy, are associated with endocrine glands (along the length of the body): adrenal, sexual, pancreas, thymus, thyroid, pineal and pitvitory.

Leading medical experts now accept that skilled Yoga practitioners can override the autonomic nervous system which controls vital functions. Yogis can change their heart rate, bring metabolism to near halt, lower blood pressure and lower body temperature.

Special People

Hinduism was not founded by one particular person or one book. However, there are a large number of significant people who have guided Hinduism at various times.

Rishis and Rishikas – great thinkers

'Rishi' is the word used by Hindus to describe a seer who understood the secrets of the Holy Vedas and helped to propagate them. 'Rishika' is a woman seer. Hindus believe that Rishis and Rishikas were great men and women to whom divine knowledge was revealed. In *Essays on the Religion and Philosophy of the Hindus*, H.T. Coolebrooke rightly called a Rishi a seer by whom the text was seen. There is an erroneous view put forward by some Western scholars and their Indian followers that Rishis are the composers whose names are mentioned in the Vedic verses (Mantras). The following extracts are brief definitions of Rishis found in Hindu scriptures:

The original seers were the men who saw or perfectly understood the Dharma.

(YASKACHARYA IN NIRUKTA, 1-91)

The Rishis are 'Mantra Drashta' – seers of Mantras.

(NIRUKTA, 2-11)

Those that after tapas or deep meditation realised the secret of the Vedic Mantras, became Rishis by the Grace of the Almighty.

(TAITTIRIYA ARANYAK, 2-9-1)

It is important to note that this divine knowledge was not revealed only to men, but also to women seers. Drs Kapildev Dwivedi and Bhartendu Dwivedi, in *Status of Women in the Vedas*, state that 224 Mantras in the Rig Veda were 'seen' by twenty-four Rishikas and 198 Mantras in the Atharva Veda were 'seen' by five Rishikas.

Hindus believe that the Holy Vedas are eternal and their knowledge was revealed to the great thinkers (Rishis and Rishikas). These thinkers and philosophers preached their teachings in various ways: some ran large residential universities called Gurukula, some established monasteries called Ashramas, while others acted as advisors/residential priests to kings. After graduation their students often started new establishments. It is estimated that there were up to 1100 different schools of scriptural knowledge in ancient India, which helps to explain why there is so much diversity in Hinduism.

Out of many Rishis whose thoughts and teachings have influenced the Hindu way of life, seven are specially mentioned in prayers. Their names and the meaning of their names, representing their qualities, are shown in the table below.

Hindu Rishis have also composed many books. The six Darshan Shastras of philosophy and several of the Upanishads recording discussions between a teacher and a disciple are some of the notable texts written by Rishis. Further details have been given earlier on pp.126, 130, 146 and 152. The contribution made by the Rishis has come to be widely known only in the post-colonial period. Academics in British universities previously thought that 'ancient philosophy' meant Greek philosophy but are now starting to appreciate the influence of the thinking of the Hindu Rishis of ancient India on other nations. During his Nehru Memorial Talk on

NAME OF RISHI	VEDIC MEANING	PHYSICAL ASPECT
Vasistha	The best	Prana (vital breath)
Bharadvaja	Bearer of knowledge	Mind
Vishvamitra	Friend of all, listens to all	Ear
Jamadagni	Protector of all, light	Eye
Angira	Source of life	Prana (vital breath)
Vishwa Karma	Doer of all work	Speech
Gautama	Remover of ignorance	Rules

the subject of 'Indian Forerunners of Greek Philosophy' delivered at the Manchester Metropolitan University, Dr David Melling stated, 'Even on the conservative datings of the early Upanishads accepted by most modern scholars, the earliest Upanishadic texts recording philosophical dialogues predate the earliest Greek philosophical texts by two hundred and fifty to three hundred years.'

Rama and Krishna
These two names are the most popular among Hindus. The story of Rama is given in the Ramayana (see pp.134–138) and the stories of Krishna are described on pp.143–146.

Mahavira Jain, Gautama Buddha and Guru Nanak
Hinduism is the foundation of Jainism, Buddhism and Sikhism, founded by Mahavira Jain, Gautama Buddha and Guru Nanak respectively (see pp.47–49).

Other religious and social reformers
In the long history of Hinduism, there have been many religious and social reformers. The founders of some of the popular modern reformist movements are mentioned on pp.49–50.

IN THE CLASSROOM

The idea of 'Rishis' and 'Rishikas' as seers of knowledge can be introduced by starting a discussion on how human beings acquire knowledge. Scientific knowledge has been accumulated over many years and is passed on by generations of teachers to their students. However, all branches of scientific knowledge can eventually be traced back to a small number of individuals who originally thought of an idea or discovered something new. This intuitive thinking or the occurrence of an idea is similar to the Hindu concept of 'seeing' knowledge, and a seer of that knowledge is called a Rishi.

Ask pupils to discuss which people are special and why they are considered special. Why do religious people believe that someone is special? This should help to clarify the concept of religious leaders and founders. It

should be explained that Hinduism has no one specific founder.

Typical questions/discussion points
1. According to Hindu belief, how was knowledge revealed to humankind?
2. How did Hindu Rishis spread this knowledge?

Sanskrit – the Common Language of Hindu Scriptures

Sanskrit is the language of the Hindu religion and culture. It originated in India. There are theories linking Sanskrit with other Indo-European, Indo-Iranian and Indo-Aryan families of languages. Some theories, which began in the nineteenth century, try to locate the original source of Sanskrit outside India, but these theories are not proven. They do, however, point out abundant similarities in structure, phonetics, grammar and vocabulary with ancient European languages such as Latin, Zend Avesta, German and Greek, and with Middle Eastern languages such as Persian and Arabic. Many words denoting the names of limbs, numerals and natural elements, for example, are identical and come from a common root. These interesting facts invite further, deeper and unbiased research in the field of linguistics and phonetics.

Sanskrit's beginning is very old and the exact date of its origin has not been discovered. The Vedas form the earliest Sanskrit literature and these are known to be several thousand years old. The Vedas, Upanishads (Vedanta), Ramayana, Mahabharata, Bhagavad Gita and Puranas are all in Sanskrit. Even the Hindu prayers used today are in Sanskrit. Many words, such as Puja, Mandir, Dev, Devi, Deepa, Havan, Yajna, names of Hindu gods and goddesses, festivals, days and months in the Hindu calendar, all come from this ancient language.

In India and abroad, Sanskrit is studied in order to gain insight into ancient scriptures, philosophy and classical literature of Hinduism.

There are several names for this ancient language of India. Some traditions hold the language to be holy as it is believed to have been created by God, hence the name 'Dev Vani'. It is also treated as sacred because all the scriptures of Hinduism are written in this language. To write in Sanskrit or to understand works written in Sanskrit is held to be prestigious and scholarly by Hindus because in ancient times it was the language of priests, royal courts, great poets and other intellectual academics.

Sanskrit is in use even today. More than 100,000 speak this language and several million people can understand it. There are some forty-five magazines and periodicals relating to Sanskrit and it is studied in schools and colleges both in India and abroad. Chanda Mama is a monthly digest, popular throughout India for stories and comic strips. In a court case in 1994, the Supreme Court in India passed the judgement that Sanskrit is the cultural language of India. In addition, several radio stations in India and Germany broadcast daily news in Sanskrit.

Other regional languages developed from the fifth century BCE and have gradually replaced Sanskrit. Attempts are being made by organizations like Samskrita Bharati to revive this ancient, pure and perfect language through daily conversation. Sanskrit homes and villages have been formed where people are introduced to the language and learn to speak it. The participants in these projects – Sanskrit Conversation Camps – for popularizing spoken Sanskrit, say that, in their experience, it takes a mere ten days (of two hours daily) to learn this so-called 'dead language'.

Some salient features of Sanskrit
1. It is India's most ancient language, yet also a living language of today. Its name literally means 'well polished', 'refined' or 'perfected'.

2. It is the fountainhead of all the basic Hindu scriptures and is considered to be the root of the entire Indian culture.

3. It is the mother of all the Indian languages. As a root language it has also influenced enormously many world languages.

4. Most of the basic and original scriptures – treatises of Hindu religious rituals, prayers,

Indian philosophy, old Indian sciences, arts and culture – are found in Sanskrit literature.

5. In grammar and etymology, Sanskrit is held to be perfect and the most suitable for computers. Research is under way to adopt Sanskrit for computer use.

6. Sanskrit is very flexible in style. It is known for its brevity and clarity. It is also remarkable for long, compound sentences. Poet Bana's single sentence runs to thirteen printed pages and one word of his (in the Kadambari novel) runs for twenty-one printed lines! Such compound words and sentences are one of the wonders of Sanskrit. Yet the language is also known for clarity in expression.

7. Sanskrit is well known for its logical grammar. Panini, who lived in the sixth century BCE, built this edifice of grammar. It was after his finishing touches that the language came to be called Sanskrit – polished, refined, perfected. Surprisingly, it has remained literally unchanged since Panini formed its perfect grammatical skeleton, retaining its pure form for over 2600 years.

8. The language is basically musical. Each syllable in any Vedic word, for example, is invariably spelt in a prescribed note or accent. The five different notes in the Vedic recitation contain the seeds of classical Indian music, one of the principal styles in the musical world.

9. The script used for writing Sanskrit is called Devanagari. This script is used to write Hindi, Nepali and Marathi languages and they also are written from left to right. Many Indian languages, such as Gujarati, Punjabi and Bengali, are written in scripts which bear a resemblance to the Devanagari script.

10. The thirty-three consonants of the Devanagari script represent the thirty-three Devatas (qualities of God) mentioned in Hindu scriptures.

IN THE CLASSROOM

Language is needed to convey ideas and pass on knowledge. Ask pupils to find out the

एकम् सत् विप्रा बहुधा वदन्ति

Ekam sat vipraa bahuda vadanti

Truth is one, wise men call it by different names.

असतो मा सद् गमय ।
तमसो मा ज्योतिर्गमय ।
मृत्योर्मा अमृतं गमय ।

Asato maa sad gamaya.
Tamaso maa jyotir gamaya.
Mrityorma amritma gamaya.

Lead us from untruth to truth,
from darkness to light
and from death to immortality

Some examples of Sanskrit text with their pronunciation and meaning; both are from Hindu scriptures.

languages in which holy books of various religions are written. Since the holy books are usually very old, their language must also be of ancient origin. Ask pupils to try to find out the names of the oldest holy books of Hinduism and the language they are written in.

Typical questions/discussion points
1. What does the name 'Sanskrit' mean?
2. What are the other names of Sanskrit?
3. Why is the Sanskrit language believed to be holy by Hindus?
4. Which is the oldest book in world literature?
5. Which is the longest literary work in the world?

Geometry in Hindu Scriptures

Area of a triangle: Aryabhata in 476 AD stated that the area of a triangle is the product of 1/2 of any side and the perpendicular from the opposite vertex.

Baudhayana Sutra Pythagoras Theorem) This theorem now known as Pythagoras theorem was stated in the Shulva Sutras 1000 years before Pythagoras. The Sanskrit script states that the diagonal of a rectangle produces by itself both the areas produced separately by its two sides.

Pi: Aryabhata gave the value of Pi by the formula, 'Add 4 to 100, multiply by 8 and then add 62000; the result is approximately the circumference of a circle of diameter of 20000. This gives the value of Pi = 3.1416

CHAPTER SIX
SOCIAL AND MORAL ISSUES

*T*his chapter is intended for use at Key Stage 4 and for students taking Religious Studies GCSE and A-Level examinations. At this stage, some syllabuses place emphasis on the development of critical skills in the evaluation of the responses of various religious beliefs to contemporary issues, with particular reference to moral, personal and social areas of human life.

Topics recommended in various RE syllabuses have been selected and researched to find the appropriate response from the Hindu point of view. It is not always easy to find a direct reference to an issue because of the enormity of the scriptural texts available in Hinduism. Furthermore, present-day issues are by definition spelt out in modern language; this means that a certain amount of interpretation is needed, which, for the purposes of education, is best left to Hindus who are practising in the faith. While teachers and pupils are of course free to make up their own minds about how Hinduism tackles the issues, the material in the following sections provides the typical response expected from a Hindu. Suggestions for classroom work can be found at the end of the chapter.

Marriage and Family

Marriage
Marriage is one of the most popular and important of the sixteen Hindu sacraments or Sanskaras (see p.65). The religious conception of marriage is that it is a union of two souls enjoying peace and prosperity at home. Marriage bonds the bride and bridegroom in spiritual ties of love and liberty, equality and integrity. They become one soul living in two bodies. This is reflected in the following verse traditionally recited by the bridegroom whilst addressing the bride:

> *I am what thou art, Thou art what I am*
> *I am the psalm and Thou art the verse*
> *I am the heaven and Thou art the earth*
> *May we live together, to produce progeny.*
>
> (ATHARVA VEDA, 14-2-71)

Marriage is a sacred duty incumbent upon every normal, healthy person. According to Taittiriya Brahmana (Chapter11, pp.4–7): 'Marriage is a sacrifice and one who does not enter the married life is an incomplete person. He on his own is a "half man", the second half is his wife.'

Both husband and wife enjoy equal rights. Both are masters of one house and are equal owners. Both enjoy the same prestige, power and position and neither is subordinate to the other. For the performance of religious duties, such as Yajna, both are required to sit together.

According to the Hindu view, marriage is based on noble sentiments of love, self-sacrifice and self-denial that help to uplift the human race. The primary function of marriage is to fulfil one's obligations towards society and provide continuity of the human race by giving birth to children.

Hindu marriages are solemnized in front of the sacred fire. Offerings made to the fire symbolize the vows taken to perform selfless service based on mutual give and take. The wedding ceremony is described on p.67.

Marriage and family life
Marriage marks the start of the second and most important stage (Ashrama) of life called the Grihastha Ashrama (family life). At this

stage, as a householder, a person is at his or her most productive stage and is meant to participate in the economic life of the country. The other three stages – student life, retirement and renunciation – depend on this one. The Manu Smruti (6-90) states: 'Just as the waters of tributaries and rivers ultimately come to rest in the ocean, the three other ashramas depend for their support on the Grihastha ashrama.'

Arranged marriages

This time-honoured and well-tested tradition of Hinduism is often misunderstood and misrepresented. The most common misunderstanding is that the arranged marriage is mistakenly thought of as a forced marriage, and then wrongly criticized for lack of freedom and lack of choice. In a properly arranged marriage, agreement is sought from everyone involved and the question of force does not arise. If a person is suitably prepared to accept the responsibility of marriage, then lack of freedom or choice does not matter.

Hindu law-givers, such as Manu, Gautama and Yajnavalkya, define the following eight forms of marriage, of which only the first four were preferred and considered lawful.

1. Brahma Vivah: the most sacred and cultured form. The bride, duly clad and adorned with ornaments, is given to a compatible bridegroom in the presence of friends and relations.

2. Prajapatya Vivah: a simpler form of Brahma Vivah. Vows of inseparable companionship and performance of duties are emphasized.

3. Daiva Vivah: the marriage performed between a bride and the priest at the altar. This tradition is now obsolete.

4. Arsha Vivah: a form in which gifts to the father of the bridegroom are given. This is now avoided because it could be construed as a disguised sale of the daughter.

5. Gandharva Vivah: a form of marriage by mutual consent, generally consummated in secret without the presence of parents and without any rites or ceremonies.

6. Asura Vivah: involves the purchase of a bride.

7. Rakshasa Vivah: forced marriage in which the maiden is forcibly abducted.

8. Paishacha Vivah: involves marriage by deceiving the bride.

Among these eight types of marriage, only the first two are highly rated because they are solemnized with the proper consent of the parents and the bride and the bridegroom. This system of marriage is therefore a common practice among Hindus. The choosing of a husband by a woman is known as 'Swayamvara' (self choice) and has been the tradition since the period of the epic Ramayana. Under this system, the elders or wise members of the family help the bride/bridegroom to seek a partner in his/her life. They compare the age, education, health, physique, temperament, likes and dislikes and other qualities of prospective persons. If found compatible, they can become future partners, but it is their 'yes' or 'no' that counts. The advantages of this system are that the wisdom and experience of elders who are deeply interested in the welfare of the couple are made available to them. The elders do not force their decision on the couple. In practice this system has worked and helped to establish stable families and long-lasting relationships.

Divorce

The Hindu view has always stressed that marriage is a long-lasting relationship based on love, affection and mutual give and take. It is not a temporary contract which can be terminated by either side. Promiscuity is not encouraged since it is not conducive to the creation of happy and stable families and the upbringing of children. The problem of divorce generally arises because of incompatibility and lack of mutual adjustment. Every effort is made in Hindu families to minimize and if possible remove the basic causes leading to a divorce. The prayer is that the wife enters her husband's house as its ideal mistress to enjoy a full life of a hundred years. This is what is said when the newly wedded bride enters her husband's house:

Remain awake
As intelligent and alert woman
Enjoying full life of a hundred years
Enter the house as its ideal mistress
May the creator bestow on thee long life.

(ATHARVA VEDA, 14-2-75)

In cases where divorce occurs then remarriage is allowed, as it is after the death of a partner.

Sexuality

In Hinduism human sexuality has a clear purpose. Sexual union is intended to express and foster love's beautiful intimacy between husband and wife with the prime objective of procreation. The earliest Vedic records indicate that Hindu society had a very natural and healthy attitude towards sexuality. Its power was recognized and considered as the origin of all living things.

Hindu seers have always recognized that the sexual instinct in man is natural. It should not be denounced, so long as it is within the limits and laws of nature. Attraction between the sexes is also natural and cannot be curbed by force. Suppression of sex is detrimental to health but unrestrained indulgence in sex is poisonous. The Hindu seers proposed a balanced and well-planned system of life. They divided the life of a person into four stages called Ashramas (see p.64), roughly corresponding to about twenty-five years each. The first stage is one of learning, called Brahmacharya. During this stage, individuals are required to concentrate on learning and building a strong mind and body by remaining celibate. During the second stage of life – the stage of householder, called Grihastha Ashrama – the individual can marry. Only during this stage is sex allowed between husband and wife. There are ethics and morals on sexual behaviour; if sex is divorced from ethics, the consequences will be disastrous.

There are a number of ancient texts in Sanskrit in which human sexuality has been seriously studied and the rich variety of expression of the emotion of love has been explained. The best-known text is the Kama Sutra. The word 'Kama' in the Vedic texts is used in the sense of desire, the first impulse for creation. It is sad that through reinterpretation these texts have been turned into cheap erotic books.

Male and female roles

In Hinduism certain patterns of behaviour and conduct have been set for both men and women.

Men

1. Sex outside marriage is not allowed.

2. A man should be loyal to his wedded wife.

3. A man should consider all women except his wife as mother.

4. The main purpose of sex in married life should be the procreation of children.

Women

1. A woman should keep her chastity before marriage.

2. A woman should be loyal to her wedded husband.

3. As mother, a woman is considered to be the first teacher (guru) of a child.

4. A woman is an equal partner with her husband not only in sexual life but also in other fields, in Dharma (duties), Artha (wealth, its acquisition and protection) and Moksha (salvation). According to the law-giver Manu, 'Where women are honoured, there the Gods are pleased; but where they are not honoured, no sacred rites yield rewards.'

5. Woman is considered as the personification of beauty. Famous Sanskrit poets and playwrights such as Valmiki, Vyasa and Kalidas have described the physical charms of their heroines in their respective works.

6. Woman's role as sister is given a very special status in Hinduism. The festivals of Raksha Bandhan and Bhaiya Dooj are dedicated to this pious relation.

7. Womanhood is believed to represent power (Shakti) behind all the functions of God. In

Hinduism, the status of woman is raised to the level of goddess.

Ravindranath Tagore recognizes two distinct aspects of womanhood: the one which allures and excites, and the other which sobers the passion and chastens the mind of man.

Homosexuality

Sexual power is one of the precious gifts of God and should be used properly. It is necessary to conserve and make healthy use of sex in a natural way. Sexual activity between persons of the same sex does not create progeny; it is therefore considered to be an improper use of a God-given gift and hence it is discouraged. Indulging in homosexuality is harmful to all parties and is now known to cause the spread of diseases like AIDS. It is also against nature and the natural order of things.

Contraception, abortion and chastity

These issues arise in the context of population control, lack of sexual restrictions and the medical grounds of modern times. Contraception and abortion are means of mitigating the bad effects of excessive or uncontrolled indulgence in sex. In Hinduism, emphasis is laid on the prevention of the root causes of these problems rather than a resort to remedies for the consequences of misuse. In the scriptures, the importance of moderation in conjugal life is pointed out.

A man is always advised to look upon all women except his wife as mothers. A woman is to endeavour to follow the ideals of chastity and undivided loyalty to her husband. The image of woman as wife is one of chastity, selfless service and devotion. At the same time, woman is worshipped as creative power – 'Shakti'. In the words of the Nobel laureate Rabindranath Tagore, 'True womanliness is regarded in our country as the saintliness of love. It is not merely praised there but literally worshipped; and she who is gifted with it is called Devi, as one revealing in herself Woman, the divine.'

Illegitimate sexual intercourse and unnecessary child-bearing are generally avoided by following certain basic rules of conduct. Many stories in the Hindu epics illustrate the advantages of following these codes of conduct and the disadvantages of breaking the rules. If one does not follow these rules one may be committing a sin and should be prepared to suffer its consequences.

The Hindu view is that life starts at the time of conception; abortion, therefore, involves taking a life and this is a sin which will bring about its inevitable consequences, if not in this life then in the coming lives. Hinduism makes no attempt to condone or make anyone feel sorry for undergoing an experience of this kind because the consequences are borne deep within the mind of anyone who has had such an experience. There are several specific injunctions in Hindu scriptures against abortion. For example, Krishna Yajur Veda (6-5-10) says, 'Therefore, a slayer of an embryo is like the slayer of a priest.'

However, scriptures do provide an answer to this ethical quandary by considering the various reasons or causes leading to abortion. Kautilya, in his famous Arthashastra (verse 229), says, 'When a person causes abortion in pregnancy by striking, by medicine, or by annoyance, the highest, middle and lesser punishments shall be imposed respectively.'

The ancient Ayurveda medical text mentions one situation where abortion may be allowed. It is described in Sushruta Samhita, Chikitsasthana (15-1-11): 'In an irredeemable situation, it is best to cause the miscarriage of the foetus, for no means must be neglected which can prevent the loss of the mother.'

Creation

Hindus do not believe that human beings were created or born out of an original sin. They are always regarded as offspring of divine immortals (Amrutasya putrah). According to the Vedas, the dawn of creation began without cohabitation. The origin of human beings is always traced to a great Rishi (sage) and each Rishi has created a Gotra (persons hailing from the same ancestor) of people.

There are many creation stories in Hindu mythology. The most popular one is from the Puranas which refers to Brahma creating pairs of opposites – good and evil, light and dark, etc. – from his body. The real theories of creation are given in the Vedas and the Upanishads. The Atharva Veda (4-2-7) says:

*In the beginning was Hiranyagarbha
    (Golden Womb),
  the seed of elemental existence.*

The word 'Hiranyagarbha', also meaning womb of energy, suggests that at the beginning all energy was concentrated at a point. This idea is remarkably similar to the 'Big Bang' theory which is now universally accepted. The Hindu view about the creation of the universe is fully described on pp.156–158.

Death

Life after death

According to Hindu scriptures, the union of the soul with the body is called birth. Birth takes place when the soul enters a body. Severance of the link between the body and the soul is death. It is only the body that dies, not the soul. The soul is immortal, it continues its journey. It is said in the Gita (Chapter 2, verse 23): 'No weapon can cut it, no fire can burn it, no wind can dry it and no water can drench it.'

The Hindu concept of reincarnation has already been described on pp.26–28. This concept explains life after death and is summarized in the Gita (Chapter 2, verse 22): 'As a man casting off old worn-out garments takes new ones, so the embodied self having cast off old bodies assumes new ones.' The soul thus passes through a cycle of births and deaths until it attains salvation (Moksha). Salvation consists of the total absorption of the soul into the existence of God, the Absolute. It is the emancipation of the soul from the cycles of births and deaths.

The passing of the soul through a succession of births is called the doctrine of rebirth (Punarjanma). The transmigration into another body is governed by the Law of Action (Karma). This means that the future of the soul is determined by its own past actions. It has to reap what it has sown. Whilst undergoing the fruits of its past actions, the soul is free to act in each birth and can determine its future. By adopting a proper course of action, it can achieve salvation earlier.

Suffering

The explanation for human suffering and misery is accounted for in Hindu philosophy by the Law of Action (Karma). As stated earlier, the soul cannot avoid the fruits of its past action. If it has performed good deeds in the past it is bound to enjoy happiness. In the same way if it has performed bad deeds, it has to suffer. Thus current suffering arises because of evil actions done in the past. The fruits of one's actions will occur in this birth, and if not completed in this birth will be carried forward to the succeeding birth or births until it is completed. By surrendering oneself to God it may be possible to mitigate the suffering but it cannot be entirely avoided. This is illustrated by the story of Yudhishthira in the epic Mahabharata.

The reason for suffering is thus explained. Hinduism asserts that it is the duty of good people to help relieve the suffering of others by sharing their pains and sorrows. This view is reflected in a Sanskrit saying: 'We have to look upon others as we look upon ourselves' ('Atmavad sarvabhuteshu yah pashyati sa pashyati').

Bereavement

The loss of near and dear ones always brings distress to anyone, but nothing can be done to bring back the dead. It is through sympathy extended by others and true knowledge that one gets over the pain of separation. Hindu scriptures look upon death as inevitable, explaining it as the passage of a soul to another body. The soul is deathless, so wise men do not cry or yearn for those who have departed. The Gita says: 'Wise are they who mourn neither for the dead nor for the living' (Chapter 2, verse 11). In Hindu philosophy, pondering over death is darkness.

The bereavement process involves funeral rites (see Antyeshti Sanskar on p.68) which include preparing the body, cremation, bone-gathering, the dispersal of the ashes, home purification and commemorative ceremonies. The involvement of the whole family and the community in general helps the bereavement process.

No one can explain the happenings between death and rebirth, but the happenings between birth and death can be explained. Furthermore, death is certain to be followed by rebirth or salvation: it is not the end of everything.

Suicide and euthanasia

The chief motives for suicide are a sense of defeat, frustration, helplessness or failure. Hindu philosophy always urges people to strive and to act but to leave the results or fruits of action in the hands of God. One has to strive for one's salvation, and try to achieve the four goals of life (duty, wealth, happiness and salvation) constantly. Suicide is therefore not sanctioned. The Yajur Veda (40-3) clearly states: 'The one who tries to escape from the trials of life by committing suicide will suffer even more in the next life.'

The Hindu scriptures offer a way of avoiding frustration and defeatism whilst facing the struggles of life. They advocate Nishkama Karma (action without desire for the fruits of the action). One has to use every moment of one's life and all opportunities to achieve the goals of life. Nothing is achieved by committing suicide for one is not avoiding the fruits of one's past actions. In ancient times, in very exceptional cases, a person was allowed to give up life by renouncing food and water, generally as a form of spiritual penance. This, however, is at the stage in life when the person has fulfilled all their obligations to society and their fellow beings. There is a very

distinct qualitative difference between such self-willed death and suicide. Even then, cases of such self-willed death were extremely rare. In modern times this term is used as a euphemism to describe the gradual deterioration of a patient's condition.

Since suicide itself is not encouraged, the question of permitting euthanasia does not arise. Instead of helping a person to die, one must endeavour to relieve his suffering as much as possible and build up his morale to face the suffering. The fundamental Hindu view is that life on this earth is a gift from God and he alone can take it back.

Work and Leisure

There is nothing higher than human dignity.
(MAHABHARATA)

Work and leisure are essentially economic issues and these matters have been addressed in Hindu scriptures, in particular in the four Vedas, some of the Upanishads, Vidur Niti in the Mahabharata, Manu Smruti, Yajnavalkya Smruti and Kautilya's Arthashastra. Some of the texts are very ancient; indeed, in a book entitled *Hindu Economics – Eternal Economic Order*, Dr M.G. Bokare has asserted that the first book on economics was written in India. The basic terminology of economics – such

The Story of Yudhishthira's Suffering Recorded in the Mahabharata

In the epic Mahabharata, Yudhishthira is presented as a righteous and truthful character. However, in the middle of the fierce battle, in which the Pandavas were fighting against the Kauravas, he was involved in a plot to demoralize the commander of the enemy forces, Dronacharya. The scheme was to convey a false message to Dronacharya that his son Ashwathama had been killed. On hearing the news, Dronacharya sought confirmation from Yudhishthira whom he knew always spoke the truth. Yudhishthira knew that it was an elephant called Ashwathama that had been killed. As he said this to Dronacharya however, Krishna blew his conch so loudly that Dronacharya could not hear the word 'elephant'. This led him to believe that his own son had died. Dronacharya was disheartened and gave up fighting. Because of this event, and the part he played in deceiving Dronacharya, Yudhishthira had to undergo the sorrow of seeing hell and the suffering therein.

words as resources, consumption, production, exchange, distribution, taxation and laws – can be found in the Vedas.

Work

It is said in the Hindu scriptures that every man should work. A Sanskrit quotation from the scriptures, 'Udyogam Purusha Lakshanam', meaning the characteristic of human beings is work, conveys the message of the work ethic in Hinduism. Ideally, every person should earn his living through honest means. A social system was therefore devised so that everyone could be employed or self-employed. Thus we have a system of economics and social organization which has evolved over time. It is based on the principle that no one should be greedy and selfish and amass wealth beyond their need, nor should anyone snatch the wealth which belongs rightfully to another person. 'Work is worship' say some of the saints in Hinduism. It should be regarded as an act of worship of God.

Unemployment

There are two types of unemployment. The first one is where a person cannot work because of age, sickness, disability or other such reasons. The second one is where a person is able and willing to work but cannot find employment. In any social and cultural system it is desirable to make provision to deal with both these cases.

In Hindu society provision was made for the inability to work through the system of joint families, a kinship structure wider than the family (and known as the caste system) and through public charity from individuals, temples, monasteries and political rulers. In respect of the latter type of unemployment, Hindu sages worked out a social and economic system in which persons seeking work would find work. The object of the system is to ensure that everyone is happy, healthy and prosperous ('Sarve bhavantu sukhinah, sarve santu niramayah, sarve bhadrani pashyantu, ma kascid duhkhabhag bhavet'). One solution offered by Vidura, considered to be the epitome of wisdom in the Mahabharata, is self-employment. He says, 'Self-employment is the best status for men in

society.' This idea is currently being pursued by the economist and labour leader D.B. Thengadi, in his movement of industrial workers in India.

Retirement

In the Hindu system, this corresponds to the third stage in life, called Vanaprastha (see the description of the Ashramas on p.64). At this stage of life, a person should delegate his or her responsibilities in the family to children and grandchildren and gradually reduce involvement in running the family. More time is devoted to selfless service to society, giving advice and guidance to younger people and to spiritual advancement. It was designed to be a purposeful and useful stage of life with the aim of preventing the stress, worries and depression associated with stopping work. The younger members of the family had a duty to look after the elders and care for their health and happiness. The elders at this stage would also impart Hindu culture and Dharma to the children and see that they were brought up well. With suitable adaptations, this system is still valid and useful in the present day.

Voluntary and community work

Swami Vivekananda, the great Hindu monk, said that service to humanity is service to God. In this way he put in a few words the essence of Hindu philosophy on voluntary and community work. All branches of Hinduism have stressed the need to serve other human beings and society in a selfless manner. This concept does not end with human beings but extends to all living things – animals, birds, plants, trees and the environment. It is also stressed in Hindu Dharma that this service should be performed without expectation of any return, but treated as a service to God.

Service should be carried out with love and regard, with compassion and understanding, and without hurting the dignity or self-respect of the beneficiary. There is a tradition of voluntary and community work in Hindu society – work done anonymously without any desire for fame, praise or honour. The beneficiary should acknowledge the service done with gratitude and remember it always. He or she should not ask for more than is necessary and should endeavour to stand on his or her own feet as soon as possible.

There are numerous stories in Hindu epics, history and literature focusing on selfless service.

Wealth and Poverty

Hindu economics

The moral issue of wealth and poverty affects both individuals and nations. Poverty occurs because of an unequal distribution of wealth. Hindu economics, as disclosed in the Holy Vedas, is the economics of abundance, whereas Western economics is the economics of scarcity. This is the fundamental difference. In the world today wealth and resources are enjoyed by a few individuals and a few nations but most of the remaining people are suffering from want and other privations. In the Hindu view of life, God provides all the natural bounties and gifts which all human beings, animals and plants have an equal right to enjoy. The policy should be 'live and let live'. In practice, however, wealth and resources are accumulated in the hands of a few who try to exploit the others for their own benefit.

Hindu scriptures have laid down that a man may keep for himself what he needs. To hoard more than what he needs and deny its use to others is a sin. One should not be greedy since greed leads to evils. It is said in Yajur Veda (40-1) that everything in the universe belongs to God, that a person should enjoy what is bestowed on him and should not covet the wealth which is gifted to others. One should not consider oneself as the owner of God-given wealth but only as a trustee. One may amass wealth with hundreds of hands but should distribute it with thousands of hands. ('Shatahasta samahara sahasrahasta sankira', Atharva Veda, 3-24-5). To live is to give and give as long as you live. A spirit of contentment and renunciation leads to peace of mind. If these principles are put into practice, a lot of the problems of the world, such as poverty and misery, would not arise. It is also said that the happiness of the individual lies in the collective happiness of the society in which he lives. One should have warmth of love for all. What applies to individuals applies to nations also.

First and Third World relationship

In the modern world, wealth is concentrated in a small number of countries, known as the 'First World'. They use the major part of nature's bounties. The 'Third World', on the other hand, is poor and is generally exploited by the First World. The existing relationship centres on the selfish interests of nations and often upon their greed. Hindu sages have said that the whole world is one family (Vasudhaiva kutumbakam) and the relationship between First and Third Worlds should be based on this principle. If such a relationship is not developed, everyone will suffer sooner or later.

Aid

It is often pointed out that the developed nations are giving aid to developing nations and charities functioning in the developed countries are helping those who live in the Third World in various ways. Although this aid is a laudable objective, in practice what happens is that aid given is conditional and is based on certain advantages or returns to the donor. Owing to those conditions, the debt burden on developing countries is increasing. The Hindu view about aid is as follows:

1. All aid or help should be rendered without expectation of any returns or profit.

2. When giving aid, it should go to the most deserving persons/nations.

3. If someone keeps all that he accumulates for himself and does not give it to others, the hoarded wealth will eventually prove to be the cause of ruin (Rig Veda, 10-117-6).

4. Real charity is that which provides a permanent source of honest earning to the poor person, enabling him to stand on his own feet in the future. It should not result in encouraging the habit of begging.

5. Charity of any kind is good but the best is that of imparting knowledge. 'Sarveshameva Dananam Brahmadanam Vishishyate' (Manu Smruti).

These principles apply not only to individual charity but also to aid-giving nations. The greatness of a nation's character can be judged from the modes of its charity giving and receiving. Real charity elevates the lowly, enables the destitute to fend for themselves and reduces the differences between 'the haves' and 'the have nots'. Those who have learnt not to receive but to give achieve immortality (Dakshinavanto Amritam Bhajante).

Religiously inspired aid organization

All major world religions stress the importance of giving in charity. An individual is asked to give to charity from his earnings. Many Hindu temples organize aid projects. A new trend is emerging whereby funds are collected and distributed by religious organizations which employ professional staff. The motives of such cash-rich charities are often questioned. If charitable giving is used as a means of, or as an allurement to, conversion to a particular faith, the charity loses its real significance. The aim of religiously inspired charity organizations should not be proselytizing, nor should their giving be conditional on the recipient conforming to their line of religious thinking. The Hindu concept of Nishkama Karma (action without expecting anything in return) should be the guiding principle. Aid should not result in loss of self-respect, or destruction or uprooting of people's culture and values of life. Many Hindu organizations in India, like the Kalyan Ashram Trust, have expressed deep concern about the conversion of poor tribal people to Christianity or Islam as a direct result of the work of some religiously inspired aid organizations.

The purpose of charity should be to help the beneficiary help themselves in the future. If this is not the case, the basis of charity descends to the level of profit and advantage and no longer elevates either the giver or the receiver. It should be selfless and based on love and respect for the needy and for their faith.

Religion and Politics

The true source of rights is duty. If we all leave our duties unperformed, and run after rights, they will escape us like a will-o'-the-wisp. The more we pursue them, the farther will they fly.

(MAHATMA GANDHI)

Citizenship

According to Hindu scriptures, citizenship of a nation is a stage of the development of an individual. The individual belongs to a family and is part of it. However, one should not think only of the family but expand one's concern to think of the village, city, community, nation and ultimately the entire universe. An individual has certain duties (Nagarik Dharma) to discharge towards the nation, such as payment of taxes, defence of the country and Dharma (Desh and Dharma), and concern for the welfare of all citizens. The individual cannot achieve happiness all alone but needs a society and a nation. This concept is elucidated in the epic Ramayana, in which it is said that the mother and motherland are far superior to heaven.

Modern Hindu thinkers have made a distinction between state and nation. The state has a well-defined geographical boundary and is governed by certain laws. As a citizen of the state, one must obey the laws of the state and take a full part in its activities. The nation is associated with culture, history and ancestral links which are not bound by geographical limits. Membership of such a nation is permanent whereas citizenship of a state is not. One can migrate from one state to another but one cannot change one's ancestors and culture. In the Hindu view, there is no conflict between the two; one can be a good Hindu and still be a faithful citizen of one's chosen state. A story in the Mahabharata illustrates this point.

The five Pandav brothers were living incognito in another state during their exile. One night they discovered that their host village was being blackmailed by a demon and one member of their host's family had to be sacrificed. The Pandav brothers offered to help. Their help was refused on the grounds that they were just guests.

The Pandavs quoted the scriptures to convince the villagers that they had chosen to stay in the village, and it was their religious duty to share the villagers' problem. One of the Pandavs, Bhim, went and killed the demon.

Obedience

The ruler, whether he is the king or the head of state, whatever his title, should rule in accordance with the precepts of Dharma, Raja Dharma. The interests of his subjects should be his own and should prevail over his personal interests. Loyalty and obedience to the laws made by such a ruler are binding on all citizens. The citizens should be free to express their views and have certain rights and duties. If a ruler is wicked, selfish or tyrannical, the citizens should be able to change the ruler. There are various stories in the Hindu epics about wicked kings being deposed.

O King! the people have elected you.
Be a true king, shine in all splendour
The sole ruler of the people
All men bow to you.

(ATHARVA VEDA, 3-4-2)

Responsibilities and freedom

In the Hindu scriptures, stress is laid on freedom of thought and expression. The spirit of questioning is encouraged. At the same time the freedom of individuals is subject to certain restraints. The balance between responsibilities and freedom is very aptly described in the following Sanskrit verse:

Tyajedekam Kulasyarthe, gramasyarthe
kulam tyajet, gramam janapadasyarthe
atmarthe prithveem tyajet.

Where there is a clash between a greater good and a smaller one, the interest of greater good prevails. In the interest of the family, one individual may be given up. In the interest of the village, one family may be dis-regarded. In the interest of the nation one village's interest may be disregarded and for the sake of Atma the whole world may be given up.

If everyone does his or her duty, the rights of everybody are guaranteed. In Hindu Dharma, the emphasis is on everyone doing his or her duty. Those who clamour for their rights without performing their duties are

like a farmer who desires to reap without ploughing and sowing the field. Discharge the duty first and then reap the fruits. Rights and duties complement each other.

Hasteshu swadhischa krutishcha sandadhe.
I hold both right and duty in my hand.

(RIG VEDA, 1-168-3)

Secular leadership

In the Hindu view of life, only a person who is unselfish and upholds Dharma can become a true leader. Dharma does not refer only to religion, it implies the performance of duties and righteous conduct in all aspects of life. If a person wishes to become a leader for selfish purposes or for the fame it will bring, he will not succeed in the long run. It does not matter in what ways and forms a person wishes to approach God. As long as he is following the path of Dharma and is unselfish and working for the good of others and the good of all, he acquires the worthiness to become a leader (Bahujana Hitaya, Bahujana Sukhaya). A leader should not work for the promotion of a particular denomination or set of people but should have the good of all, the majority, at heart.

Separation of religion and politics

Hindu sages have always asserted that political leaders should not advocate or work for the good of one particular denomination or sector of people. What matters is the welfare of society as a whole. Leaders are bound not by a religious doctrine but by the rules of Dharma which hold society together. Every religious faith should be looked upon with equal respect and regard. The leader may have a personal faith in a particular denomination (Panth) but he should be tolerant of all other denominations.

The Hindu emperors in the past did not indulge in religious persecution. All Panths in their kingdom were protected, while religious persecution was the order of the day elsewhere. In India (Bharat) persecuted people came seeking shelter. In his book entitled *Om*, Geoffrey Moorhouse describes the Jewish settlement in Cochin (south India). It is believed that about a thousand of their forefathers fled from Palestine to India after the destruction of the second temple in 135 CE, and were welcomed by the Hindu ruler of the time, who allowed them to settle wherever they pleased. Other minorities seeking shelter in India were also allowed to settle freely and thrived along with other faiths and denominations. The administration was impartial and laws applied to all equally. The governing factor in politics was Dharma rather than a particular Panth (denomination).

Religion and Race

The essence of Hindu Dharma is that God exists in all creation, animate and inanimate. 'Eswarah sarvabhutanam hriddeshe pratitishthati' – since the divine spark exists in all souls there is thus a common bond among all. No one is superior or inferior. The noblest way of looking at others is to look upon everyone as one would look upon oneself – 'Atmavat sarvabhuteshu yah pashyati sa pashyati'. Although human beings have outward differences like colour and racial features, all have the same divinity in them, either apparent or potential. Discrimination based on colour and race is therefore a sin against God. For the same reason, domination or exploitation of one race by another is also wrong. God's gifts and natural bounties are not for the exclusive enjoyment of any particular race or nation but for the benefit of all, including the animal kingdom and the plant kingdom.

Racial prejudice and apartheid

In mankind, nobody is higher or lower nor is anybody of middle status. Everybody with concerted effort toils along the path of progress.

(RIG VEDA, 5-59-6)

There is no room for feelings of superiority or prejudice in Hindu philosophy. Negative attitudes like racial prejudice arise out of selfishness, greed, egotism or lack of understanding. Hinduism has always preached that these evils should be avoided. The nobility of selfless service, helping others without desire for reward, and recognition of

the same divinity in all are the ideals which are repeated again and again in Hindu scriptures.

Sometimes, it is said that there is racial prejudice in Hinduism on account of the alleged superiority of Aryans over Dravidians or because of the existence of the caste system and untouchability in India. This is mainly due to lack of proper understanding of the situation. The historian David Frawley has made the following points which are worth looking at in this context:

1. The Vedas speak of a battle between light and darkness which is the symbolic conflict between truth and falsehood. European scholars have wrongly interpreted this as a war between light-skinned Aryans and dark-skinned Dravidians.

2. Researchers like Max Muller and Dr Ambedkar have concluded that 'Aryan' is not a racial term. It was never used as such in the Vedas (see the discussion on the myth of Aryan invasion on pp.8–10).

3. The idea of Aryan and Dravidian races is the product of an unscientific, culturally biased form of thinking that saw race in terms of colour. Aryans and Dravidians are related branches of the Caucasian race.

4. Some scholars have wrongly tried to separate the northern and southern Indian religions. It is incorrect to say that some Hindu gods are Aryan and some are Dravidians.

5. Aryan and Dravidian languages are all derived from one language, Sanskrit.

6. The long cruel Islamic assault on north India turned the south of India into the land of refuge for Vedic culture. The best Vedic chanting, rituals and other traditions are preserved in the south. This may explain some apparent differences between the north and the south.

Hindu scriptures, history and Sanskrit literature all point to the basic unity existing among all Hindus. The Varna Vyavastha (class system) was not intended to promote a policy of apartheid or the exploitation of one class by another. As explained on pp.69–72, it was a system for organizing society, a kind of kinship structure larger than a family unit. Some undesirable mutations to the system crept in during the long period of foreign subjugation that Hindu society had to endure. In modern times, great Hindu leaders like Mahatma Gandhi, Dayanand Saraswati, Mahatma Phule, Dr Ambedkar and many more have fought against the idea of apartheid and racial prejudice or caste prejudice.

Anti-racism and international organizations
The contribution of Hindu thinkers to the fight against racism is considerable. Mahatma Gandhi's struggle against racism in South Africa is a well-known fact of history and has inspired many world leaders to tackle the problem of racism.

Among Hindu international organizations, special mention may be made of the Vishwa Hindu Parishad (World Council of Hindus). This organization has a work base in many countries. It has not only worked to consolidate and unify Hindu society, but is also helping to remove divisions along narrow lines of caste and language. Through its work in countries outside India, it has shown how harmonious relations can exist between different faiths. It has exposed racial discrimination and expressed strong views against it. It has held international conferences in various countries to promote the Hindu view, seeking tolerance, co-operation and friendship between different faiths and races.

Other Hindu organizations working in the same field in Britain are: Brahamakumaris, ISKCON, Satya Sai Baba Movement, Swami Narayana Mission, Ramakrishna Mission, Swadhyaya Parivar, Bharatiya Vidya Bhavan and Arya Samaj.

War and Peace

Violence
Hinduism professes the existence of God in all creation, hence hurting any living being is going against God. Non-violence is one of the five spiritual principles (see the discussion on Yamas on p.52 and Ahimsa on p.53). 'Ahimsa

paramo Dharma', meaning that non-violence is the greatest Dharma, has been preached by many Hindu saints and scholars for centuries. Whatever one's strength and power, the inclination to use violence should be controlled. At the same time, defence of oneself when attacked is considered to be the right conduct.

May your weapons be strong to drive away the attackers.
May arms be powerful enough to check the foes.
Let your army be glorious, not the evil-doer.
(RIG VEDA, 1-39-2)

Hindu scriptures also specify punishment for crimes (Dandaniti).

It is important to understand the meaning of the word 'violence' in the Hindu context, because one may get the impression that Hinduism preaches non-violence but at the same time permits the use of violence. In his book *Heritage of Vedic Culture*, Satyavrata Siddhantalankar explains, 'It is generally thought that to kill an animal for eating its flesh, to commit murder for any reason whatsoever, or to be engaged in unjustifiable warfare are some of the grossest forms of violence. But Vedic culture understood violence in a much wider sense. The feelings of divergence, disunity, separateness, I-ness, my-ness, that set man against man and nation against nation, are the finer forms of violence. To live and let others live for us is violence, to live and let others live for themselves is non-violence.'

Mahatma Gandhi was a devout Hindu who gave practical shape to the ideology of non-violence. He used non-violence against the British Raj to win India's freedom, but when armed tribesmen and other Pakistani nationals invaded the state of Kashmir, Gandhi openly advocated military action against the invaders.

Holy wars and just wars
World history is full of instances where wars have been waged on the basis of religion. There have been crusades and jihads which were justified as holy wars and defended as just wars. Believers of one faith fought with the

believers of another faith. There have been fights between different groups belonging to the same faith; Catholics and Protestants, Shia and Sunni Muslims have clashed with each other on religious grounds and quoted their respective scriptures to justify their cause.

No Hindu scripture allows the waging of war as a means of spreading religion or imposing it on others. Recorded history reveals that Hinduism is free from such religious wars. The great Hindu king Ashoka, after his victory over Kalinga, realized his folly and gave up arms to preach non-violence. Stories from the Mahabharata and the Ramayana demonstrate that a Hindu warrior never engineers a battle but when he has no choice, he fights valiantly. The warrior title refers to Kshatriya, a martial caste of Hinduism. These warriors are allowed to fight only righteous wars which must be waged honourably. The code of conduct is given in the Rig Veda:

He is not allowed to poison the tip of his arrow, he must not attack the sick or old, or someone who is asleep or does not want to fight. Attacking a child, a woman or from behind are sinful acts, and lead to hell even if the warrior is the winner.

(RIG VEDA, 6-75-15)

Anwar Shaikh, editor of the Humanist Quarterly *Liberty*, declares that unlike a Muslim, a Hindu does not fight for the glory of Allah; a Hindu's God is described by several names and is universal in character, therefore a Hindu is above sectarianism and the need to search for glory. Hinduism believes in the universality of religious experience, truth and goodness, asserting that the same God can be found in every faith. So a holy war to please God does not exist. Hinduism is not a missionary religion. It does not force its belief on others, hence religious crusades do not exist. If this is so, then why are references to

brave warriors found in Hindu scriptures? The answer is given succinctly in the Rig Veda: 'A true devotee is faithful to mankind and fights to defend it' (1-52-9 to 15).

Pacifism

Hinduism preaches and prays for world peace. The main teaching is that one should not use one's strength to attack the weak but should use it for the protection of the weak and for upholding righteousness or Dharma. The Hindu belief in pacifism is not based on cowardice or weakness, but on the self-restraint of the strong. The dialogue between Krishna and Arjuna in the Bhagavad Gita elucidates the principle of using power to establish peace.

The ultimate goal of Hinduism is to establish peace. All Hindu prayers end with a special prayer for peace: 'AUM Shantih, shantih, shantih', meaning peace, peace and peace. The first word seeks peace and protection from mental suffering such as worries, jealousy and insanity. The second seeks protection from bodily pains and diseases. The third and final word of the prayer seeks peace from natural disasters and wars.

Conservation and Environment

The relation between God, humans and nature

The Hindu scriptures state that God created the entire world, including all human beings, plants and animals. It is also acknowledged that life depends on the five basic physical elements (Panch Bhoot): earth, water, fire, air and space. Humans are endowed with consciousness and powers of thinking; they study nature through scientific investigation and make use of the natural elements to satisfy their needs. This interaction is summarized as follows:

ELEMENT	PROPERTY	SENSORY ORGAN
Earth	Smell	Nose
Water	Taste	Tongue
Fire	Light/heat	Eye
Air	Touch	Skin
Ether/medium for propagation of waves	Sound	Ear

The central Hindu thought is that macrocosmically matter (Prakriti) exists but it is not all there is; there is some spiritual reality behind it which animates it and is called 'Param atma tattva' (world consciousness or the universal life principle). Microcosmically, the body (Sharira) is also a reality but not the ultimate reality because even here there is Atma tattva animating the body; this is known as Jivatma or Purusha (human consciousness or the individual life principle). There is the same ultimate reality behind everything and the physical world is an interplay of the forces of Prakriti and Purusha.

In the Hindu scriptures, much thought has been given to the relationship between the three entities: God, soul and matter. Are they all the same or are they different entities? Many principles have been enunciated and set out in the Darshana Shastras (see pp.46–47 and 158–160).

Concern for the created world

The care and protection of the environment is considered a religious duty in Hindu scriptures. Evidence is found in the ancient Vedic verses: 'Do not cut trees, because they remove pollution' (Rig Veda, 6-48-17). 'Do not disturb the sky and do not pollute the atmosphere' (Yajur Veda, 5-43).

Mankind is urged not to exploit but to lovingly milk mother nature. Plants and animals like the cow are given the status of mother. The scriptures prescribe the daily practice of Bhoot Yajna; 'Bhoot' is a sentient being or one that has life and 'Yajna' here means service. This is performed by looking after the health and welfare of farm and domestic animals. In environmental matters, importance is placed on observing rules designed to prevent wastage and pollution.

Hinduism recognizes the inevitable consumption of natural resources for the basic needs of human beings. The Holy Vedas state that there is an abundant supply of resources, the only requirement is that humanity must develop the knowledge of using them correctly and efficiently. This is made clear in the first stanza of Isha Upanishad: 'Resources are given to mankind for their living. Knowledge (Isha) of using them is necessary.'

In this context, Hinduism sees no conflict between science and religion. The study of nature is promoted so that a better understanding of the created world can be achieved.

Health Issues

Body, mind and soul

In order to appreciate the response of Hinduism to health issues, it is essential to understand the Hindu concept of body, mind and soul, because its approach to health is holistic.

The soul (also known as Atman or Purusha) has three aspects: (a) unmanifest, pure consciousness, unchanging absolute reality; (b) semi-manifest, nebulous; (c) manifest nature as an individual being conscious of the universe. The three bodies of the soul are: (a) physical body when one is awake; (b) subtle body when dreaming; (c) causal body when in deep sleep. Further discussion on the soul can be found on pp.35–37.

Similarly, the mind has three states: instinctive (Manas), intellectual (Buddhi) and superconscious (Karan chitta). Manas is the seat of desire and controls the sensory and motor organs of the body.

The physical body is made from the five elements: earth (solids), water (liquids), fire (energy), air (gases) and space. These five elements are controlled by three qualities (Gunas): Rajas (activity), Tamas (inertia) and Satva (purity – the balancer of the others). Reference to these Gunas appears on p.41.

Now it will be understood why the Hindu scriptures place so much emphasis on having a clean and healthy body. They state that 'the body is the instrument for achieving all Dharma'. Because of the importance of maintaining a healthy body and mind, the scriptures have specified rules about abstentions and observances called Yamas and Niyamas respectively (see p.52 for further details). These rules deal with personal hygiene and self-discipline. It is believed that an unclean body or mind, apart from becoming disease-prone, cannot make spiritual progress.

The Ayurveda, a branch of the Rig Veda, is the scripture that is concerned with the well-being of the physical body. This is now recognized as medical science, helping to harmonize the body with mind and soul. Yoga (now very popular in the West) was developed to enable the body and mind to be harmonized with the soul. Tantra uses the mind to balance the demands of the body and soul. The balance between these three is called health (Svastha, meaning self-established).

Drugs

Hindu scriptures recommend that all food eaten should be 'Satvic', that is the quality which is conducive to good thoughts and feelings. Nothing should be taken that results in the loss of self-control or that overburdens the body mechanisms. Hence the use of intoxicating drugs (including alcohol and smoking) is strictly prohibited. The Hindu view is that intoxicating, addictive drugs should be avoided because they may result in serious ailments, disturb and agitate the mind, lead to wicked or evil actions and retard spiritual progress.

Instances of Hindu holy men using drugs are sometimes quoted. The intake of drugs does not lead to salvation or peace of mind so no true holy man will ever advocate the use of drugs.

The use of the word 'Soma' in many Hindu scriptures has also been misconceived by some interpreters. A very common mistake is to relate it to some hallucinating drug leading to an experience of ecstasy. The correct meaning of Soma is 'elixir of divine love'. Pandit Satyakam Vidyalankar gives the following translation in his book *The Holy Vedas – A Golden Treasury*:

> *Soma, the Elixir of Divine Love,*
> *Cleanses the heart of all unwanted and*
> *   undesirable tendencies.*
> *The soul then is free of fear, sorrow and*
> *   ignorance.*
> *Thus liberated, full of divine faith and*
> *   spiritual joy,*
> *The brave soul discovers God in all His*
> *   splendorous forms.*
>
> (RIG VEDA, 9-1-10)

AIDS

Scientists have still not discovered the root cause of AIDS, which is related to the presence of a virus called HIV, but one fact that has been established is that it is more widespread among drug addicts and homosexuals. Hindu sages anticipated the hazards of drug abuse and improper indulgence in sex, as explained in the sections above. What is relevant now is the view of Hinduism on prevention and on the care of sufferers.

Hinduism teaches that in all cases of human suffering, whether self-inflicted or not, it is the moral duty of healthy and wise people to help minimize the suffering and to help the sufferers return to the right path. For the prevention of such diseases, advice is given in the Rig Veda: 'Cultivate the strength of will-power to conquer the passionate urges of thy sense organs' (5-31-3).

Spiritual healing

Healing refers to the process of curing diseases of the body or the mind. It is now recognized as a medical fact that in the healing process the attitude of the mind plays an important role. As explained in earlier sections, Hinduism has a holistic approach to health, involving body, mind and soul. Spiritualism helps to create a healthy mind, free from anxieties, worries, evil passions and evil thoughts. Spiritual practices such as prayers, meditation, reading of scriptures and Japas (repetition of the name of God or a Mantra) are beneficial because they relieve stress and improve the inner strength that is needed to fight or prevent disease. Such spiritual practices in the long term become effective in curing diseases, particularly those related to stress, such as hypertension, cardiac problems, ulcers and so on. In most cases, these practices should be accompanied by orthodox medical treatment. In Hinduism, spiritual practices have a scientific basis and therefore help in the healing process; miracles do not.

IN THE CLASSROOM

Marriage and Family

1. What in your view is the importance of marriage?

2. Why is the basic building block of society considered to be the family unit? What do you think will happen to society if family units break down?

3. What makes a happy family? Why do some families break down?

4. What is the difference between 'arranged marriage', 'forced marriage' and 'love marriage'?

5. Why are chastity and loyalty considered to be important by religious people?

6. How can a religious faith and traditions help to keep a family together?

7. In Hinduism, woman is worshipped as creative power (Shakti). How does this compare with the modern view of womanhood?

8. What do various religions advise on population control and contraception?

9. What is the Hindu point of view on abortion?

10. The sexual instinct is natural, so what is a moral and responsible way of dealing with it? If sexual activity is devoid of morals and ethics, what will be the consequences?

11. Many religious ideas on creation require pairs of opposites (man/woman, day/night, etc.). Does that mean that homosexuality and lesbianism are unnatural?

Death

1. How does religious belief help us cope with death?

2. Do death rites serve any purpose?

3. Is there life after death? Was there life before birth?

4. When does life begin? Who owns it? Can it be ended by choice?

5. Why do some people seem to suffer more than others? How does Hinduism explain this?

Work and Leisure

1. What can retired and older people contribute to family and social life?

2. Is it acceptable to earn one's living by exploiting others?

3. Should we do voluntary and community work to help others?

4. What is your view on 'work is worship'?

5. Do religions teach or promote the right balance between work and leisure? Who should work and who should not?

6. Who do you think should look after the disabled and the unemployed?

Wealth and Poverty

1. What do most religions teach about helping the poor and disabled?

2. What is the best way to use one's wealth?

3. Can you become trapped by your own wealth?

4. What do you think is more important than money?

5. What responsibilities do developed countries have towards underdeveloped countries?

6. Do you think it is acceptable for religiously inspired aid organizations to try to convert those being helped?

7. What motivates a Hindu to give aid?

Religion and Politics

1. Should religion be separate from politics?

2. How should a government treat religious minorities?

3. What is more important, rights or duties?

4. Should you be free to do whatever you want to do irrespective of your responsibility towards fellow citizens?

5. What should a religious person do when the law of the state conflicts with his or her religious beliefs?

6. What do you understand by the terms 'orthodox', 'fundamentalist' and 'fanatic'.

7. Hinduism has no founder, is not based on any one book and allows freedom to worship God in any manner. Can a Hindu be called 'fundamentalist'?

Religion and Race
1. Is there prejudice based on race, colour or religion in our society?

2. What causes racial prejudice?

3. Are all human beings equal? Can one race be better than another?

4. How can the world's religions help to remove prejudice?

5. What problems do Hindus face in following their religion in the UK?

War and Peace
1. Is it wrong for religious people to quarrel and fight?

2. Can you explain why religion seems to be the cause of many conflicts?

3. How can religious people who promote non-violence protect themselves when attacked? Can injustice be tolerated?

4. Is it ethical to wage a war to spread or impose one's religion on others? Why was it done in the past?

5. Can religion bring world peace? What kind of religion is it likely to be?

6. What qualities would be needed in a universal religion which is acceptable to all? Evaluate Hinduism and its concepts like 'universal brotherhood' and 'freedom of worship'.

7. Are pacifism and non-violence the same as cowardice?

8. What is a just war? Who decides whether it is just or unjust?

Conservation and Environment

1. How do the various religions view the role of nature? Which religions teach respect for nature?

2. Can spiritual experience be gained by living close to nature?

3. Is the advancement of science bringing us closer to an understanding of God and creation?

4. Our planet has limited natural resources. For how long can an unlimited consumption continue? What guidance is given by Hindu scriptures?

Health Issues

1. Why do some people become drug addicts?

2. Can religious faith help in the healing process?

3. Which religions promote vegetarianism and why?

4. Stress and anxiety are now known to be the root causes of many ailments. What role can Yoga and meditation play in curbing these stress-related problems?

GLOSSARY

Preferred form	Main variants	Explanation
Acharya	Acarya	One who teaches by example. Usually refers to a prominent or exemplary spiritual teacher.
Advaita	Adwaita	Non-dual. Refers to the philosophy of the absolute which unqualifyingly unifies God, soul and matter.
Ahimsa	Ahinsa	Non killing, non-violence; respect for life.
Artha		Economic development. The second aim of life.
Arati	Arti	Welcoming ceremony in which auspicious articles such as incense and lamps are offered to the deity or to saintly people.
Aryan		Noble. Refers to those who know the spiritual values of life.
Ashram	Asram	(i) A place (hermitage) set up for spiritual development. (ii) A stage of life (of which there are four) adopted according to material considerations, but ultimately as a means to spiritual realization.
Atharva Veda		The fourth of the Vedas.
Atman	Atma	Self. Can refer to mind or soul, depending on context. Ultimately, it refers to the real self, the soul.
AUM	Om	The sacred symbol and sound representing the ultimate; the most sacred of Hindu words.
Avatar	Avatara, Avtara	One who descends. Refers to the descent of a deity to earth, most commonly Vishnu. Sometimes it is translated as incarnation.
Ayodhya		Birthplace of Rama.
BCE		Before the Common Era, i.e. before the birth of Christ in the Western calendar.
Bhagavad Gita		The Song of the Lord. Spoken by Krishna, this is the most important scripture for most Hindus. Tradition dates it to 3000–5000 years BCE. Considered to be an Upanishad.
Bhajan	Bhajana	Devotional song.
Bhakti		Devotion. Love of God.
Bhakti-yoga		The path of loving devotion, aimed at developing pure love of God.
Brahmaa		A Hindu deity, considered one of the Trimurti, and in charge of creative power. Not to be confused with Brahman or Brahmin.
Brahmacharya		The first stage of life, the learning stage, during which the student remains celibate. One who is in this stage is called Brahmachari, a student of Vedic knowledge.
Brahman	Brahma	The ultimate reality, or the all-pervading reality; that from which everything emanates, in which it rests and into which it is ultmately dissolved.
Brahmin		The first of the four Varnas, the principal social groupings from which priests are drawn. Should not be confused with the words 'Brahmaa' and 'Brahman', mentioned above.

Preferred form	Main variants	Explanation
CE		Common Era; the same as AD in the Western calendar.
Darshan Shastras		Six systems of Hindu philosophy: Nyaya, Vaisheshika, Sankhya, Yoga, Mimamsa and Vedanta.
Dussera	Dussehra, Dashara, Dushera (other variants are also found)	Also called Vijay Dashmi. Celebrates the victory of Rama on the tenth day of the bright half of the lunar month of Ashwin. As is often the case with Hindu festivals, followers may interpret the festival differently, e.g. in connection with Durga (see Navaratri).
Dharma		Literally it means the intrinsic quality of the self or that which sustains one's existence, but religion or religious duty is the usual translation in English.
Dhoti		A garment made of natural fibre (usually cotton or silk), worn by males, which covers the lower body and legs.
Diwali	Divali, Dipavali, Deepavali	Festival of lights celebrated on new year's day of one of the Hindu calendars, called Vikram Samvat.
Durga		Female deity. A form of the goddess Parvati, wife of Shiva.
Dvaita	Dwaita	Dual. Refers to the personalistic philosophy that differentiates between God, soul and matter.
Dwarka	Dvarka, Dwaraka	Pilgrimage site on the west coast of India.
Ganesh	Ganesa	Hindu deity, portrayed with an elephant's head and believed to remove obstacles.
Ganga		Ganges. Most famous of all sacred rivers of India.
Gangotri		Source of the River Ganges.
Gotra		Exogamous group within Jati.
Grihastha	Grhastha Grthastha	The second stage of Hindu life; one who belongs to that stage, i.e. the householder.
Guna		Rope; quality. Specifically refers to the three qualities of Sattva (goodness), Rajas (passion) and Tamas (ignorance) which permeate and control matter.
Guru		Spiritual teacher, preceptor or enlightener.
Hanuman		The monkey warrior who faithfully served Rama and Sita. Also called Pavansuta (son of the wind god, Maruti).
Havan		The part of many Hindu sacraments used at weddings and on other ceremonial occasions; the ceremony or act of worship in which offerings of ghee and grains are made on the fire.
Havan kund		The container, usually square or pyramid-shaped, in which the sacred fire is lit.
Hitopadesha		An ancient text written by Narayana containing moral stories about birds, beasts and man.
Holi		The festival of colours, celebrated in spring.
Homa		Term often used interchangeably with Havan.
Janeu	Jenoi	Sacred thread worn by Hindus. Three strands of the thread represent three vows.
Janmashtami	Janmasthami	The birthday of Krishna, celebrated on the eighth day of the waning moon in the month of Badra.
Japa	Jap	The quiet or silent repetition of a Mantra as a meditative process.
Jaati	Jati	Caste is the usual translation, meaning occupational kinship group.

Preferred form	Main variants	Explanation
Jnana	Gyan	Knowledge.
Jnana-yoga	Gyan-yoga	The path of knowledge, that aims at liberation.
Kaali		Name given to the destructive power of God; often represented by the goddess Kaali (a form of Durga).
Kali yuga		The fourth of the ages; the iron age or the age of quarrelling and hypocrisy.
Kama		The third of the four aims of life: a regulated sense of enjoyment.
Karma		Action. Used to refer to the law of cause and effect.
Karma-yoga		The path of self-realization by unattached (selfless) work.
Kirtan	Keertan	Songs of praise; corporate devotional singing, usually accompanied by musical instruments.
Krishna		A lovable lad, a hero, a statesman, a philosopher and a teacher, personified as a fully integrated life. An avatar of Vishnu. His teachings are elaborated in the Bhagavad Gita.
Kshatriya	Khatri	Second of the four Varnas of traditional Hindu society, the ruling or warrior class.
Lakshmi and prosperity.	Laksmi	Power of wealth; often represented by the Hindu goddess of wealth
Mahabharata		The longest Hindu epic; relates the story of the five Pandava princes. It includes the Bhagavad Gita.
Mala	Maala	Circle of stringed beads of wood or glass (rosary) used in meditation and repetition of God's name.
Mandir		Temple.
Mantra		That which delivers the mind. Refers to a short sacred text or prayer, often recited repetitiously.
Manu Smruti		The laws of Manu. An ancient and important text on Dharma, including personal and social laws.
Marg		Path (see yoga).
Mata		Mother. Often associated with Hindu goddesses who represent Shakti (power).
Mathura		Holy place, birthplace of Krishna.
Maya		Illusion; particularly where the permanent soul identifies itself with temporary matter, e.g. the body. It can also mean divine potency.
Moksha	Moksa	Salvation or ultimate liberation from the process of transmigration, the continuous cycle of birth and death.
Mundan		The head-shaving ceremony. Performed in the first or third year of life and also at special occasions.
Murti	Moorti	Icon. The scared image or deity used as a focus of worship.
Navaratri	Navaratra	The Nine Nights Festival preceding Dussera, and held in honour of the goddess Durga.
Nirvana	Nirbana	The cessation of material existence. See Moksha.
Panchatantra		An ancient text, including animal stories with a moral.
Parvati		The consort of Shiva; also known by other names such as Durga or Amba.
Prahlada	Prahalada	A great child devotee of Vishnu, connected with the festival of Holi.

Preferred form	Main variants	Explanation
Pranayam	Pranayama	Regulation of breath as a means of controlling the mind.
Prashad	Prasad, prasada, prashada	Sacred or sanctified food often distributed after offering to the deity.
Pravachan		A lecture or talk, usually based on the scriptures.
Puja	Pooja	Worship. General term referring to a variety of practices in the home or Mandir.
Purana		Part of the ancient Hindu scriptures. Contains mythological stories.
Raja Yoga	Raj Yoga	Path of self-control and meditation to realize God.
Rajas		Passion or creative potency, one of the three Gunas (qualities of material nature).
Rakhi	Rakhee	A sacred thread usually made out of silk or cotton, tied as a promise to protect and to strengthen the bond of mutual love.
Raksha Bandhan		The festival when women tie a Rakhi on their brothers' wrists.
Rama	Raam	Personification of righteousness usually considered an avatar of Vishnu. The hero of the Ramayana (avoid using the variant 'Ram' for obvious reasons). An ideal son, brother, husband and king.
Ramayana	Ramayan	The great Hindu epic that relates the story of Rama and Sita, composed by the sage Valmiki thousands of years ago. A moral text for millions of Hindus all over the world.
Ramnavami	Ramanavami	The birthday festival of Rama.
Rig Veda	Rg or Rc Veda	The first scripture of Hinduism, containing spiritual and scientific knowledge. The most ancient of the world scriptures.
Rishi	Rsi, Risi	A spiritually wise person. Also refers to the seven seers who received the divine wisdon.
Sadhana	Sadhan	Regulated spiritual practices or discipline.
Sadhu	Sadhoo	Holy man. An ascetic who has renounced the world.
Sama Veda		The Veda of chanting; material mainly from the Rig Veda, arranged for ritual chanting in worship.
Samsara	Sansara	The world; the place where transmigration (the soul's passage through a series of lives in different species) occurs.
Samskar	Sanskar, Samskara	Sacraments designed to initiate a new stage of life. There is usually a total of sixteen such rites of passage (though many schools of thought do not practise them all).
Sanatan Dharma		The eternal or imperishable religion; also known as Vedic Dharma. Adherents often prefer this term to Hinduism since it characterizes their belief in the revealed and universal nature of religion.
Sanatanist		Adherent of ancient Hindu traditions (generally non-reformist).
Sanyasa	Sanyaas	The state of renunciation, the fourth stage of life.
Sanyasi	Samyasin, Samnyasin	A renunciate who, having given up worldly affairs and attachments, has entered the fourth stage of life, often as a mendicant.
Sanskrit	Samskrit	Sacred language of the Hindu scriptures. One of the most ancient languages in the world.
Saraswati		Power of knowledge, often represented by the goddess Saraswati, the goddess of learning.
Satsang		Meeting for spiritual songs, prayers or discourses.
Sattva	Sattwa	Goodness, or the potency to sustain and nourish; one of the three Gunas.

Preferred form	Main variants	Explanation
Seva	Sewa	Service, either to the divine or to humanity.
Shaivism	Saivism	The sect of Hindus who are devotees of Shiva.
Shakti	Sakti	Energy or power, the term used especially in relation to a Hindu feminine deity.
Shiva	Siva (many other variants including Civa)	Means kind or auspicious. Name of one of the Trimurtis, in charge of destructive power.
Shivaratri	Sivaratri	The annual festival celebrated in February/March in honour of Shiva. Also called Mahashivaratri.
Shraaddha	Sraddha, shradha	Ceremony in which sanctified food is offered in memory of departed ancestors.
Shri	Sri	Illustrious. Used as a title of respect, e.g. Shri Krishna. Also a respectful title for men. The feminine form is Shrimati (Mrs).
Smruti	Smriti	That which is remembered. Generally Hindu scriptures which give codes of conduct.
Sita	Seeta	The divine consort of Rama.
Shruti	Srti	That which is heard. A term specifically applied to the four Vedas, including the Upanishads.
Sutra	Sutta	Short sayings or verses relating to various rituals, or encapsulating profound philosophical meaning.
Swami		Controller or master. Sometimes, more specifically, Goswami (one who controls his/her senses). An honorific title applied to a religious teacher or holy person, particularly the Sanyasi.
Swastika	Svastika	From the Sanskrit for well-being; a mark of good fortune. The four arms signify the four directions (space), the four Vedas (knowledge), and the four stages (time) in the life-cycle. Not to be confused with the Nazi symbol.
Tamas		Ignorance or destructive potency; the lowest of the three Gunas.
Trimurti		The three deities. Refers to Brahmaa, Vishnu and Shiva (Mahesh), who personify the control of the three functions of creation, preservation and destruction. 'Trinity' should be avoided.
Upanayana		Ceremony when the sacred thread is worn to mark the start of learning with a guru.
Upanishad	Upanisad	To sit down near. A sacred text based on the teaching of a guru to a disciple. The Upanishads are the end portion of the Vedas and contain deep philosophical truths.
Vaishnavism	Vaisnavism	The sect of Hindus who are devotees of the god Vishnu.
Vaishya	Vaisya	The third of the four Varnas of Hindu society, composed of merchants, traders and farmers.
Vanaprastha		The third stage of life, typified by retirement and asceticism. One who is in the third stage of life is called Vanaprasthi.
Varanasi	Banares, Benares, Kashi, Kasi	City on the holy River Ganges, sacred place of Shiva. It is one of the holiest pilgrimage sites and also an ancient centre of learning.
Varna		Colour. The four principal divisions of Hindu society. It is important to note that the word 'caste' refers strictly to sub-divisions within each Varna, and not to the Varnas themselves.
Varnashrama	Varnasrama-Dharma	The system whereby society is divided into four varnas (divisions), and life into four ashramas (stages).

Preferred form	Main variants	Explanation
Varsha Pratipada		The day of Creation, celebrated as New Year's Day by all Hindus.
Veda		Knowledge. Specifically refers to the four Vedas, though any teaching which is consistent with the conclusions of these scriptures is also accepted as Vedic.
Vijaya Dashmi	Vijaydashmi	Another name for the festival of Dussera.
Vishnu	Visnu	A Hindu god. With Brahma and Shiva forms the Trimurti.
Vishwa Hindu Parishad		World Council of Hindus.
Vrat	Vratam	Vow. Often including absention from certain foods.
Vrindavan	Brindavan, Vrindavana	The sacred village connected with Krishna's pastimes as a youth.
Yajur Veda		One of the four Vedas, dealing with the knowledge of ritualistic aspects while performing sacraments.
Yamuna	Jamuna, Jumna	Tributary of the River Ganga (Ganges), considered by many Hindus to be equally sacred.
Yatra	Jatra	Pilgrimage; usually to important sacred places in India.
Yoga		Communion; union of the soul with the Supreme, or a process which promotes that relationship. The English word 'yoke' is derived from yoga.
Yuga		Age or extended period of time, of which there are four: Satya, Treta, Dwapar and Kali.

Guide for Pronunciation

The word Rama is to be pronounced as Raam (not emphasising the last 'a' in Rama). Similarly, in the pronunciation of the following proper nouns, the last 'a' is not emphasised:- Krishna, Dharma, Yoga. In the feminine words such as Yamuna, Ganga etc. the last 'a' is stretched longer as 'aa'.

BIBLIOGRAPHY

Amar Chitra Katha, *Hitopadesha – Choice of friends*, Vol. 556, India Book House Pvt. Ltd., Bombay, India.

Amar Chitra Katha, *Jataka Tales: Monkey Series*, Vol. 543, India Book House Pvt. Ltd, Bombay, India.

Amar Chitra Katha, *Panchatantra*, No.163, India Book House Pvt. Ltd, Bombay, India.

Aurobindo, Sri, *India's Rebirth*, Institute for Evolutionary Research, Paris, 1994.

Bokare, M.G., *Hindu Economics*, Janaki Prakashan, New Delhi, 1993.

Burghart, R., *Hinduism in Great Britain*, Tavistock Publications, London, 1987.

Chandrasekharendra Saraswati Swami, *Hindu Dharma – The Universal Way of Life*, Bharatiya Vidya Bhavan, 1995.

Children's Book Trust, *Treasury of Indian Tales, Books 1 – 3.*

Chinmayananda Swami, *The choice is yours*, Central Chinmaya Mission Trust, Bombay, 1991.

Dayananda, M., *An Introduction to the Vedas*, Sarvadeshik Arya Pratinidhi Sabha, New Delhi, 1984.

Eliot, C., *Hinduism and Buddhism*, Vols I, II & III, Routledge and Kegan Paul, 1954.

Elst, Koenraad, 'Ram Janmabhoomi vs Babri Masjid', Voice of India, New Delhi, 1990.

Farquhar, J.N., *Modern Religious Movements in India*, Munshiram Manoharlal Publishers Pvt. Ltd., 1977.

Frawley, D., *From the river of heaven – Hindu and Vedic knowledge for the modern age*, Morson Publishing, Utah, 1990.

Frawley, D., *Hinduism – the eternal tradition*, Voice of India, New Delhi, 1995.

Glover, J.T., *Vedic Mathematics for Schools – Book 1*, 11 Beverley Gardens, London SW13 0LZ, 1993.

Griffith, R.T.H., *The Hymns of the Rig Veda*, 3rd edition, E.J. Lazarus & Co., 1920.

Iyer, B.K., *Hindu Ideals*, Bharatiya Vidya Bhavan, Bombay, India, 1969.

Jitatmananda Swami, *Modern Physics and Vedanta*, Bharatiya Vidya Bhavan, Bombay, 1992.

Jois, M.R., *Supreme Court Judgement on Hindutva – An Important Landmark*, Suruchi Prakashan, Keshav Kunj, New Delhi, 1996.

Jois, M.R., Dharma the Global Ethic, Bharatiya Vidya Bhavan, Mumbai, 1996.

Kanitkar, V.P. *What We Believe: We Are Hindus*, Saint Andrew Press, Edinburgh, 1987.

Mathur, R., *Woman in Hindu Society*, Sudhanshu Bandhu, New Delhi, 1989.

Modi, B.K., *Hinduism, the Universal Truth*, Brijbasi Printers Pvt. Ltd, New Delhi, 1993.

Naik, *Ramayana (Parts 1 & 2) and Bhagawada Gita*, Anada Book Depot, Ahmedabad, India.

Paarinder, G., *Avatar and Incarnation*, Faber and Faber, London, 1970.

Parthasarthy, A., *The Symbolism of Hindu Gods and Rituals*, Vedanta Life Institute, Bombay, 1994.

Prabhavananda, Swami, *The Spiritual Heritage of India*, Vedanta Press, Hollywood, California, 1969.

Rajagopalachari, C., *Stories for the Innocent*, 1988, and *Ramayana*, 1982, Bharatiya Vidya Bhavan, Bombay, India.

Ryder, Arthur W., *Panchatantra*, translated from Sanskrit, Jaico Publishing House, India, 1989.

Sarma, D.S., *A Primer of Hinduism*, Bharatiya Vidya Bhavan, 1984.

Seshadri, H.V., *Our Festivals*, Hindu Council of Kenya, 1983.

Shah, U., *Basic Introduction to Hindu Religious Education*, Shanti Publications, Kenya.

Shastri, V.N., *Sciences in the Vedas*, Sarvadeshik Arya Pratinidhi Sabha, New Delhi, 1970.

Siddhantalankar, S., *Heritage of Vedic Culture – A Pragmatic Presentation*, D.B. Taraporevala, Sons & Co. Pvt. Ltd, Bombay, 1969.

Sister Nivedita, *Cradle Tales of Hinduism*, Advaita Ashrama, Calcutta, 1981.

Sivananda, S., *Ethical Teachings*, Divine Life Society of South Africa, Durban, 1995.

Sivananda, S., *Yoga Lessons for Children*, Divine Life Society of South Africa, Durban, 1984.

Stein, B. (ed.), *South Indian Temples*, Vikas Publishing House Pvt. Ltd, 1978.

Talageri, S.G., *Aryan Invasion Theory and Indian Nationalism*, Voice of India, New Delhi, 1993.

Talreja, K.M., *Philosophy of Vedas*, Talreja Publications, Ulhasa Nagar, Bombay, India, 1982.

Tirtha Maharaja, B. K., *Vedic Mathematics*, Motilal Banarsidas Publishers Pvt. Ltd, Delhi, 1992.

Yeats, W.B., *Ten Principal Upanishads*, Faber and Faber, London, 1937.

Veda, Niketan, *Basic Teachings of Hinduism – Book 2*, 1992; *Elementary Teachings of Hinduism – Book 1*, 1992; *Essential Teachings of Hinduism – Book 3*, 1979; *Spiritual Teachings of Hinduism – Book 4*, 1985, Arya Pratinidhi Sabha, South Africa.

Vidyalankar, S., *The Holy Vedas – A Golden Treasury*, Clarion Books, New Delhi, 1986.

Vivekananada, Swami, *Hinduism*, Ramakrishna Math, Madras, India, 1976.

The books listed here are available from:
Hindu Sahitya Kendra (Hindu Literature Centre)
46/48 Loughborough Road
Leicester LE4 5LD
Tel: 01162-611303
Fax: 01162-611931

The Natraja temple at Chidambaram built by Chola dynasty.

The concept of Gopuram, a richly decorated multi-storey gateway to a Hindu temple, was introduced by the Chola dynasty who ruled in South India during 12th century.

Hindu temple built by ISKCON in New Delhi which was inaugurated by India's Prime Minister, Atal Bihari Vajpayee in 1998.

A magnificient Gopuram (gateway) as the temple entrance in Kanchipuram

Five chariots, one for each of the Pandavs, carved out of a single rock (monolithic) by the Pallavas at the Shore Temple in Mahabalipuram.

World's largest basrelief, 27m by 9m, at Mahabalipuram depicting Arjuna's Penance and the Descent of the Ganga with various characters from the epic Mahabharata.

Entrance to the Brihadeesvara temple at Thanjavur (Tanjore).

Lord Vishnu's statue at the ISKCON temple in New Delhi.

Statue of Saraswati carved in stone

Swami Vivekananda Memorial built at the Southern most tip of mainland India at Kanyakumari.

Hindu women decorate their home with rangoli on Diwali

Dandia (stick dance) is performed with a rhythmic beat of dholaks (drums) around the sacred image of Durga during the navratri Celebrations.

A traditional Hindu temple (Mandir) of Swaminarayana Hindu Mission in Neasden, London. It is the largest marble temple outside India. It has been constructed in accordance with the ancient scriptures, the Shilpa Shastra, depicting the mandir as a living body (see p.111).

*Architectural Inscription of Hindu Art on Part Ceiling of Famous
Jain Temple, Leicester, U.K.*

Creation and Evolution of Life

Modern Science

Known physical laws cannot describe the initial state. It was too hot and too dense.

Energy converts to matter $(E = M C^2)$

3 types of elementary particles : electron neutrino, muon neutrino, tau neutrino

Elements form by fusing neutrinos,

Atom - Electron

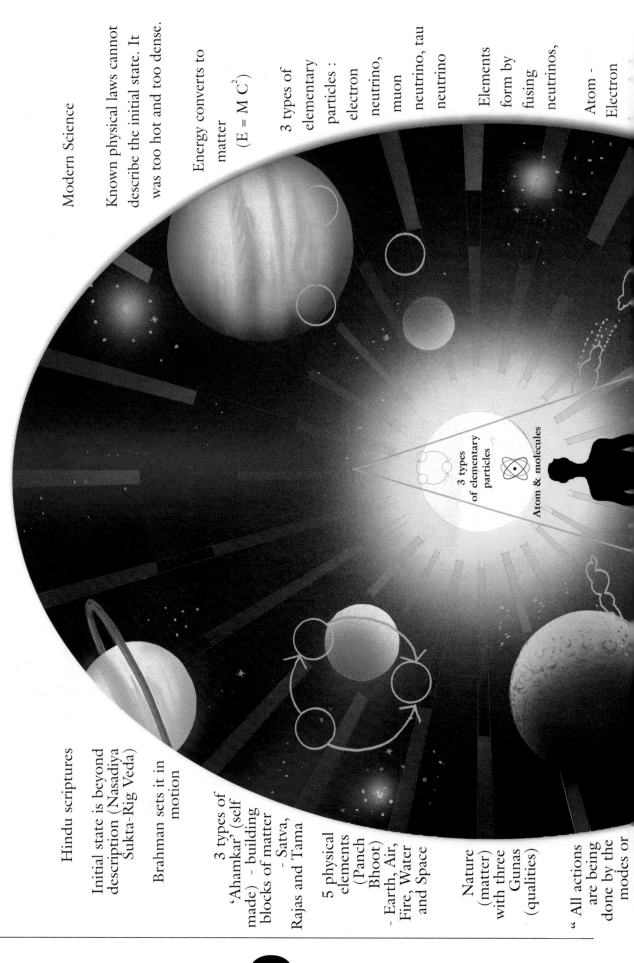

3 types of elementary particles

Atom & molecules

Hindu scriptures

Initial state is beyond description (Nasadiya Sukta-Rig Veda)

Brahman sets it in motion

3 types of 'Ahamkar' (self made) - building blocks of matter - Satva, Rajas and Tama

5 physical elements (Panch Bhoot) - Earth, Air, Fire, Water and Space

Nature (matter) with three Gunas (qualities)

" All actions are being done by the modes or

(positive)-

- Gita
(Ch.3 verse 27)

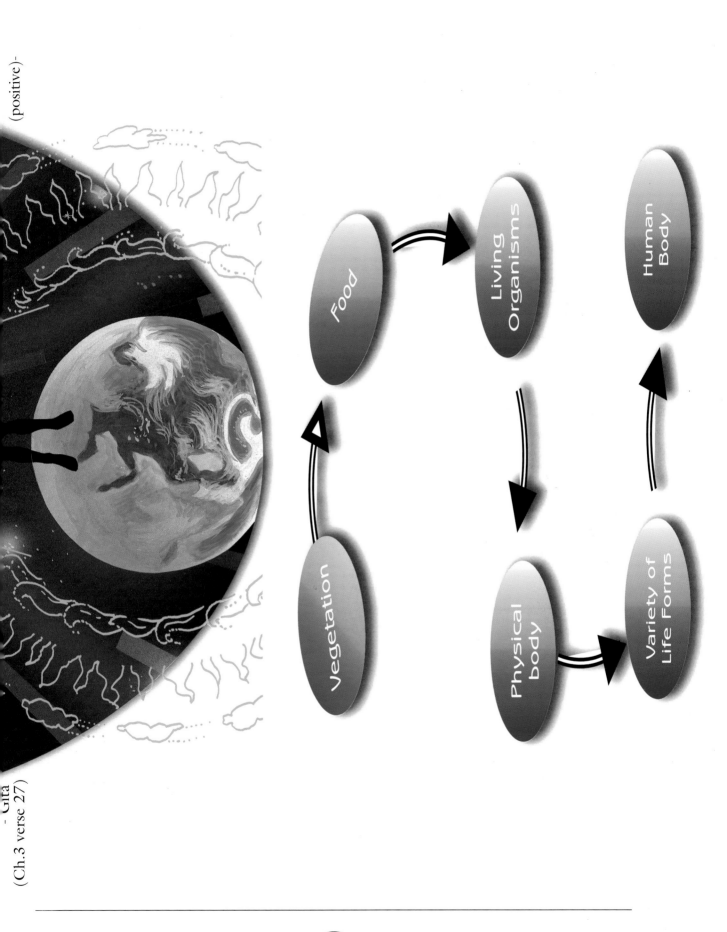

Krishna and Arjuna sounding their transcendental conchshells as the battle of Kurukshetra was about to commence

Hindu concept of Cyclic Creation and Cycle of Life and Death

Shri Krishna guiding Arjuna on the Mahabharata battlefield at Kurukshetra

Devotees making a wish by tying red cloth to a holy tree at Mansa Devi temple dedicated to Durga.

Childless couples wishing to start a family tie toy cradles around a pair of holy trees.

Holy elephants at the temple entrance giving blessings (Asheervad) to a devotee.

Bronze statue of Ganesha.

A Hindu priest in traditional attire.

201

INDEX

Worldwide Distributors

United Kingdom & Europe

1. Vishwa Hindu Parishad, Karam House, 79 Lever Street, Manchester M1 1FL.
    Tel: +44 (0)161 236 8621 / Fax: +44 (0)161 228 0056

2. Vishwa Hindu Parishad, Keshav Pratishthan, 46/48 Loughborough Road, Leicester LE4 5LD.
    Tel: +44 (0)116 266 5665 / Fax: +44 (0)116 261 193/ e-mail: admin@hss-leic.demon.co.uk

3. Vishwa Hindu Parishad, Madhav Sadan, 52 Rugby Place, Bradford BD7 2DF.
    Tel: +44 (0)1274 577395 / Fax: +44 (0)1274 521211

Bharat (India)

Vishwa Hindu Parishad, Sankat Mochan Ashram, Ramkrishna Puram - 6,
New Delhi - 110 022, Bharat (India).
Tel: 00 91 11 610 3495 & 617 8992 / Fax: 0091 11 619 5527
e-mail: sangam@nda.vsnl.net.in

Australia

Vishwa Hindu Parishad (Australia), 11/43, Sheffields Street, Merry Lands, Sydney,
NSW 2160. Australia.
Tel & Fax: 00612 9824 1517 / e-mail:ravi@bb.com.au & vhp@bb.com.au

America

Vishwa Hindu Parishad of America
37 Kimberly Road
West Hartford
CT 06107
USA

Africa

1. Hindu Council of Kenya, Muranga Road, P O Box 44831, Nairobi, Kenya.
    Tel: 00 254 2 749911 / 760075 - Fax: 00 254 2 764423
2. c/o Shri Anith Maharaj
    P.O. Box 5462
    Durban - 4000
    Republic of South Africa